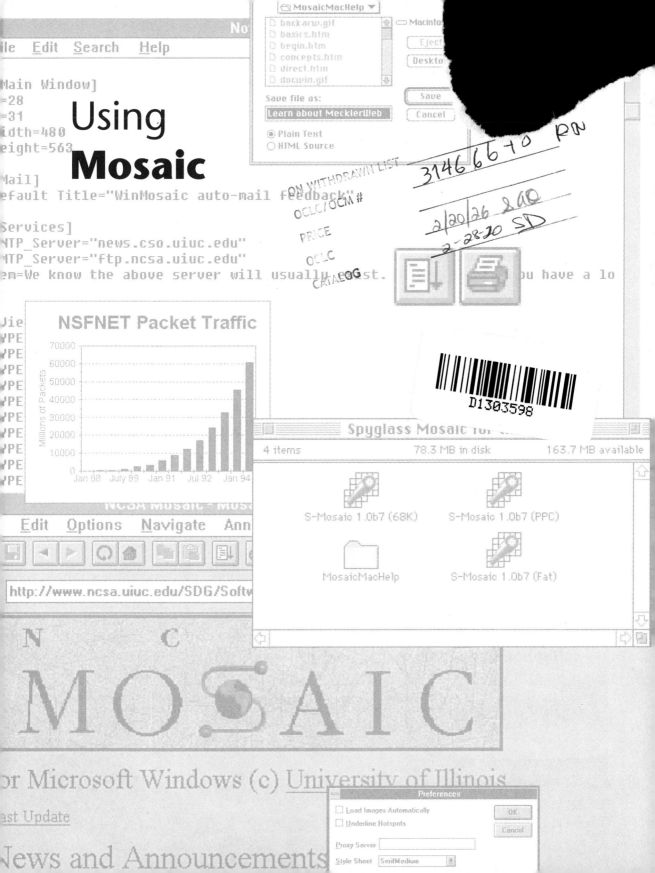

Using
Mosaic

File   Edit   Search   Help

[Main Window]
=28
=31
idth=480
eight=563

[Mail]
efault Title="WinMosaic auto-mail feedback"

[Services]
NTP_Server="news.cso.uiuc.edu"
NTP_Server="ftp.ncsa.uiuc.edu"
em=We know the above server will usually ... st. ... ou have a lo

MosaicMacHelp ▾
backarw.gif
basics.htm
begin.htm
concepts.htm
direct.htm
docwin.gif

Macinto...

Eject
Desktop

Save file as:
Learn about MecklerWeb

Save
Cancel

● Plain Text
○ HTML Source

NSFNET Packet Traffic

70000
60000
50000
40000
30000
20000
10000
0

Millions of Packets

Jan 88   July 89   Jan 91   Jul 92   Jan 94

NCSA Mosaic - Mos...

Edit   Options   Navigate   Ann...

http://www.ncsa.uiuc.edu/SDG/Softw...

Spyglass Mosaic for ...

4 items   78.3 MB in disk   163.7 MB available

S-Mosaic 1.0b7 (68K)   S-Mosaic 1.0b7 (PPC)

MosaicMacHelp   S-Mosaic 1.0b7 (Fat)

N   C
MOSAIC

or Microsoft Windows (c) University of Illinois

ast Update

News and Announcements

Preferences
☐ Load Images Automatically   OK
☐ Underline Hotspots   Cancel
Proxy Server
Style Sheet   SerifMedium

PLUG YOURSELF INTO...

The MCP Internet Site

Free information and vast computer resources from the world's leading computer book publisher—online!

Find the books that are right for you!

A complete online catalog, plus sample chapters and tables of contents give you an in-depth look at *all* our books. The best way to shop or browse!

- ✦ **Stay informed** with the latest computer industry news through discussion groups, an online newsletter, and customized subscription news.

- ✦ **Get fast answers** to your questions about MCP books and software.

- ✦ **Visit** our online bookstore for the latest information and editions!

- ✦ **Communicate** with our expert authors through e-mail and conferences.

- ✦ **Play** in the BradyGame Room with info, demos, shareware, and more!

- ✦ **Download software** from the immense MCP library:
    - Source code and files from MCP books
    - The best shareware, freeware, and demos

- ✦ **Discover hot spots** on other parts of the Internet.

- ✦ **Win books** in ongoing contests and giveaways!

Drop by the new Internet site of Macmillan Computer Publishing!

To plug into MCP:

World Wide Web: http://www.mcp.com/
Gopher: gopher.mcp.com   **FTP:** ftp.mcp.com

GOING ONLINE DECEMBER 1994!

Using
Mosaic

Mary Ann Pike

Peter Kent

Kamran Husain

Dave Kinnaman

David C. Menges

que

Using Mosaic

©1994 by Que® Corporation

Library of Congress Catalog Number: 94-68835

ISBN: 0-7897-0021-2

96 95 94   4 3 2 1

Interpretation of the printing code: The rightmost double-digit number is the year of the book's printing; the rightmost single-digit number, the number of the book's printing. For example, a printing code of 94-1 shows that the first printing of the book occurred in 1994.

Screen reproductions in this book were created with Collage Complete from Inner Media, Inc., Hollis, NH.

Publisher: David P. Ewing

Associate Publisher: Corinne Walls

Managing Editor: Michael Cunningham

Product Marketing Manager: Greg Wiegand

Associate Product Marketing Manager: Stacy Collins

Credits

Publishing Manager
Jim Minatel

Acquisitions Editor
Lori A. Angelillo

Acquisitions Coordinator
Ruth Slates

Production Editor
Linda Seifert

Copy Editors
Danielle Bird
Charles Bowles
Kelli M. Brooks
Noelle Gasco
Theresa Mathias

Editorial Assistant
Andrea Duvall

Technical Editors
Discovery Computing, Inc.
Paul McIntire
Dave Taylor

Technical Specialist
Cari Ohm

Book Designer
Paula Carroll

Cover Designer
Dan Armstrong

Production Team
Stephen Adams
Angela Bannan
Amy Cornwell
Chad Dressler
Terri Edwards
DiMonique Ford
Karen Gregor
Debra A. Kincaid
Bob LaRoche
Malinda Lowder
Steph Mineart
Victor Peterson
Kris Simmons
Donna Winter

Indexer
Charlotte Clapp

Composed in *Stone Serif* and *MCPdigital* by Que Corporation

About the Authors

Mary Ann Pike has a B.S. in electrical engineering and an M.A. in professional writing from Carnegie Mellon University. She has experience in software design and development, and is currently working as a technical writer at the Software Engineering Institute at Carnegie Mellon University.

Peter Kent is the author of *The Complete Idiot's Guide to the Internet* (Alpha Books).

Kamran Husain is an independent consultant with experience in UNIX systems programming, X Windows, Motif, Microsoft Windows and specializes in Real Time systems applications. He is a University of Texas at Austin alumni. Kamran offers training and consulting services through his company, MPS Inc., in the Houston area. He can be reached at mpsi@aol.com.

Dave Kinnaman in a systems analyst for a state agency in Austin, Texas. His work entails labor market and economic analysis to improve coordination and planning in education and training programs.

A strong believer in lifelong learning, Dave actually enjoys scholarship, and helping others to discover. His formal education includes degrees in biology, psychology, curriculum and instruction, and cognitive psychology. He is a member of the Austin Central Labor Council, (AFL-CIO), Self Help for the Hard of Hearing (SHHH), and a mass-media criticism group called the Council for Public Media.

David C. Menges is an Internet consultant in the Denver area. He joined the on-line community back in 1975, when it was based on UUCP. David gained his experience designing and maintaining LANs and WANs at Indiana University, Bell Labs, US West, and Colorado SuperNet. His current interests center around electronic storefronts.

Acknowledgments

Trademark Acknowledgments

All terms mentioned in this book that are known to be trademarks or service marks have been appropriately capitalized. Que cannot attest to the accuracy of this information. Use of a term in this book should not be regarded as affecting the validity of any trademark or service mark.

Contents at a Glance

Contents

11 Other Versions of Mosaic for Mac   219

12 Other Ways to Access the World Wide Web   231

V WWW Resources   287

13 Hot Home Pages   289

Introduction

In the past 18 to 24 months, the Internet has exploded on the computer scene as a topic of national interest. What used to be a computer network reserved for a select few scientists, government workers, and educational institutions became available to corporations—large and small—and even individual users.

If you bought, or are considering buying, *Using Mosaic*, chances are you know what the Internet is and all of the powerful capabilities it promises to bring to your computer. (You can retrieve files, search for information, exchange e-mail, keep up to date on current events, and chat with other users anywhere in the world.)

Sure, that's what your friends and neighbors tell you anyway. But as you struggle for hours, then days, and even weeks and months to understand File Transfer Protocol (FTP), Gopher, Wide Area Information Search (WAIS), and other hideous Internet creations, you begin to wonder if there is any substance to those promises. Are you disillusioned with all of the hoops you had to jump through (with a computer tied to your back!) to get anything accomplished on the Net?

Don't feel alone. You aren't the only one who is disillusioned. In fact, a group of scientists realized that the Internet just wasn't providing what they needed either. They wanted an easy-to-use system that links documents and files all over the world. They wanted a system that ate FTP and Gophers for breakfast.

So, in their spare time, they created the World Wide Web. The Web is a powerful addition to the Internet that simplifies the way users interact with the Net. Documents of many types can be linked together in a common framework; hypertext links remove the need to understand arcane UNIX commands; and graphics, movies, and sound are as easily handled as text.

By itself, this did not create much of a stir outside the scientific and computing world. However, soon after the creation of the Web, a group of researchers in Illinois created software to use the Web—Mosaic. Mosaic is powerful, easy to use, and makes the Web visual and fun.

What really grabbed the attention of a lot of computer users (over 2,000,000 in the first year) is that it's FREE!

Mosaic turns the Web, and the Internet, into something that any computer user can easily learn, be productive on, and master.

Mosaic features an easy-to-use point-and-click interface that, in Windows and on Macintosh, is familiar to users. Graphics and color make the documents come alive on-screen.

This introduction is the briefest of overviews of Mosaic and the Web. The Internet, the Web, and Mosaic are explored in more depth in the body of this book.

What This Book Is

This book is intended to provide a comprehensive reference and guide to using Mosaic. Both the Windows and Macintosh versions are covered fully.

While there are now several versions of Mosaic available (see chapters 10, "Other Versions of Mosaic for Windows," and 11, "Other Versions of Mosaic for Mac"), most of the commands and procedures in the book are essentially the same—regardless of the version you use. Chapters 10 and 11 are provided to point out any substantial differences. If you use the free version, a commercial version, Windows, or a Mac, this book has all the information you need.

Here is a brief glimpse at the contents of the book with short descriptions of each chapter:

- *Chapter 1, "What is the Internet?"* This chapter provides a brief history of the Internet and an overview of Internet services. It is assumed that you have at least some minimal exposure to the Internet—it is not a comprehensive guide to the Internet.

- *Chapter 2, "Introduction to the World Wide Web."* This chapter introduces you to the exciting world of the Web and tells you how to get more information about it. You see how computer programs, graphics, movies, netnews, and information of any kind can be transferred and found on the Web.

■ *Chapter 3, "Getting Mosaic for Windows Running."* Mosaic is the primary focus of this book, so getting the software installed properly is important. This chapter shows you how to do this for Windows.

■ *Chapter 4, "Getting Mosaic for Mac Running."* Mosaic is also a popular application on the Mac. This chapter walks you through installation on a Mac.

■ *Chapter 5, "Navigating with Mosaic."* After you have Mosaic running, you'll want to start exploring. This chapter shows you how to open documents from anywhere on the Web.

■ *Chapter 6, "Shortcuts to Favorite Places."* This chapter is one of the most useful in the book. If you want to save time on the Web, be more productive, and find resources faster, don't miss this chapter.

■ *Chapter 7, "FTP with Mosaic."* Mosaic easily integrates the anonymous FTP standard into the Web. In this chapter, you see how easy it is to find and transfer a file with Mosaic.

■ *Chapter 8, "Gopher with Mosaic."* Gopher is another old standard for finding and transferring files on the Internet. The Web includes access to all the Gopher sites in the world and this chapter makes it easy for you to use them on the Web.

■ *Chapter 9, "Using Mosaic to Access Other Internet Services."* If you are familiar with the Internet, you probably know of Telnet, Usenet, and WAIS, although you may never have used them. Usenet is one of the most popular Internet services, and Mosaic incorporates access to this as well as other Internet services.

■ *Chapter 10, "Other Versions of Mosaic for Windows."* As wildly popular as the free version of Mosaic is (over 2,000,000 copies were downloaded in less than a year), there are reasons to consider a commercial version. This chapter introduces some of these versions and gives you a quick tour of their features and how to use them.

■ *Chapter 11, "Other Versions of Mosaic for Macintosh."* While there aren't many options for Mosaic on the Mac, the free version isn't the only one out there. This chapter takes a look at what else is available.

■ *Chapter 12, "Other Ways to Access the World Wide Web."* This chapter provides you with some basic information about several other programs that access the World Wide Web.

- *Chapter 13, "Hot Home Pages."* If you want to find the most interesting, unique, or useful special sites, this chapter provides addresses and descriptions of the best of the best. (If you want to find even more sites, take a look at Que's *Using the World Wide Web*, a comprehensive listing of WWW sites arranged by category.)

- *Chapter 14, "Hot FTP and Gopher Sites."* Because Mosaic can be used to access FTP and Gopher archives, this chapter is included to help you find the most useful FTP and Gopher sites.

What This Book Is Not

This book is not an introduction to the Internet. If you go to your local bookstore, you can find dozens of such introductions. If you have no previous experience with the Internet, you really should read a book such as *Easy Internet, Using the Internet,* or *Internet Quickstart* (all from Que), *Internet Unleashed* (from SAMS Publishing), or *The Internet Starter Kit* (from Hayden Books).

If you have Mosaic, chances are you can get on the Internet, or already have been on the Internet, and are now ready to learn to use Mosaic.

Conventions Used in This Book

The conventions used in this book help you learn to use Web software quickly and easily, and help you easily locate Web resources.

The book uses several type enhancements to indicate special text. URL address of Web sites are set in **bold**. (Don't worry if you don't know what a URL is, they are explained in chapter 2, "Introduction to the World Wide Web.") Bold is also used for other electronic addresses mentioned, such as FTP sites, e-mail and others. Text that you need to type is set in special `computer type`.

Because this book covers both the Windows and Macintosh versions of Mosaic, we use a small icon in the margin (like the one beside this paragraph), to indicate procedures or features that are different in the Mac version. (Sometimes there are entire sections devoted to a Mac feature that is very different from Windows, but that isn't usually necessary.)

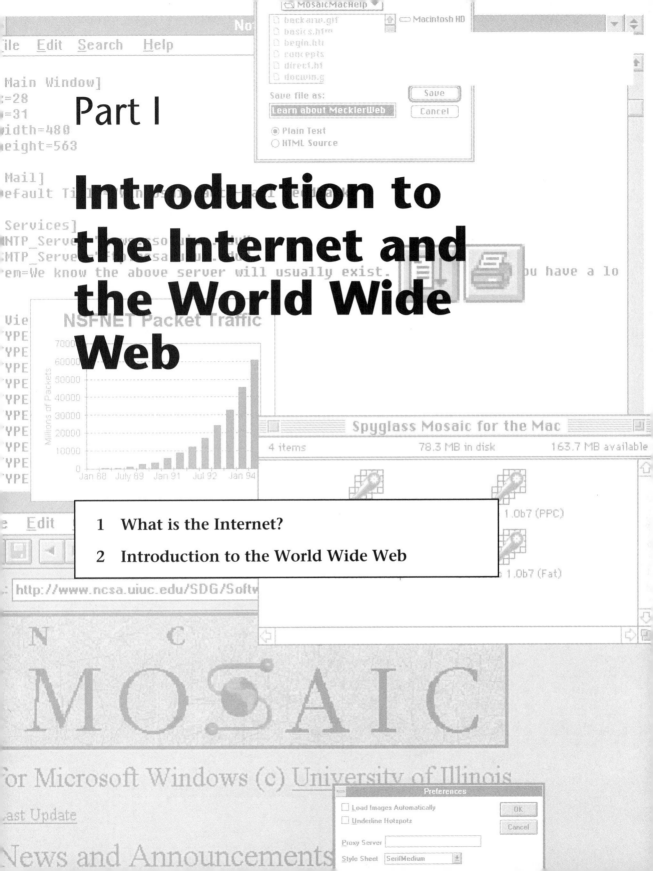

Part I

Introduction to the Internet and the World Wide Web

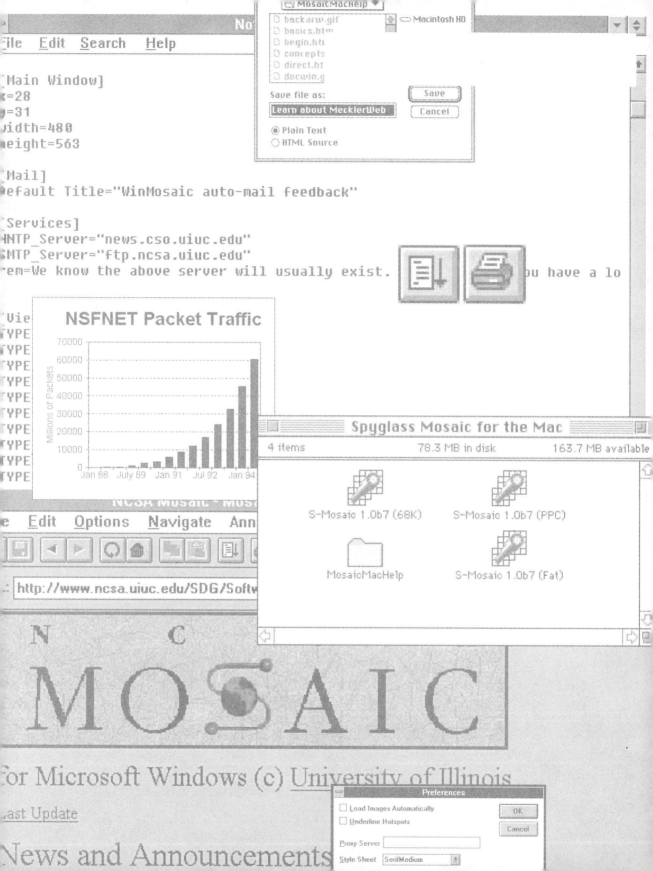

Chapter 1

What Is the Internet?

Today, the use of remote computer resources is commonplace. There are commercial on-line services, such as CompuServe and Prodigy; there are automatic teller machines that communicate with banks in other states; and there are companies with nationwide (or even worldwide) offices that transfer information between distant sites. What is common to all of these situations is that they involve accessing a *network*, communicating over long-distance lines (often phone lines) to allow remote computers and terminals to send information back and forth.

The Internet is the oldest long-distance network in the country, if not the world. Rather than limiting remote computing to terminals accessing a central computing site (as the on-line services of today do), the Internet provides a way for remote computer centers to communicate and share services and resources.

A number of different services have developed over the years to facilitate the sharing of information between the many sites on the network. Because the Internet was originally research-oriented, many of these services were hard to use and poorly documented. Now that the Internet is opening to commercial sites, new services are being developed that are easier to use. One of these new services is the *World Wide Web* (WWW), a hypermedia service provided by many Internet sites. *Mosaic* is a GUI (Graphical User Interface) application that gives you easy access to the WWW and many other Internet services. Mosaic lets you access the WWW and other Internet services by using your mouse to select items on your screen instead of having to type in text commands.

This chapter discusses the history and growth of the Internet, and some of the services that have developed over the years, including the following topics:

- A brief history of the Internet

- The culture of the Internet

- The growth of the Internet

- Internet services

A Brief History of the Internet

Almost as soon as computers were developed, the need to transfer information between machines became apparent. Initially, this was done by writing the information to an intermediate medium (such as magnetic tape or punched cards) and physically carrying that medium to the new machine.

In the early 1960s, scientists across the country began exploring ways of directly connecting remote computers and their users. In the mid- to late-60s, the United States government began to realize the impact computers would have on education and military research and development. So, the government decided to fund an experimental network that would allow remote research and development sites to exchange information. This network, funded by the U.S. Advanced Research Projects Agency, was christened the ARPANET.

The Development of the ARPANET

One of the main goals of the ARPANET research was to develop a network whose communications would not be seriously impaired if physical sections of the network were lost. Also, the network needed to allow the addition and removal of new nodes with minimal impact, and allow computers of many different types to communicate easily.

One of the major impacts of the ARPANET research, and the one that lead to today's Internet, was the development of the TCP/IP (Transmission Control Protocol/Internet Protocol) *network protocol*, the language that computers connected to the network use to talk to one another. During the 1970s, TCP/IP became the standard network protocol for the ARPANET. Also during this time, the government began encouraging the educational community to take advantage of the ARPANET. The increasing number of users led to the development of many of the services available on the Internet today, including electronic mail (e-mail), file transfer, and remote login.

The Structure of the Internet

During the early 1980s, all the interconnected research networks were converted to the TCP/IP protocol, and the ARPANET became the backbone (the physical connection between the major sites) of the new Internet, which comprised all TCP/IP-based networks connected to the ARPANET.

When the Internet first came into existence in the early 1980s, there were only 213 registered *hosts* (computers that provided services) connected to the network. By February of 1986, there were 2,308 hosts. Today, the Internet is undergoing tremendous growth, with several million hosts connected worldwide.

Internet Administration

The Internet is not "owned" by anyone, in the usual sense of the word. The backbone in the U.S. is funded by the National Science Foundation (NSF). There are regional and international segments of the network that have their own funding and administration. But, any network connected to the Internet agrees to the decisions and standards set forth by the Internet Architecture Board (and anyone who is willing to help may participate in the process of devising and setting standards). The reports of the IAB are made public through the publication of Request for Comment (RFC) documents. Some of these RFCs document Internet standards, but many of them are meant to introduce new ideas and stimulate discussion about future developments on the Internet. Past and current RFCs can be found at the sites identified in chapter 14, "Hot FTP and Gopher Sites."

The NSF Manages the Internet Backbone

In the mid-1980s, the National Science Foundation (NSF) established a number of supercomputer centers around the country. To give universities and research centers remote access to these supercomputer centers, NSF funded a backbone network (NSFNET) that connected these supercomputer centers, and also provided funding for connections to the backbone for regional networks.

In the late 1980s, NSF awarded a contract to a single organization to be responsible for maintaining and upgrading the physical network and the network administration for the NSFNET. In the early 1990s, this organization

Tip

You can learn a lot about the Internet by reading the informational RFCs (also known as FYI documents). These documents do such things as discuss the culture of the Internet, give a glossary of Internet terms, and answer commonly asked questions about the Internet.

proposed allowing the Internet to carry commercial traffic. Initially, the NSF was opposed to the conveyance of commercial traffic on what was intended as an educational and research network. An agreement was reached that required the profits from commercial traffic to be used to improve the national and regional network infrastructure.

Current Internet Management Structure

NSF is in the process of awarding new agreements to various organizations for the management of the NSFNET. The administration of this latest manifestation of the NSFNET will be substantially different from the current version.

Network Traffic Conveyance Services. The NSF envisions the new configuration of the NSFNET as a number of networks connected to a new high-speed backbone. In this arrangement, regional networks would pay connection fees to use the high-speed backbone, and commercial and educational institutions who wanted to connect to the regional networks would pay network usage fees. Rather than the NSF directly funding the network, they would instead provide funds for NSF-sponsored research projects to pay for the projects' network usage fees. The NSF's goal is to remove itself from the direct funding of the NSFNET.

Network Information Services. In April of 1993, the NSF awarded three five-year cooperative agreements for the management of the Network Information Services. The recipients of these agreements together manage the InterNIC (Internet Network Information Center). They are responsible for providing information about getting connected to and using the Internet.

Network Solutions was chosen to provide the Internet registration services, including the assignment of IP addresses and registration of domain names. AT&T was chosen to maintain lists of FTP sites, lists of various types of servers available on the Internet, lists of white and yellow page directories, library catalogs, and data archives. AT&T will also offer database design, management, and maintenance services to groups for material available to the Internet community. General Atomics was selected to provide a Network Reference Desk (providing general information about the Internet) and educational services.

The National Information Infrastructure

Because the government recognized the importance of a national information infrastructure (NII), it began to set in place the funds for the development of the high-speed, cutting-edge communications network. This network is a research project involving collaboration between government and industry, and is meant to encourage the continued expansion of network technology. By developing a stable, widely used network technology, the government hopes to encourage the commercial development of similar networking technology and services.

The development of the information infrastructure of the country could be as important to the educational climate and economy as the development of the automobile highway infrastructure was in the 1950s. Eventually, connections to the Information Superhighway should be as common as telephone connections are today. The Superhighway will provide access to retail merchants, information services (such as personalized newspapers and on-line magazines), commercial databases, public information (such as library holdings and government documents), and many other services.

Access to a common network will facilitate the concept of telecommuting (working at home, using the network to access information, have video conferences, and so on) and teleschooling (having students attend classes remotely using a two-way, live video conference, in addition to video broadcasts and on-line multimedia information and exercises). Companies are already beginning to take customer complaints and inquiries by e-mail and distribute marketing materials and product updates on-line. All financial transactions could take place on-line, with currency becoming almost unnecessary. Eventually, the Information Superhighway could completely change the structure of our society.

Some of these things are already available through commercial on-line services (such as CompuServe, Prodigy, and America Online), but the potential for information access through a common network like the Internet is almost unlimited. In addition to business and educational activities, social forums could allow interaction between millions of people around the world, allowing people to explore other cultures and exchange information about topics of common interest.

The Culture of the Internet

When researchers first began to explore the concept of a large-scale network, few envisioned the uses to which the network would be put or the eventual size of the network. The initial designers of the ARPANET imagined that it would facilitate cooperation between researchers by giving them access to easy information exchange and remote processing. Most of those initial network developers were surprised when one of the most used network services turned out to be e-mail.

Before computer networks became so widespread, researchers depended on printed materials (journals, technical reports, letters, and so on), conferences, and face-to-face meetings to exchange information about their research. Researchers were very isolated, having infrequent contact with anyone but their close colleagues. Researchers in different parts of the country could be pursuing the same goal, with no way of knowing that their efforts were being duplicated, or sharing the information that might have allowed them to collaborate or compare results.

One of the main goals of the ARPANET was to allow researchers to exchange information in a much more timely and convenient manner. Through the file exchange facilities, reports and data could be easily transferred from one researcher to another within a matter of hours, if not minutes. Programs that were developed at one site could be shared with others who were doing similar work. The resources of a powerful computer could be made available to labs that were too small to be able to afford to purchase such a machine for themselves.

All of this has become a reality on the Internet. But the Internet has become something much more than this.

The Community Expands

Back in the early days of the ARPANET (even as late as 1981), the Internet community was so small that people literally knew almost everyone on the network. Most of the sites were either government or university research centers. If a researcher received a request for information from a colleague at another site, he or she generally would know the colleague (or know of him), and would be able to spend a few hours (or more) of his/her time answering the request.

With the growth of the Internet, this type of personal response has become more difficult. It can be compared with a small town suddenly acquiring a large industry and expanding to 25 times its original size. People in the small town all used to know each other and be on speaking terms with most of their neighbors. Their children went to the same schools and grew up together. In the big city, people keep their houses shut and only come out to drive to work or for other necessities. They don't have time to know their neighbors, except perhaps for one or two with whom they have something in common.

The Internet has become like this, in a way. There are so many people on the Internet now that it is difficult to know even the people in your own organization (if it is large), let alone others on the network. Perhaps people know a few dozen others who participate in a discussion newsgroup, or other researchers they have met at conferences or whose papers they have read in journals.

Even though this smallness has been lost, there is still a community of sorts on the Internet. Right now, access to the Internet is still relatively restricted. Compared to the hundreds of millions of people in the United States, the approximately 10 million or so that have Internet access is still a small number. Most use the Internet for its intended purpose: to exchange information or use remote computer resources unavailable to them locally. Usually this is done in a friendly and honest manner.

Cultural Pitfalls

One interesting thing about communicating over the Internet is that it removes many preconceived notions that you form about people when you meet them in person. When you communicate with individuals over the network, you don't know (unless they tell you) their age, race, height, weight, or even their gender sometimes. You don't know if they're the president of a company, or a high-school student. The only thing by which you have to judge them is their words.

For this reason, it's very important to choose carefully the words you use in your Internet communications. The Internet, for the most part, is a friendly, open community. Because there is little chance of any real retribution, some people make vicious attacks on others. These people quickly lose credibility in the community, though, and may find themselves in trouble if they do need to have dealings with someone they insulted or someone who was unimpressed by their abuse. Even though this is one of the few drawbacks of the Internet community, it is one that has grown as the number of users on the Internet has grown.

The Internet community has features that physical communities have, but on a much larger scale. Two people from different parts of the country may strike up a friendship that eventually leads to a romantic relationship, or even marriage. There are on-line, real-time conferences using services such as the Internet Relay Chat, that allow many people to converse in real-time about subjects they have in common. There are all types of people on the Internet: shy people, aggressive people, friendly people, and even abusive people. It is truly representative of society in general.

The Growth of the Internet

The growth of the Internet has been absolutely phenomenal, particularly over the last five years. The number of machines connected and amount of traffic carried has grown tremendously, and the type of organizations connected has changed.

Traffic Growth

The number of data packets that flowed through the NSFNET went from 152 million in July of 1988 to 60,587 million packets in July of 1994 (see fig. 1.1).

Fig. 1.1

Growth of NSFNET Packet Traffic from July 88 to July 94.

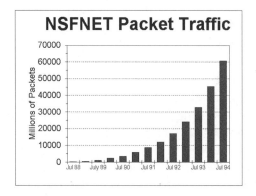

The byte traffic increased from 1,594 billion bytes of data in July of 1991 to around 12,764 billion bytes of data in July of 1994 (see fig. 1.2).

Fig 1.2

Growth of NSFNET Byte Traffic from July 91 through July 94.

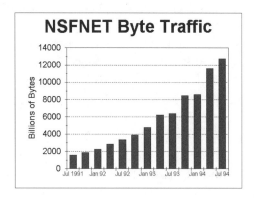

Approximately 35 percent of the network traffic involves file exchange (FTP activity). Approximately 15 percent involves e-mail and Usenet traffic, although this has dropped considerably from a high of almost 30 percent four years ago. The interactive traffic (including Telnet) has remained almost constant, averaging about six percent of the traffic. Gopher traffic runs about four percent of the total, and the WWW traffic is at six percent and growing rapidly.

Host Growth

The number of hosts on the Internet has grown from 235 in May of 1982 to approximately 3.2 million hosts in July of 1994 (see fig. 1.3). The edu domain, which is for educational and research organizations, has the most hosts (about 850,000). The commercial domain now has almost as many hosts (about 775,000). (Domains are groupings of addresses explained later in this chapter in the section "What is a Host Name?")

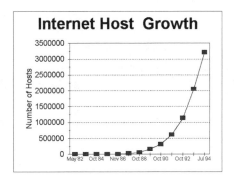

Fig. 1.3
Internet Host Growth from May of 82 to July of 94.

Internet Services

A number of different Internet services exist, and many of them can be accessed through Mosaic. This section familiarizes you with the common Internet services, and discusses host names and addresses (which you need to understand to use the services).

Internet Addresses

Internet *addresses* are the key to using the Internet. You use *mail addresses* to send messages to other Internet users, and you use *host addresses* (or *host names*) to retrieve files and connect to hosts that provide Internet services. This section discusses what makes up an Internet address.

What Is a Host Name?

All Internet sites are identified by a unique domain name (such as "bigcorp.com"). The *domain name* is made up of several pieces that identify the organization and the domain hierarchy to which it belongs. A host name contains the domain name in addition to a name identifying the particular host and any subdomain it may be associated with at its Internet site. This section describes the various parts of a host name.

Host names are found in e-mail addresses and also are used when connecting to Internet hosts to use Internet services (such as WWW) or retrieve files. A host name is made up of several words separated by periods. You can examine these words to find out information about the host. The host name **bigmachine.bigcorp.com** is used here to illustrate the parts of a host name. The rightmost word, for example, specifies the *domain* of the machine. In this case, the word **com** means that the machine belongs to a commercial entity—a company of some kind. Some other domains are **edu** for educational institutions, **mil** for military sites, and **gov** for sites that are part of the government. Also, each country that is connected to the Internet has a domain assigned to it; for example **fr** is the domain name for France.

> **Note**
>
> You can find a listing of country codes in several files on the Internet. These files can be retrieved by anonymous FTP or Gopher (these services are discussed later in this chapter). Two of the files you can look at for this information can be found at the address **nic.merit.edu** in the directory internet/connectivity. The files in this directory are nets.by.country and world.list.txt.

Working to the left in the host name, you come to the word **bigcorp**. This part of the host name defines the institution that owns the machine. When an institution connects to the Internet, they must register the name of their organization with the Internet registration services. In this case, the name **bigcorp.com** has been registered to a fictitious company called Big Corporation (this name can be used only for machines connected to Big Corporation's network). Examples of real-life institution names (including the domain name) are **ibm.com** for International Business Machines, **mit.edu** for the Massachusetts Institute of Technology, and **nasa.gov** for the National Aeronautics and Space Administration.

Any words to the left of the institution name are assigned within the institution. Small organizations usually have only a single word (specifying the name of an individual machine at the organization) to the left of the institution name. Sometimes, the host name for large organizations has more words, which usually designate departments within the organization. For example, you may see a name such as **amachine.cs.mit.edu**, which indicates that the machine **amachine** is in the **cs** (probably Computer Science) department at MIT, an educational institution. With host names, the leftmost word is always the name of a machine.

What Is an IP Address?

Host names are used to access individual hosts on the Internet. The host name is really just a convenient way for people to refer to hosts. The host name represents the IP address (or host address) of the host, which is the address that Internet software needs to get information to or from the host. The *IP address* is a unique number assigned to identify a host on the Internet. This address is usually represented as four numbers between 1 and 254 separated by periods, for example, 192.58.107.230.

Most software translates automatically between the host name and the IP address so that you don't have to remember which numbers represent which machine.

File Transfers—Downloading with FTP

One of the first Internet services developed allowed users to move files from one place to another—the *file transfer protocol* (*FTP*) service. This service is designed to allow you to connect to a computer on the Internet (using an FTP program on your local machine), browse through the programs that are available on the computer, and retrieve files.

▶ See "FTP with Mosaic," p. 133

What Are Anonymous FTP Servers?

The FTP service is an example of a *client-server system*. In this kind of system, you use a program on your local computer (called a *client*) to talk to a program on a remote computer (called a *server*). In the case of FTP, the server on the remote computer is designed to let you download and upload files, but many other services are also available on the Internet. Some of these, such as Gopher and Archie, are discussed in the section "Archie, Gopher, and Other Information Retrieval Systems" later in this chapter.

To connect to a computer system using an FTP program, the system must be running an FTP server. This server must be set up by the administrators of the machine, and the administrators decide which files and information are made available on the FTP server.

Tip

It is common courtesy on the Internet to use your e-mail address as the password when logging in at an anonymous FTP site. Many FTP sites request you to do this when you connect to the site.

Tip

When you use Mosaic to access anonymous FTP sites, you do not actually need to log in to the site—Mosaic does it for you.

One common type of FTP server is an *anonymous* FTP server. This server allows you to connect and download files without having an account on the machine. If an FTP server is not anonymous, when you connect to the server you have to provide a user name and password, just as if you were logging into the machine. On an anonymous FTP server, you use the special user name "anonymous" when you connect. This "anonymous" user name lets you log in by providing any password you want.

Anonymous FTP servers are one of the major means of distributing software and information across the Internet. There is a large amount of software available on anonymous FTP servers, and this software is often provided free of charge. Software is available for many different types of computer systems, such as UNIX, IBM PC, and Macintosh systems.

Locating Files at FTP Sites

One of the most frustrating problems with the Internet is the difficulty of finding information such as FTP sites, host resources, sources of information, and so on. Imagine that you went into your local public library and found that rather than the books being arranged on shelves according to a book classification scheme, the books were simply in piles all over the floor. Rather than a central card catalog, there were notes placed on some of the piles stating what people had found in that pile. Well, this is how the Internet has been for most of its existence; there are many resources, but no way to easily locate them.

Most FTP sites do not have a listing of all of their available files. Sometimes, the only way to locate a file or find interesting files is to click on the folders to show the contents of the directories, and look through them.

Because the format of the file and directory names depends on the machine that is being used as the FTP server, what you see depends on the type of system to which you connect. If the server is running on a UNIX system, for example, the file names will appear with any combination of uppercase or lowercase letters, and can be of any length.

If, on the other hand, the system you connect to is a VMS system (from Digital Equipment Corporation), the file names will be only uppercase. Other systems, such as PCs and Macintoshes, display files and directory names in their standard formats.

On some machines (especially the very large archive sites), the site maintainers keep an index of available files with brief descriptions of what the files contain. This is very useful, and makes finding useful files much easier. When you enter a directory, you should look for a file called INDEX (either in uppercase or lowercase). You should also look for a file called README (or perhaps readme, or read.me). These README files are generally descriptions of the contents of the directories, or information about the server system. You should always download the README files and read the contents—the files are put there for a reason.

If you have a question about an FTP server, or about the contents of the files there, you should send an e-mail message to the "postmaster" of the FTP machine. For example, if you connected to the machine **rs.internic.net**, you should send e-mail to the address **postmaster@rs.internic.net**. Some FTP servers have a different person to contact; in this case, the name of the contact person is displayed when you connect to the machine, or is in a README file in the first directory you see when you connect.

Locating Files Using Archie

Information retrieval systems are being explored as a way to locate information resources on the Internet. Even though a complete central list of all the resources on the Internet does not exist, the various information retrieval systems go a long way towards making a resource easy to find.

Archie was the first of the information retrieval systems developed on the Internet. The purpose of Archie is simple—to create a central index of files that are available on anonymous FTP sites around the Internet. To do this, the Archie servers periodically connect to anonymous FTP sites that agree to participate and download lists of all the files that are on these sites. These lists of files are merged into a database, which then can be searched by users.

To use Archie, you have to use the Mosaic Telnet protocol to connect to one of the Archie machines and search the database there. See chapter 9, "Using Mosaic to Access Other Internet Services," for more information on how to use Archie through Telnet.

When you have connected to one of the Archie database machines, you can search the database for a program or file. Because the database only knows the names of the files, you must know at least part of the file name for which you are looking. For example, if you are looking for a program that will compress files (make them smaller), you would search the database for the word "compress." The Archie program will return the location of all the files that are named "compress."

Now, this search only returned those files exactly named "compress," so it wouldn't return the location of a file named "uncompress" (which undoes the work of the compress program). Archie, though, lets you search for a string of characters that is anywhere in the file name. If you tell the Archie program that you want to do a "substring" search, it looks for files that have your search string anywhere in the file name. Similarly, you can tell the Archie program to match the file name even if it has different capitalization than your search string.

The Archie server provides the machine name and location of the files that match the string for which you are searching. This allows you to use the FTP program to connect to the machine and download the file to your local machine. The main limitation of Archie is that you have to know at least something about the name of the file to search for it; if you don't have any idea what the file is called (for example, you want a program that searches for viruses on your machine and don't know that it is called scanv), you may have to try several searches using different strings before you find something that looks useful.

Another limitation of Archie is that not all sites on the Internet that have anonymous FTP participate in the Archie database. There may be a file that fits your specifications at a non-participating site, but Archie will not be able to find it because it is not in the database. Despite these limitations, however, Archie is a very useful tool for locating files to download through FTP.

Retrieving Information Using Gopher

▶ See "Gopher with Mosaic," p. 147

Gopher is another information distribution service within the Internet. Sites on the Internet that want to distribute information through the Gopher system set up and run Gopher servers that allow people with Gopher clients to display and download files and directories.

The functionality of Gopher is very similar to FTP, but the Gopher can connect you to other Internet services in addition to displaying and retrieving directories and files. Displaying or downloading a file is as easy as selecting an item from a menu. This ease of use, plus the ability to put descriptive titles on the menu items, makes Gopher a much easier method of browsing files than simply using FTP.

One of the big advantages of the Gopher system is that you can include menu items on a server that, when selected, move the user to other servers on other machines on the Internet. For example, one menu item on machine A's Gopher server may say "Connect to Machine B Gopher." When that menu item is selected, your Gopher client connects to machine B's Gopher server, just as if you had connected to it when you ran the Gopher client.

What is Gopherspace?

This ability to link Gopher sites together makes it very easy to examine the files available at one site then move to other interesting Gopher sites. All Gopher servers are interconnected at some point—this network of Gopher servers is known as Gopherspace. When a new Gopher site becomes available on the Internet, the administrators send a mail message to the maintainers of the Gopher software (at the University of Minnesota) to have their site included in the master list of all Gopher sites worldwide. Many organizations run Gopher servers; universities and colleges, companies, and government agencies all have information available through Gopher.

The Gopher maintainers run a Gopher site (located at the address **boombox.micro.umn.edu**) that lists all the known Gopher sites and lets you connect to them. This gives you a very good starting place to browse through all the Gopher sites and discover the wealth of information available on the Internet. Even though there are many interesting Gopher sites listed in chapter 14, "Hot FTP and Gopher Sites," the main Gopher site at **boombox.micro.umn.edu** is always the best place to begin exploring the information on Gopher.

Locating Files Using Veronica

With all the Gopher sites available, though, it may be hard to locate a site that carries the information and files you want. You probably want to search the Gopher sites for a document you want. A service, called Veronica, is available to do this.

Just as Archie is a service that allows you to search file names and directories on anonymous FTP servers, Veronica allows you to search menu items on Gopher servers. To use Veronica, you have to be connected to a Gopher server that gives you access to a Veronica server. The Veronica database is built by scanning the Gopher menus on servers around the world, and can be searched by selecting "Search Gopherspace using Veronica," which is found on the Gopher site **gopher.tc.umn.edu**.

Locating Documents Using WAIS

Whereas Gopher is a good system to use for exploring the files and systems available on the Internet, suppose you want to find all documents available on a particular subject? The WAIS (Wide Area Information Server) is a system that allows you to search for your subject through documents on servers all over the world. WAIS allows you to search a set of databases that have been indexed with keywords, and returns addresses where you can locate documents that would be of interest to you.

▶ See "Using WAIS to Search for Information," p. 173

Intro to Internet & WWW

The heart of the WAIS (pronounced "ways") system is the use of client software running on your local computer that lets you ask for information in a simple, English-like language. The client takes your question and sends it off to the WAIS server you select. The server takes your question and searches all the documents it knows about for the information you want. If it finds documents that match your question, it returns indexes to these documents, which you can then use to download the documents and display them on your local system.

One of the key features of the WAIS system is the ability of a WAIS server to have indexes which actually point to other WAIS servers. A central site on the Internet maintains indexes to all known WAIS servers on the Internet; you can use this central site as a starting point for your searches. For example, let's say you want to find out all the times that President Clinton mentioned the city of Atlanta, Georgia.

You can set your search database to be "directory-of-servers," which is located on the machine **quake.think.com**. As a quick example of how WAIS works, using this database, you search for "president clinton," and it returns (among others) a database resource marked "clinton-speeches." You now can use this database to search for "atlanta georgia." This search returns some number of documents, and the first ones are the ones that best match your question. These speeches, when retrieved, are the ones which mention Atlanta, Georgia.

Connecting to Host Resources Using Telnet

▶ See "Using the Telnet Protocol from Mosaic," p. 165

Just as a computer system can run an FTP server to allow you to transfer files, a computer on the Internet can run other servers to let you do other things when you connect. There is a wide variety of these services (also called *host resources*) on the Internet, and they provide everything from information about agriculture to space research. Some of these host resources are similar to bulletin board systems, which you may be familiar with. But instead of dialing into one of these systems using a telephone line and modem, you can connect to these systems over the Internet using a program called Telnet.

Telnet is a method used to connect two computers together; it provides a terminal connection to the remote machine. This connection allows you to type commands to the remote machine, just as if you had a terminal hooked right into it. You are probably already familiar with the idea of a terminal program; if you have a modem connected to a personal computer that you use to dial into computer systems, you use a terminal program to talk to the modem and remote system.

Just as you use a local FTP program to connect to an FTP server on another machine on the Internet, you use a Telnet program on your local machine to talk to the Telnet server on another machine anywhere on the Internet. The main difference between FTP and Telnet is that when you connect to the remote machine with FTP, the FTP server only lets you do things connected with transferring files. When you connect to a machine using Telnet, what you see really depends on what the host resource provides. You may see a bulletin board menu system, or a simple command line interface, or you may just receive some output without typing anything. It all depends on what the resource expects.

World Wide Web (WWW)

The World Wide Web (WWW) is one of the newest Internet services. In the late 1980s, CERN (the European Laboratory for Particle Physics) began experimenting with a service that would allow anyone to easily access and display documents that were stored anywhere on the Internet. To do this, they developed a standard format for the documents that allowed them to be easily displayed by any type of display device, and allowed links to other documents to be placed in documents.

▶ See "Introduction to the World Wide Web," p. 31

Although the WWW service was initially developed for the CERN researchers to use, after the service was made public it became tremendously popular. A number of different client applications (the ones that actually display the documents on-screen) were developed to read WWW documents. One of the most popular of these clients is Mosaic, the topic of this book. Not only does Mosaic provide quick graphical access to WWW documents, but it also lets you use the same GUI to interface to other Internet services.

The remaining chapters in this book tell you how to install and use Mosaic, and where to find some interesting collections of WWW documents.

Electronic Mail (E-Mail)

E-mail was one of the first Internet services developed. Although the original intent of having a network connecting physically remote sites was to allow the exchange of files and remote use of computing resources, the designers of the network discovered that one of the most popular services involved personal communications (e-mail). Today, e-mail is an important service on any computer network, not just the Internet.

E-mail involves sending a message from one computer account to another. There are many different e-mail standards, which can make it difficult to write an application that has a general e-mail interface. At this time, Mosaic does not support an e-mail protocol, although it may at some time in the future. (A few other WWW clients—mostly UNIX based—currently support an e-mail protocol.)

Internet Relay Chat (IRC)

Internet Relay Chat is a service that was developed in the late 1980s, originally as a replacement for the UNIX talk program. IRC allows multiple people to "talk" simultaneously (by typing, of course) about a particular topic. Like many other Internet services, IRC is a client/server application. People who want to talk together must be running an IRC client, and they must connect to an IRC server. After they are on the server, they select the *channel* on which they want to talk (channels often are named for the topic they discuss, if they restrict themselves to a particular topic).

At this time, Mosaic does not directly support the IRC protocol. To learn more about IRC, use FTP or Gopher to retrieve the IRC Primer, a basic IRC user's manual. It is available in plain text, PostScript, and LaTeX from **cs-ftp.bu.edu:/irc/support**. There are also IRC tutorials avaliable via anonymous FTP from **cs-ftp.bu.edu:/irc/support/tutorial**. For answers to a number of questions about IRC, read the FAQ, available for FTP from either of the following two sites: **cs-ftp.bu.edu:/irc/support/alt-irc-faq** or **ftp.kei.com:/pub/irc/alt-irc-faq**.

Internet News Groups (Usenet)

▶ See "Using Mosaic to Access Usenet News Groups," p. 169

Internet *newsgroups* are on-line discussions (via posted messages) on thousands of different topics. In addition to the mechanics of reading and posting to newsgroups, you should be aware of some of the social aspects of participating in newsgroup discussions.

What Is Usenet?

Usenet (which is short for users' network) is made up of all the machines that receive network newsgroups, which are computer discussion groups or forums. The network news (commonly referred to as *netnews*) is the mechanism that sends the individual messages (called *articles*) from your local computer to all the computers that participate in Usenet.

While you don't have to understand the exact details of how Usenet works, a broad outline will help you to understand what makes Usenet a very powerful means for reaching lots of people. The basic idea with Usenet is that when you post an article on your local computer, the article is stored on your computers' disk, and then the article is sent to other computers that have agreed to exchange netnews articles with your computer. These machines, in turn, send your article to other machines, who send it to others; this continues until your article has reached every computer that participates in Usenet. Because each machine can send articles to many other machines, your article can reach the majority of Usenet computers in a few hours.

A news article is very similar to an e-mail message. It has some information at the top of the article in the *header* lines and the content of the article in the *message body*. Just as in an e-mail message, the header lines give information to the netnews software that allows it to put the article in the right news-group or groups (an article can appear in more than one group at the same time—this is called *cross-posting* the article) and to identify the sender of the article.

The message body of the article contains the information that the sender of the article wrote. In many cases, the article ends with a *signature*; this is often a witty comment or some information about the author. Many news readers allow you to set up a file that contains your signature; the contents of this file are automatically tacked onto the end of each article you post. See the section, "Usenet Etiquette," later in this chapter for more information about these signature files.

To give you a better idea of what a netnews article looks like, see the example article in figure 1.4. In this example, the first line (starting with the word `Newsgroups:`) indicates which newsgroup the article is posted in. The line starting with `From:` gives the author of the article, while the line starting with `Subject:` gives the topic of the article. The rest of the header lines (everything up to and including the line `Lines:`) give additional information about the article. The message body is after the first blank line. Everything after the line of dashes is the users' signature.

```
Newsgroups: comp.sys.mac.hardware
Path: bigcorp.com!tgp
From: tgp@bigcorp.com (Tod Pike)
Subject: Re: recent prices
Message-ID: <1993Nov30.134422.4009@bigcorp.com>
Sender: netnews@bigcorp.com (Netnews)
Date: Tue, 30 Nov 1993 13:44:22 EST
Lines: 10
Recent prices should be posted to this news group soon - keep
an eye out!
            Tod Pike
-----------------------------------------------------------------
To reach me send mail to tgp@bigcorp.com
Disclaimer: I don't speak for the boss!
```

Fig. 1.4
An example
Usenet article.

Newsgroups and Topics

The information carried by Usenet is divided into *newsgroups*, which are areas of discussion that can be compared to bulletin boards (the cork kind) with messages tacked all over them. Each newsgroup is devoted to a particular topic, although the discussion in these groups can be far-reaching. There is a newsgroup for almost every topic you can imagine—many large Usenet sites carry well over 5,000 newsgroups!

To get an idea of how discussion happens in newsgroups, you might think of Usenet as a large building, and each newsgroup is a room in that building. Each room has a name on the door, and a brief description of the topic of discussion in that room. In some of these rooms, you can find a small number of people politely discussing a serious topic. You can come in, ask a question, and join in the discussion.

In other rooms, you may find a loud, raucous group of people discussing a heated topic. Each person is shouting out his or her opinion loudly, with little regard for the shouting from the people around them. You try to enter the conversation, but you either find that your opinions are ignored or you are insulted. Both of these conditions happen everyday (sometimes in the same newsgroup at different times!) on Usenet.

How Newsgroups Are Organized

Newsgroups are named in a *hierarchical* manner. The name of a newsgroup is made up of several words separated by periods. In the name, the words on the left side of the name are the most general—they specify the hierarchy that the newsgroup belongs in. As you move along the name to the right, the words become more and more specific about the topics that are discussed in the group. For example, a valid newsgroup name is **comp.sys.mac.hardware**. The first word, "comp," gives the hierarchy; groups under "comp" are for discussions about computers. The next word, "sys," indicates that we are talking about computer systems, as opposed to languages or editors. The next word, "mac," tells us that we are talking about Macintosh computer systems. The final word, "hardware," lets us know that the group talks about hardware issues relating to Macintosh computer systems.

The left-most word in the group name defines the so-called *top level hierarchies*. In the current scheme of Usenet, there are seven top level hierarchies. These hierarchies are listed in table 1.1, with a description of the topics included in them.

Table 1.1 Major Usenet Newsgroup Hierarchies	
Name	**Description**
comp	Computer related topics
rec	Recreational topics
sci	Related to sciences
soc	Social issues
news	Topics of interest to people who run Usenet sites
talk	Conversational topics, often controversial
misc	Miscellaneous topics, not covered elsewhere

In addition to these hierarchies, there are a few other hierarchies. Most of these were created in response to a specific need or to discuss a topic that is of limited interest. The system that you use to read netnews may not have any of these, but most of the major Internet service providers carry these hierarchies. Some of these alternative hierarchies are listed in table 1.2.

Table 1.2 Other Usenet Newsgroup Hierarchies	
Name	**Description**
alt	A hierarchy with relaxed rules for creation of groups
vmsnet	Devoted to Systems running the VMS operating system from Digital Equipment Corporation
bionet	Devoted to biological sciences
k12	Devoted to education in grades kindergarten through 12

The Culture of Usenet

Because Usenet reaches a large number of people (current estimates are that more than a million people read netnews), you should be prepared for somewhat of a culture shock when you begin reading netnews. Usenet reaches people in all 50 states and in many countries around the world. Quite a few of the people reading netnews don't speak English as a native language; certainly many will have a different cultural background than you. So an article you post may seem reasonable and understandable to you, but others may completely misunderstand it. This section tries to give you an idea of the culture of Usenet and what to expect when you read and post news articles.

Going back to the analogy of a newsgroup as a room with people in it, you can imagine stepping into a group of people and trying to understand their culture. You probably spend a few minutes listening to the conversation and trying to understand the basic rules of the group—how the people interact, what information has been covered before you joined, and how you should enter into the conversation.

In a similar way, when you decide to read a newsgroup, reading the group for a while—a few weeks, if you can—is a good idea before you post an article to the group. In this way, you can determine the tone and character of the group, what topics have been discussed recently (topics that probably won't be welcome if brought up again), and what topics are now being discussed. You might want to try to discover who the "regulars" in the group are—those people who post regularly and are generally respected by the people in the group. In some cases, sending an e-mail message to one of these regular post-ers to ask about the culture of the group is a good idea; a person who has been participating in a group for a while can give you a good history of the group and some pointers on working effectively with the people in the group.

Many groups maintain a list of frequently asked questions (called a *FAQ*, pronounced "fak"), which is posted periodically for the newsgroup (generally once a month). You might want to read a newsgroup long enough to see the FAQ and look through it before you make your first post, or you can send e-mail to one of the regular posters asking if they know if there is a FAQ and how to get a copy of it. This way, you may have some of your questions an-swered without having to waste network resources on information that is already available. The FAQ may also give you ideas of what topics would be good ones to discuss in the newsgroup.

As a general rule, newsgroups in the comp and sci hierarchies tend to be ori-ented toward "serious" topics; emphasis is more likely to be placed on dis-cussing facts rather than opinions, and the group participants are likely to be tolerant of new posters. On the other hand, groups in the soc, rec, and news hierarchies tend to be oriented toward people's opinions on topics and are more likely to be argumentative. People often listen to the opinions of a new-comer, but be prepared to receive other people's opinions in turn.

Finally, groups in the talk and misc hierarchies definitely lean toward being argumentative. Many groups are devoted to discussing topics that generate strong opinions, and you should be ready to defend your position if you post to one of these groups. Remember, politeness and accuracy will gain you more respect than responding in kind to other people's attacks.

Usenet Etiquette

One important thing to remember when communicating via Usenet is that the only thing other people see from you are the words you type. If you are trying to be witty or sarcastic, the reader of your words can't see the expressions on your face or hear the tone of your voice. Remembering this fact, and accurately expressing your feelings when writing, can avoid many misunderstandings.

> **Note**
>
> The etiquette of communicating in Usenet newsgroups is discussed here to give you an idea of how to interpret what you read. At this time, you cannot post to newsgroups using Mosaic. Of course, if you have some other news reading/posting mechanism at your site, you can use that to post and these etiquette comments apply to those posts as well.

You can use a number of common ways to express emotions in your articles. You can emphasize what you are saying by typing in uppercase—for example, THAT IS NOT TRUE! This is considered "shouting," so you shouldn't use uppercase in a normal post. You also can provide emphasis by using asterisks around your text, such as *do this step first*. You also can express emotions by using small text symbols called *emoticons*. The most basic of these is the *smiley*, typed by using **:-)**. (If you turn your head sideways, you see that :-) is a smiling face.) The smiley is used to indicate humor or sarcasm. Many variations of smileys exist, and you will certainly run into them when reading news.

When you compose your article, make sure that your post is worded carefully to avoid misunderstandings. Make sure that your intent is clear; remember that some of the people reading your post may not be native speakers of English. If you use slang or local expressions, people outside your community (or country) might not understand you.

When you read an article, it's a good idea to read the entire article before responding to it. Reading a few other peoples' replies before responding is also a good idea; other people may have made the same point you want to make, and you should avoid duplicating what other people have said. In any case, if you read an article that makes you want to respond angrily, it's a good idea to wait a few hours before replying, so that you can calm down first.

Some news readers allow you to quote text from the article to which you are responding. You may want to quote only the parts of the original text that are pertinent to your response for clarity, and delete the rest of the material to avoid wasting network resources. Also, if a person is requesting information that might not be of general interest to the group, you should respond with e-mail to the author of the post, if possible, rather than posting your reply to the entire newsgroup.

Another thing to keep in mind when posting is that the way you format the article can make it easier to read. These are some of the guidelines you might want to follow:

- Try to keep the Subject: line of your article relatively short, but informative.

- Don't use anything but text characters. Control characters do odd things to different types of displays.

- Keep your line lengths under 80 characters, which is the maximum line length of some displays, and put a return at the end of each line.

- Break up your text into medium size paragraphs with blank lines between them. This is much easier to read than long, solid blocks of text.

One of the best ways to avoid problems when posting to Usenet is to remember that many people read news; someone you know, such as your boss, friend, or future spouse, quite possibly may read something you post. A good rule of thumb is never post something that you wouldn't want your mother to read!

From Here...

To learn more about using the WWW and Mosaic, refer to these chapters:

- Chapter 2, "Introduction to the World Wide Web," gives you background information about the WWW.

- Chapter 3, "Getting Mosaic for Windows Running," tells you how to set up Mosaic for Windows.

- Chapter 4, "Getting Mosaic for Mac Running," tells you how to set up Mosaic on your Macintosh.

- Chapter 5, "Navigating with Mosaic," tells you how to use Mosaic to find and view documents on the WWW.

Chapter 2

Introduction to the World Wide Web (WWW)

The World Wide Web (WWW or W3) is one of the newest Internet services. It allows you to explore Internet sites that have set up WWW servers to give access to hypermedia documents provided at those sites. Not only does it provide quick graphical access to hypermedia documents, but it also allows you to use the same GUI to interface to other Internet services.

In this chapter, you learn the following:

■ History of the WWW

■ Important WWW concepts

■ How to access the WWW

History of the WWW

The history of the WWW is fairly short. In 1989, some researchers at CERN (the European Laboratory for Particle Physics) wanted to develop a better way to give widely dispersed research groups access to shared information. Because research was conducted between distant sites, performing any simple activity (reading a document or viewing an image) often required first finding the location of the desired item, making a remote connection to the machine where it resided, then retrieving it to a local machine. Each activity required running a number of different applications (such as Telnet, FTP, and an image viewer). What the researchers wanted was a system that would allow them quick access to all types of information with a common interface, removing the need to execute many steps to achieve the final goal.

Over the course of a year, the proposal for this project was refined, and work began on the implementation. By the end of 1990, the researchers at CERN had a text-mode (non-graphical) browser and a graphical browser for the NeXT computer. During 1991, the WWW was released for general usage at CERN. Initially, access was restricted to hypertext and Usenet news articles. As the project advanced, interfaces to other Internet services were added (WAIS, anonymous FTP, Telnet, and Gopher).

During 1992, CERN began publicizing the WWW project. People saw what a great idea this was, and began creating their own WWW servers to make their information available to the Internet. A few people also began working on WWW clients, designing easy-to-use interfaces to the WWW. By the end of 1993, browsers had been developed for many different computer systems, including X Windows, Apple Macintosh, and PC/Windows. By the summer of 1994, WWW had become one of the most popular ways to access Internet resources.

Important WWW Concepts

Like the word "Internet," which seems to imply a well-defined entity (which, of course, it isn't), "World Wide Web" seems to imply a fixed (or at least defined) set of sites that you can go to for information. In reality, the WWW is constantly changing as Internet sites add or delete access to information. Learning about some of the basic concepts of the WWW will help you to understand the nature of the Web.

Browsers

To access the WWW, it is necessary that you run a WWW *browser* on your computer. A browser is an application that knows how to interpret and display documents that it finds on the WWW. Documents on the WWW are *hypertext* documents (see the next section, "Hypertext (and Hypermedia)" for more information about hypertext). Hypertext documents are not plain text. They contain commands that structure the text by item (different headings, body paragraphs, and so on). This allows your browser to format each text type to best display it on-screen.

For example, if you connect to the Internet using a simple VT-100 compatible terminal, you have to run a text-based WWW browser like Lynx. This browser would format any documents that you receive so that they can be displayed in the fonts available on a terminal, and would let you move between keywords in the document using the arrow keys.

If you have a more sophisticated terminal like an X terminal, you can use a graphics-based browser like the X version of Mosaic. If you are running on a PC or Macintosh, you can use the PC or Macintosh version of the Mosaic browser, or one of the other WWW browsers that have been developed for these computers. These browsers are GUI applications that take advantage of the graphic abilities of these terminals and computers, allowing you to use different sizes, fonts, and formatting for different text types.

In addition to displaying nicely formatted text, browsers can also give you the ability to access documents that contain other media besides text. For example, if you have a sound card in your PC, or a *driver* (a program that controls a piece of hardware) for your PC speaker, you can hear sound clips that are included in WWW documents. Some other media that can be accessed in WWW documents are still pictures and animations. The section "Multimedia Viewers" in chapter 3 discusses drivers that you can install on your PC to access other media.

Not only can you access different media in WWW documents, but some browsers can be set up so that appropriate applications will be started to display a document of a particular type. For example, if a WWW document contains a reference to a document that is in Microsoft Word for Windows format, you can set up your browser so that it automatically starts up Word for Windows to display that document when it is retrieved.

Some browsers also give you access to other Internet services. With Mosaic, for example, you can access anonymous FTP servers, Gopher servers, WAIS servers, and Usenet news servers. You also can do remote logins using the Telnet protocol. Using these Internet services from Mosaic is discussed in more detail in Part III, "Advanced Mosaic Features."

Hypertext (and Hypermedia)

When you use the WWW, the documents that you find will be *hypertext* documents. Hypertext is text that contains links to other text. This allows you to quickly access other related text from the text you are currently reading. The linked text might be within the document that you are currently reading, or it might be somewhere halfway around the world.

In addition to text, many of the documents you retrieve may contain pictures, graphs, sounds, or even animations. Documents that contain more than just text are called *hypermedia* documents, because they contain multiple media.

HTML

When you retrieve a document from the WWW, the text that you read on-screen is nicely formatted text. To do this, the documents that you read on the WWW cannot be plain text, or even text with specific formatting information in it (because the person who places a document on a WWW server doesn't know what type of computer or terminal is being used by the person reading the document).

To assure that everyone sees documents displayed correctly on-screen, it was necessary to come up with a way to describe documents so that they are displayed in whatever was the best format for the viewing terminal or computer. The solution to this problem turned out to be HTML.

HTML (hypertext markup language) is used when writing a document that is to be displayed through the WWW. *HTML* is a fairly simple set of commands that describes how a document is structured. This type of markup language allows you to define the parts of the document, but not the formatting, so the browser that you run when reading the document can format it to best suit your display.

HTML commands are inserted around blocks of text in a document to describe what the text is. So, for example, within a document you have text that is marked as the various heading levels, simple paragraphs, page headings and footers, bulleted items, and so on. There are also commands that let you import other media (images, sounds, animations), and commands that let you specify the links to other documents (or text within the same document). Your browser gets the document and interprets the HTML commands, formatting each structure in the document (headings, bullets, plain paragraphs, and so on) in a way that looks best on your display. Figures 2.1a and 2.1b show the HTML code for a Mosaic help file and the corresponding file displayed in Mosaic for Windows.

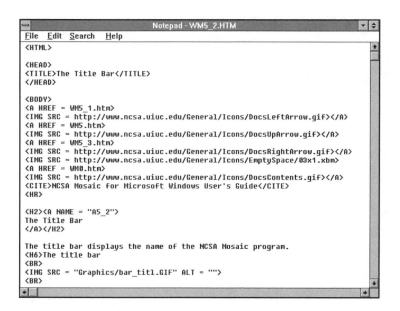

Fig. 2.1a
The HTML code
for a help file from
Mosaic for
Windows.

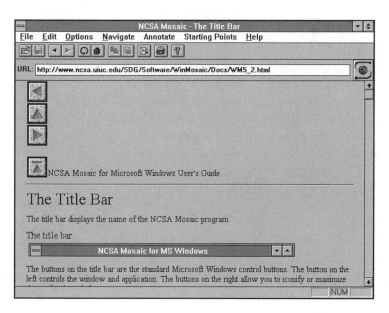

Fig. 2.1b
The same help file
as it is displayed
by Mosaic.

> ### Note
>
> HTML is an easy format to learn. If you want to learn about it and create your own Web documents, see *Using the World Wide Web* from Que. (This book also contains extensive categorized listings of good Web sites.)
>
> There are also several on-line documents to help you learn HTML. "A Beginner's Guide to HTML" can be found at:
>
> **http://www.ncsa.uiuc.edu/demoweb.htmlprimer.html**
>
> This document also can be accessed from the Other Documents menu under the default Starting Points menu that is distributed with Mosaic. The "HTML Quick Reference" is found at:
>
> **http://www.ncsa.uicu.edu/General/Internet/WWW/ HTMLQuickRef.html**
>
> This document also can be accessed from the World Wide Web Info menu under the default Starting Points menu.

Links

One of the defining features of any hypertext documents are *links* (also known as *hyperlinks*). Links are simply references to other documents. But they aren't just stated references like "see page 2-3 for more information." They are actual live links, where you can activate the link and cause the thing it references to appear on your screen. When someone writes a hypertext document, he or she can insert links to other documents that have information relevant to the text in the document.

WWW documents are all hypertext documents. Besides document description commands, HTML contains commands that allow links in a document. Many of them are hypermedia documents, containing links to pictures, sounds, or animations, in addition to document links.

There are two parts to a hypertext link. One part is the reference to the related item (a document, picture, movie, or sound). In the case of the WWW, the item being referenced could be within the current document, or it could be anywhere on the Internet.

The second part of a hypertext link is the *anchor*. The author of a document can define the anchor to be a word, a group of words, a picture or any area of the reader's display. The reader may activate the anchor by pointing to it and clicking with a mouse (for a graphical-based browser) or by selecting it with arrow keys and pressing Enter (for a text-based browser).

The anchor is indicated in different ways depending on the type of display you are using. If it is a color display, anchor words may be a special color, and anchor graphics may be surrounded by a colored box. If you have a black-and-white display, anchor words may be underlined, and anchor graphics may have a border drawn around them. On a simple terminal, anchor words may be in reverse video (and, of course, there would be no graphics). See figures 2.2 and 2.3 for some examples of anchors on different types of displays.

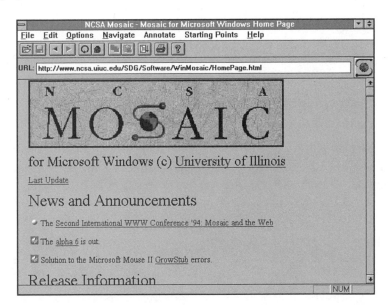

Fig. 2.2
An example of hypertext anchors in Mosaic.

Fig. 2.3
An example of hypertext anchors in a text-based WWW interface (Lynx). The anchor words are in reverse video.

Tip

One way of identifying an anchor on a graphical WWW interface is to watch the cursor. Your cursor may change to another shape when it passes over an anchor. For example, the cursor changes to a pointing hand in Mosaic.

When you activate the anchor, your browser fetches the item referenced by the anchor. This may involve reading a document from your local disk, or going out on the Internet and requesting that a document be sent from a distant computer to yours. The reference indicates what type of item is being retrieved (HTML document, sound file, and so on) and your browser tries to present the material to you in the appropriate format.

URLs

One of the goals of the World Wide Web project was to have a standard way of referencing an item, no matter what the item's type (a document, sound file, and so on). To achieve this goal, a Uniform Resource Locator (URL) was developed.

A *URL* is a complete description of an item, containing the location of the item that you want to retrieve. The location of the item can range from a file on your local disk to a file on an Internet site halfway around the world.

Tip

If you do not have the correct driver for the type of item that is retrieved (a driver for sound files, for example), the item is still retrieved by your browser. Only after the item is retrieved do you get an error saying that the driver could not be found.

A URL reference can be set up to be *absolute* or *relative*. An absolute reference contains the complete address of the document that is being referenced, including the host name, directory path, and file name. A relative reference assumes that the previous machine and directory path are being used, and just the file name (or possibly a subdirectory and file name) are specified.

> **Note**
>
> If you save a document to your local disk, you should check to see if the references in the document are absolute or relative. If the document references other documents with relative addresses, you will not be able to view those documents unless you copy them to your local disk and set them up with the same directory structure as they had at the original site. Absolute references will always work unless your Internet connection fails or the referenced documents are moved.

The URL is not limited to describing the location of WWW files. Many browsers (including Mosaic) can access a number of different Internet services, including anonymous FTP, Gopher, WAIS, Usenet news, and Telnet. (Part III, "Advanced Mosaic Features" explains how to use Mosaic to access these other services.)

A typical URL looks like this:

http://bigcorp.com/doc/progexample.html

Note

Don't try to connect to this site. It is a fictitious URL.

The initial item in the URL (the part that ends with a colon) is the *protocol* that is being used to retrieve the item. A protocol is a set of instructions that defines how to use that particular Internet service. In this example, the protocol is HTTP, the HyperText Transfer Protocol developed for the WWW project. The two slashes after the colon indicate that what follows is a valid Internet host address. In this URL, you want to find a file on that machine, so what follows after the host name is a UNIX-style path for the file that you want to retrieve.

So, the URL in the example tells Mosaic (or any other WWW browser) to retrieve the file progexample.html from the /doc directory on the Internet host bigcorp.com, using the HTTP protocol.

Other protocols that the Web can use to retrieve documents are:

Protocol	Use
gopher	Starts a Gopher session
ftp	Starts an FTP session
file	Gets a file on your local disk if followed by ///c|; or, equivalent to ftp if followed by //. Any local disk may be specified, and it must be followed by the bar character rather than a colon, because the colon has a special significance in a URL
wais	Accesses a WAIS server
news	Reads Usenet newsgroups
telnet	Starts a Telnet session

Tip
Even if you are retrieving files from a server that is running on a PC, you must use a slash (/) to indicate a subdirectory, not a backslash.

HTTP

Another of the goals of the WWW project was to have documents that were easy to retrieve, no matter where they resided. After it was decided to use hypertext as the standard format for WWW documents, a protocol that allowed these hypertext documents to be retrieved quickly was developed. This protocol is HTTP, the HyperText Transport Protocol. *HTTP* is a fairly simple communications protocol, that takes advantage of the fact that the documents it retrieves contain information about future links the user may reference (unlike FTP or Gopher, where information about the next possible links must be transmitted via the protocol).

Although it is not necessary to know anything about the HTTP protocol to view documents on the WWW, if you are interested, you can find a copy of the IETF http specification at the URL **http://info.cern.ch /hypertext/WWW/Protocols/HTTP/HTTP2.html**. This is the standard specification of the HTML protocol that has been developed and accepted by the Internet community.

Home Pages

Each person who uses the WWW can set up their own *home page*, where they can set up links to sites that they use frequently. Home pages can also be developed for groups who use the same resources. For example, a project administrator may want to set up a home page that gives links to all project-related items that exist.

> **Note**
>
> Many people refer to the primary welcome page of a site as the home page for that site. This is not really a home page, because it is for general use and is not a page that organizes information related to a single topic.

Clients and Servers

Two terms heard frequently when the WWW is discussed are *client* and *server*. A WWW client is an account on an Internet site that requests a document from the WWW. The WWW servers are the collections of WWW documents at different sites on the Internet.

Client software is a program (like Mosaic) that you use to view WWW documents. *Server software* is a program that manages a particular collection of WWW documents on an Internet host.

Learning More about WWW

The WWW, like the Internet, changes constantly. New servers become available, old ones go away. Eventually, new protocols for accessing new Internet services will be available. New browsers will be written and old ones will get new features. There is so much information changing so rapidly that anything in hard print (like this book) will become out of date quickly. (Only somewhat out of date, though! Most of the information will be current.)

There are a number of ways that you can find out more information about what is current on the WWW. This section gives you pointers to some of the most useful sources of information.

Usenet Newsgroups

If you have access to Usenet newsgroups, there are several of them that are directly related to the WWW.

comp.infosystems.www.users

This newsgroup is a general purpose one where users of WWW clients can ask questions about how to set up and use their client software, how to find and install drivers for other media (movies, sound), where on the WWW they can find information on a topic, and any other user-oriented questions.

comp.infosystems.www.providers

This newsgroup is for topics related to setting up a WWW server. Appropriate topics for this group include questions about how to get a server running, how to design the WWW documents that will be on your server, questions about security of WWW sites, and other questions related to setting up a WWW server on the Internet.

comp.infosystems.www.misc

This newsgroup is for topics not discussed in the other WWW groups; for example, discussions on the future of the web, new technologies that might impact both Web servers and clients, government use and regulation of the WWW, and so on.

Electronic Mailing Lists

There are several electronic mailing lists that are dedicated to the WWW. To subscribe to one of these groups, send electronic mail to the address **listserv@info.cern.ch** with the line subscribe <mailing list name> <your name>. (Insert the name of the mailing list you want to join in place of <mailing list name> and your first and last name in place of <your name>.)

www–announce

This mailing list discusses the current state of the WWW, new software available for the WWW (clients, server, HTML editors, and so on), introduction of commercial services available through the web, and anything else anyone wants to offer to other WWW users.

Tip
These mailing lists tend to be of a more technical or administrative nature (the newsgroups are the place to ask questions about how to do something or where to find something on the WWW).

www–html

This mailing list is a technical discussion of the design and extension of the HTML language.

www–talk

This mailing list is for technical discussions among people who are interested in the design of WWW software.

WWW Interactive Talk

WWW Interactive Talk (WIT, for short) is a new type of discussion group that has been formed for the WWW. In some ways it is similar to Usenet newsgroups. The creators of this forum, however, have tried to overcome some of the limitations of the Usenet groups by structuring the discussion of a particular topic. Each topic is presented on a form that shows the topic and proposals for discussion about the topic. Under the proposals there are arguments for and against each proposal.

Note

The designers of WIT hope that this format allows readers to see if the topic has been adequately discussed before they submit their own comments. As a comparison, often in Usenet newsgroups a point will be made over and over again because readers respond before they see if someone else has already brought up the same point.

This is a new and somewhat experimental discussion format. Currently, there is a WIT discussion area set up at **http://info.cern.ch/wit/hypertext /WWW**. This area is not limited to WWW discussions (any topic can be introduced), but it is a place where you are likely to find some people to talk to you about the WWW.

The WWW Itself

Of course, one of the best places to find information about the WWW is on the WWW itself! Here are a few URLs that will take you places where you can find out more about the WWW and what can be found on it.

> **Note**
>
> When you view a document on the WWW, you are actually retrieving it from a computer somewhere on the Internet. When you do this, you are making demands on the Internet host that is providing the information, and also on the network itself. Please try to keep your document viewing to things that are really of interest to you so that you don't make unnecessary demands on the network or individual Internet hosts.

World Wide Web Initiative
http://info.cern.ch/hypertext/WWW/TheProject.html

This URL takes you to *World Wide Web Initiative*. This document gives you pointers to WWW information to be found at CERN, the people who started it all. Some of the information you can find here includes: information about available client and server software; lists of WWW servers grouped by subject, by country, and by service; technical information about the WWW; and other background information.

NCSA Mosaic Demo Document
http://www.ncsa.uiuc.edu/demoweb/demo.html

Follow this URL to the *NCSA Mosaic Demo Document*. This document gives a brief description of Mosaic. Its main attraction, however, is a large list of interesting documents that can be found on the WWW.

InterNIC
http://www.internic.net

This URL takes you to the welcome page for the InterNIC, the main Internet Network Information Center. One of the resources offered by this project is the InfoGuide, a resource intended to help people locate information on specific topics. To access the InfoGuide, click the Information Services anchor. There are links from this document to many different lists of Internet resources. Many of these resources are in WWW format, or are accessible by one of the other Internet services that Mosaic can handle (FTP, Gopher, and so on).

Entering the World-Wide Web: A Guide to Cyberspace
http://www.eit.com/web/www.guide

This URL takes you to the document *Entering the World-Wide Web: A Guide to Cyberspace*. This document gives you a good overview of the World Wide Web, and points you to some interesting information repositories on the WWW.

From Here...

To learn more about using the WWW, refer to these chapters:

- Chapter 3, "Getting Mosaic for Windows Running," tells you how to set up Mosaic on your PC.

- Chapter 4, "Getting Mosaic for Mac Running," tells you how to set up Mosaic on your Macintosh.

- Chapter 5, "Navigating with Mosaic," tells you how to use Mosaic to find and view documents on the WWW.

Part II

Mosaic Basics

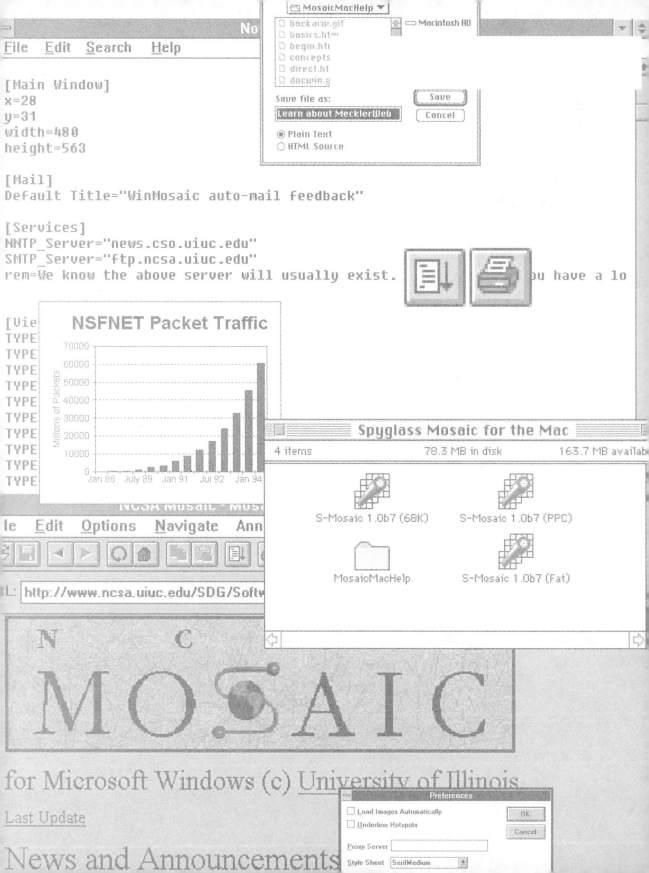

MosaicMacHelp ▾

□ backarw.gif
□ basics.htm
□ begin.htm
□ concepts
□ direct.ht
□ docwin.g

Macintosh HD

Save file as:

Learn about MecklerWeb

Save
Cancel

● Plain Text
○ HTML Source

No
File   Edit   Search   Help

[Main Window]
x=28
y=31
width=480
height=563

[Mail]
Default Title="WinMosaic auto-mail feedback"

[Services]
NNTP_Server="news.cso.uiuc.edu"
SMTP_Server="ftp.ncsa.uiuc.edu"
rem=We know the above server will usually exist.   ou have a lo

[Vie
TYPE
TYPE
TYPE
TYPE
TYPE
TYPE
TYPE
TYPE
TYPE
TYPE

NSFNET Packet Traffic

70000
60000
50000
40000
30000
20000
10000
0

Millions of Packets

Jan 88   July 89   Jan 91   Jul 92   Jan 94

NCSA Mosaic - Mos

le   Edit   Options   Navigate   Ann

L: http://www.ncsa.uiuc.edu/SDG/Softw

Spyglass Mosaic for the Mac

4 items   78.3 MB in disk   163.7 MB availab

S-Mosaic 1.0b7 (68K)   S-Mosaic 1.0b7 (PPC)

MosaicMacHelp   S-Mosaic 1.0b7 (Fat)

N C MOSAIC

for Microsoft Windows (c) University of Illinois

Last Update

News and Announcements

Preferences

□ Load Images Automatically   OK
□ Underline Hotspots   Cancel

Proxy Server
Style Sheet SerifMedium

Chapter 3

Getting Mosaic for Windows Running

Before you can try Mosaic for Windows on your personal computer, you will have to obtain the software and set it up on your computer. Depending on how your system is set up, getting Mosaic for Windows to run can be as easy as just loading the software. If your system is not already connected to the Internet, however, getting Mosaic for Windows running will require you to do some extra work.

In this chapter, you learn the following:

- Whether your computer system can run Mosaic for Windows, and what additional hardware and software you might need

- Where to get a copy of Mosaic for Windows, and any additional software you might need to run it

- How to set up Mosaic for Windows on your system

- How to set up viewer programs for images, sounds, movies, and other files

- What the Mosaic for Windows interface looks like and how you interact with it

After you read this chapter, you should be able to set up and run Mosaic for Windows on your system.

Can Your Computer System Run Mosaic for Windows?

Before you can get Mosaic for Windows running on your personal computer, you must make sure that your computer system is capable of running the software. While this might seem fairly basic, it is disappointing (not to mention annoying) to spend quite a few hours getting software and setting it up only to discover that your system does not have enough memory to run Mosaic for Windows, or that the software runs so slowly that you cannot effectively use it.

This section outlines what type of hardware and software you must have on your computer to run Mosaic for Windows.

Basic System Requirements

First of all, your computer system must be capable of running Microsoft Windows version 3.1 or later. If you do not already have Windows 3.1, you will have to purchase and install this software before you can run Mosaic.

In addition, Mosaic for Windows requires at least 4M of main memory and an Intel 80386 processor. This means that most older systems (80286 systems, for example) are not able to run Mosaic for Windows, and many newer systems may need additional memory to run Mosaic properly.

The basic Mosaic for Windows configuration requires around 5M of disk space for the Mosaic software and documentation, and the Win32s libraries. Besides this basic disk space requirement, Mosaic requires some disk space to hold temporary files while it is running, and you need disk space for any documents you want to store locally, and for any viewers that you need to display movies, image files, sound files, and so on.

If your system has a minimal configuration to run Mosaic for Windows, you can add additional hardware capacity to make Mosaic more effective and pleasant to use. A fast 80486 or Pentium system runs Mosaic much better than a slower 80386-based system. Adding more memory to a system also greatly improves the performance of Mosaic (and the rest of the system for that matter).

Network Requirements

In addition to these system requirements, Mosaic for Windows requires a direct connection to the Internet, either through an Ethernet card in your system, or through some kind of modem connection. The best configuration is with an Ethernet card which is directly connected to a local network—this provides the best Mosaic performance and requires the least additional software.

If your system does not have a direct Ethernet connection, you will have to get an account from an Internet provider to connect to the Internet. You have to obtain software that enables your system to run the "Serial Line Internet Protocol" (SL/IP) or "Point to Point Protocol" (PPP). This software allows you to connect to the Internet through a modem on your system. There are a number of different options available for obtaining the software you can use to connect to your Internet account. Some service providers will supply you with the software as part of your account start-up. You also can buy a book (such as *Easy Internet* from Que) that comes with the basic connection software, or, you can buy commercially available connection software (such as Netmanage Chameleon). There are also a few shareware programs that you can use (such as Trumpet) to connect to your Internet account.

Other Software Requirements

In addition to the basic system and network requirements, other software may be required to either set up Mosaic or enhance its capabilities. Because Mosaic for Windows comes packaged as a ZIP file, you need some software to unpack these archives. PKZIP is the software usually used for this, and it can be found on many Internet FTP sites. See Chapter 14, "Hot FTP and Gopher Sites," for more information about good FTP sites to find this software.

After Mosaic is running on your system, you may want to extend its capabilities by adding software to handle more types of documents. Mosaic for Windows comes with software which lets you display some types of images, but you may want to get software to process sound files, animation files, and additional picture formats. Obtaining and setting up these additional programs is discussed in more detail later in this chapter.

Where to Get Mosaic for Windows and Associated Software

One of the best features of Mosaic for Windows is that the basic software is free for anyone to use. The software, which is written and maintained at the National Center for Supercomputer Applications (NCSA) at the University of Illinois, is available through anonymous FTP. This section discusses exactly how to get this software and any additional software you will need to run Mosaic for Windows.

Obtaining Network Software

If your system has an Ethernet card that allows you to be directly connected to a local network, the card vendor should have provided all the software necessary for your system to use the TCP/IP protocol suite that is required by Mosaic for Windows. You may have to consult your local network administrator to get information that is required by the Ethernet software (such as your host name and number), but this network configuration is beyond the scope of this book. If the Ethernet software is running on your system (that is, you can run FTP and Telnet), then Mosaic for Windows should work correctly.

Mosaic for Windows uses the WinSock (Windows Socket) standard for talking to the network. Your Ethernet card vendor should have provided a version of the WinSock libraries for your system. If they have not, contact the vendor to determine what WinSock library is suitable for use with their Ethernet software.

If you want to get a publicly available version of the SL/IP software, there are several places where you can find it. If you have an Internet connection, you can get Netmanage's Chameleon Sampler (also included with the book *Easy Internet,* published by Que), through anonymous FTP to the machine **ftp.netmanage.com** in the directory /pub/demos/sampler. You can also get a shareware version of the SL/IP software called Trumpet Software International WinSock via anonymous FTP to the machine **ftp.ncsa.uiuc.edu**. The file you want to retrieve is /Web/Mosaic/Windows/sockets/winsock.zip.

Both of these shareware (or demo) versions of SL/IP come with the WinSock libraries that Mosaic for Windows requires.

After you have obtained the software for running SL/IP (or PPP) on your computer system, you have to configure the software for your network. You have to set up your SL/IP software with the proper phone number for your Internet provider, and might have to set up your host name and address and other network information. Read the installation instructions that came with your SL/IP software carefully. You may have to contact your Internet provider for some of the information that is needed by the software.

Where to Get the Basic Mosaic Software

The basic Mosaic for Windows software is available through anonymous FTP at the machine **ftp.ncsa.uiuc.edu**. On this machine are versions of Mosaic for several different machine types, but you are interested in the Mosaic software for PC machines running Windows. The latest version of Mosaic for Windows (as of the writing of this book) is version 2.0a7 which, although fairly stable, is still under development.

> **Note**
>
> The "a" in this version number indicates that this is an "alpha" version. Alpha versions are the early testing, pre-release versions of software. Be aware that these versions still have bugs or features that don't work.

Besides the actual Mosaic software, Mosaic for Windows version 2.0 requires the Windows 32-bit extension software which is available in the same FTP directory as the Mosaic software itself. If you are already running a 32-bit version of Windows (such as Windows NT), you do not need this software to run Mosaic for Windows. These two packages make up the basic Mosaic for Windows software.

Tip
When you download Mosaic, be sure to see if there is a more recent version. If there is, it may run better and have fewer problems.

If you have a terminal (command line) interface to FTP, you can retrieve the Mosaic and Win32a software as shown in the example that follows. After connecting to the FTP server **ftp.ncsa.uiuc.edu**, use the command **cd** to move to the directory /Web/Mosaic/Windows. Then use the **binary** command to tell the FTP program that you will be retrieving binary files (ZIP format files in this case). Finally, retrieve the Mosaic and Win32s software. Note that some of the system messages that you would see when you connect to the FTP site have been deleted in this example (indicated by . . .) to save space.

This example retrieves the Mosaic for Windows software and the Win32s software from the site **ftp.ncsa.uiuc.edu.** (The text you have to enter is indicated in boldface type.)

```
% ftp ftp.ncsa.uiuc.edu
Connected to zaphod.ncsa.uiuc.edu.
220 zaphod FTP server (Version 6.23 Thu Apr 8 06:37:40 CDT 1993)
ready.
Name (ftp.ncsa.uiuc.edu:tgp): anonymous
331 Guest login ok, send e-mail address as password.
Password: *********
```

II

Mosaic Basics

```
230-
230-Welcome to NCSA's anonymous FTP server! I hope you find what
you are
230- looking for. For questions regarding NCSA software tools,
please e-mail
230- softdev@ncsa.uiuc.edu.
...
230 Guest login ok, access restrictions apply.
ftp> cd /Web/Mosaic/Windows
250 CWD command successful.
ftp> binary
200 Type set to I.
ftp> get wmos20a7.zip
200 PORT command successful.
150 Opening BINARY mode data connection for wmosA6r1.zip (292878
bytes).
226 Transfer complete.
local: wmosA6r1.zip remote: wmosA6r1.zip
292878 bytes received in 3.8 seconds (76 Kbytes/s)
ftp> get win32s.zip
200 PORT command successful.
150 Opening BINARY mode data connection for win32s.zip (1130854
bytes).
226 Transfer complete.
local: win32s.zip remote: win32s.zip
1130854 bytes received in 12 seconds (93 Kbytes/s)
ftp> bye
221 Goodbye.
```

If you have a Windows-based FTP program such as Netmanage's Chameleon FTP (a sampler of Chameleon including FTP comes with the book *Easy Internet* from Que) or the shareware WS-FTP, the procedure is similar to this (shown for WS-FTP, the procedure varies slightly in other FTP programs):

1. Connect to your Internet provider.

2. Start the FTP program.

3. Click Connect and enter the address of the site you are using. Enter **anonymous** as the User ID and your e-mail address as the password (see fig. 3.1).

4. Navigate to the directory you need by double-clicking the directory name in the host window on the upper right (see fig. 3.2).

5. When you are at the correct directory, select the file to transfer from the lower left of the host window, and click the left arrow to transfer it (see fig. 3.3).

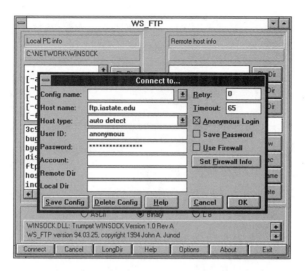

Fig. 3.1
Entering the address and user information in WS-FTP.

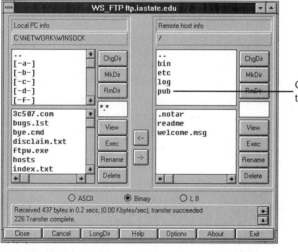

Fig. 3.2
After you are connected to the site, navigate the directories.

Click here to move to that directory

II

Mosaic Basics

Note

The transferred file is saved in the directory in the Local PC Window on the left of the screen. To change this directory, click the desired directory.

Fig. 3.3
Click the left
arrow to transfer
the file to your
local hard drive.

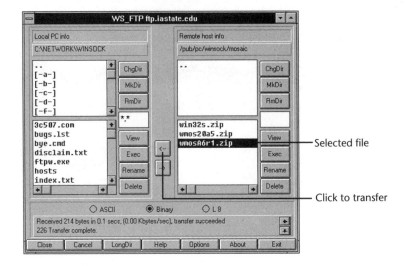

Selected file

Click to transfer

> 6. After transferring all the files you need, click Close, then Exit, to close
>   your FTP connection and exit FTP.

There is one problem you may encounter in obtaining the Mosaic and
Win32s software. Because this software is so popular, the NCSA site is often
very busy. There are limits to the number of users that can connect to it at
once; at busy times, you may not be able to connect. If this happens, be patient and try again. If you still can't get connected, don't despair. Many other
FTP sites have copies of the Mosaic and Win32s ZIP files. The following table
lists a few alternate anonymous FTP sites and the directories in which to look
for the software.

Table 3.1 Alternate FTP Sites for Mosaic and Win32

Site Address	Directory
nic.switch.ch	/mirror/Mosaic/Windows
ftp.iastate.edu	/pub/pc/winsock/mosaic
ftp.cac.psu.edu	/pub/access/test

Another thing to keep in mind when looking for this software is that just as
you move files around on your computer, the system administrators of the
FTP sites may occasionally move files or rename directories. If you can't find
the files you are looking for, look in another directory. They may be somewhere else.

Obtaining Auxiliary Software for Mosaic

Besides the standard software necessary to run Mosaic for Windows, there is some additional software which you may need to either set up Mosaic or allow Mosaic to handle certain documents.

PKZIP

First of all, because Mosaic for Windows and its accessories are packed in ZIP file format, you will need a copy of PKZIP to unpack these files. PKZIP is available through anonymous FTP at the same site you found Mosaic (**ftp.ncsa.uiuc.edu**) in the directory /PC/Windows/Contrib. Retrieve the file PKZ204G.EXE from this directory. (Make sure that the version of PKZIP that you get is 2.04 or later.)

> **Note**
>
> If you unpack the PKZ204G file in a directory that is found in the PATH statement of your AUTOEXEC.BAT file (like the DOS directory), you can just enter the commands **pkzip** and **pkunzip** anytime you are at the DOS prompt. Alternatively, you can unpack the file in any directory that you want and add that directory to the PATH statement of your AUTOEXEC.BAT file.

After you have retrieved the file, you have to run it to unpack it. Either enter the command **pkz204g** at the DOS prompt, or open the File menu and choose Run.

Table 3.2 lists alternative sites where you can find the PKZIP software.

Table 3.2   Alternate FTP Sites for PKZIP

Site Address	Directory
oak.oakland.edu	/pub/msdos/zip
ftp.cica.indiana.edu	/pub/pc/starter
ftp.uu.net	/systems/ibmpc/msdos/simtel/zip

Multimedia Viewers

While Mosaic for Windows displays normal Web documents, you may want to obtain additional software to allow Mosaic to handle things such as pictures, sounds, and animations (movies). This additional software is available through anonymous FTP at **ftp.ncsa.uiuc.edu** in the directory /Web /Windows/Mosaic/viewers. The following are some of the software packages:

- GhostScript and Ghostview, display PostScript documents

- Lview, displays GIF and JPEG images

- MPEGPLAY, displays MPEG movies

- Speak, a Windows driver which allows the speaker in your personal computer to play sound files

- WHAM, an audio file player that works with Windows-supported sound cards

- Wplay, another audio file player that works with the PC speaker driver to play sound files

There are many viewer programs that can handle the different types of media files you find on the WWW. Some of these are commercial software packages; others are shareware that you can find on the Internet. If you have more questions about viewers or can't find the viewers you need, here are some additional sources of information:

- Read the FAQ (Frequently Asked Questions) file by clicking **F**AQ Page under the **H**elp menu. If you scroll to the bottom of the document, there is a hyperlink entitled Viewer Software Information. Click this to load a document that gives you general information on how to customize Mosaic to use different viewers. This document also has links that let you load some of the more popular shareware viewers.

- Use Gopher or FTP to go to some of the big software repositories on the Internet and look around for viewer programs. Chapter 14, "Hot FTP and Gopher Sites," lists some of these servers.

- If you have Usenet access, read the newsgroup **comp.infosystems.www.users**. A discussion of viewers that work with Mosaic is an appropriate topic with this group.

> ### Note
>
> After you have Mosaic running, you can get more information about different viewers and where to find them from the URL **http://www.ncsa.uiuc.edu/SDG /Software/WinMosaic/viewers.html**.

Setting Up Mosaic for Windows on Your System

After you have obtained all the files you need to run Mosaic for Windows on your PC, you can go through the process of getting the software ready to run. This section covers the steps necessary to set up the basic Mosaic for Windows software, gives an example of setting up SL/IP software to connect your personal computer to the Internet, and discusses how to set up any auxiliary software you have retrieved to use with Mosaic.

Setting Up the Basic Mosaic Software

Setting up the basic Mosaic for Windows software consists of unpacking and installing the Windows 32-bit libraries and the Mosaic software itself. The first step is to install the Windows 32-bit libraries into your Microsoft Windows directories.

Installing the Windows 32-bit Libraries

The Windows 32-bit libraries, written by Microsoft, come with the standard Windows setup utility to do the installation. This makes the process of installing these libraries simple and almost foolproof. The following are the steps necessary to install these libraries:

> **Note**
>
> The Win32s add-ins enable Windows to run 32-bit programs such as Mosaic. 32-bit programs run faster than their 16-bit counterparts. The down side of this is that some users have complained that Win32s is not 100 percent stable. There have been complaints that it is buggy and won't work reliably with many existing applications. So, many Windows users have been reluctant to upgrade to Win32s.
>
> Most software vendors whose programs have had trouble under Win32 have released updates and fixes so that their programs work in Win32. Microsoft also has released several updated versions of Win32s and these have dramatically reduced the problems with Win32 incompatibilities.
>
> The authors and development staff of this book all have worked using the latest version of Mosaic, which is a 32-bit version. We have not experienced any problems with Win32s—with only one exception noted later in this section. The best advice we can give you is to back up your Windows directory and subdirectory before installing Win32s. That way if you have problems, you can restore from your backup.

1. Move the ZIP file you retrieved from the FTP site to a temporary directory on your hard drive.

2. Use the PKUNZIP command to unpack the ZIP file. For example, if the file name you retrieved was called WIN32S.ZIP, the command to unpack this file is **PKUNZIP WIN32S.ZIP**.

> **Note**
>
> This assumes that you have the PKZIP utilities in your standard path for executables on your system. You can put these utilities into your C:\DOS directory so the system can find them.

3. The temporary directory now contains the original ZIP file and several other files. One of these files is another ZIP file that contains the actual Windows libraries. If this file is called W32S115A.ZIP, use the command **pkunzip -d W32S115A.ZIP**.

> **Caution**
>
> The -d in the above PKUNZIP command is very important because it creates the correct directories to hold the distribution files. The setup program will not be able to find the files if the -d switch is not used.

4. The temporary directory now contains two directories called DISK1 and DISK2 that hold the Windows 32-bit library distribution files.

5. Start up Microsoft Windows.

6. Open the **F**ile menu and choose **R**un.

7. If the temporary directory you used is called C:\TEMP, type the following command in the Run dialog box: **C:\TEMP\DISK1\SETUP**. Select OK to run the setup program.

8. The setup program displays where it thinks your standard Windows directories are and asks you to confirm that you want to load the 32-bit libraries. Select Continue to load the libraries.

9. After setup has loaded the 32-bit libraries, it asks if you want to load a 32-bit version of the game FreeCell to test that the libraries were loaded correctly. If you have enough disk space to do this (less than 1 megabyte of space is required) you should select Continue to load this

software—it allows you to make sure that the 32-bit libraries are running correctly.

10. After setup is complete select Exit to leave the program. The 32-bit libraries should be completely loaded.

11. You can remove the files in the temporary directory, as they are no longer needed.

This completes the process of loading the Windows 32-bit library software. You can now proceed with loading the Mosaic for Windows software.

If you have a LaserMaster printer or printer accessory you may have a little work to do before you can install Win32s. For years, LaserMaster has used the term *Winspool* for their printer ports. For example, if you have a WinJet800—a modification that makes a LaserJet III print at 800 dots per inch—you have a print driver that is named *LM WinJet 800 PS on WINSPOOL*. The term WINSPOOL, then, is a protected one—after you've started Windows you cannot create a file called WINSPOOL, in the same way that you cannot create a file in DOS called LPT1 or COM1.

Unfortunately, Microsoft picked the name WINSPOOL.DRV for one of the Win32s files. So if you have installed a LaserMaster product, when you try to install your Win32s system, the setup program locks up when it tries to copy and extract the WINSPOOL.DR_ file off the disk.

That's if you have the Win32s files on a disk—if you are getting the ZIP file off the Internet and are trying to extract the archived files out of the ZIP file, you won't even be able to get as far as the installation procedure. You'll be able to extract all of the files out of the ZIP file except for one—WINSPOOL.DR_.

Luckily, the fix is fairly easy. Just follow these steps:

1. At the File Manager or Program Manager, open the **F**ile menu and choose **R**un. Type `sysedit` and press Enter. The Windows System Configuration Editor appears. This contains several document windows, one of which contains the SYSTEM.INI file.

2. Maximize the SYSTEM.INI document window.

3. In the SYSTEM.INI file, find these lines:

```
device=LMHAROLD.386
device=LMCAP.386
device=LMMI.386
```

4. Place a semicolon (;) at the beginning of each line (`;device-LMHAROLD.386`, for example).

5. Exit Windows.

6. Restart Windows.

7. Now you can continue. If you got the Win32s files off the Internet, extract them from the ZIP file into the directory you created for that purpose, and run the installation program.

8. When you have finished installing the Win32s system, go back to the SYSTEM.INI and remove the semicolons that you placed. The next time you open Windows you'll be able to use both your 32-bit Mosaic *and* your LaserMaster printer.

Installing the Mosaic for Windows Software

After you have loaded the 32-bit libraries, loading the Mosaic for Windows software is very straightforward. To set up the software, follow these steps:

1. Create a directory to hold the Mosaic for Windows software. (For example, you might create a directory called C:\MOSAIC.)

2. Move the Mosaic for Windows ZIP file you retrieved from the FTP site into this directory.

3. If, for example, the ZIP file is called WMOS20A7.ZIP, you can use the command **pkunzip WMOS20A7.ZIP** to unpack this file.

4. Copy the file MOSAIC.INI from your Mosaic directory to the directory C:\WINDOWS. This file contains configuration information used by Mosaic for Windows.

5. After you install the Mosaic software, you will probably want to create a program item in the Program Manager so that you can start Mosaic by clicking an icon. You may want to create your Mosaic program item in an already existing program group. However, you might want to go to the Program Manager and create a new program group for Mosaic.

    To create a new program group, open the **F**ile menu and choose **N**ew. In the New Program Object dialog box, select Program Group, then select OK. Enter the name of the program group in the Description: field of the Program Group Properties dialog box, then select OK. A window for the new program group opens.

Now you have to create a new program item. Select the program group where you want to put Mosaic. To create a new program item, open the **F**ile menu and choose **N**ew. In the New Program Object dialog box that appears, select Program Item, then select OK. In the Program Item Properties dialog, select Browse; select the Mosaic EXE file in the browser; then select OK (or double-click the EXE file). This fills in the Command Line: field of the Program Item Properties dialog box. You can now select OK in this dialog box. The Mosaic icon appears in the program group.

6. The setup of the Mosaic for Windows software is now complete. You can remove the Mosaic ZIP file if you want—it is no longer needed.

While there are some customizations that can be done to the Mosaic for Windows software to personalize it to your needs, you can run the Mosaic software without any further work. You will, of course, need to set up your software to connect to the Internet before using Mosaic for Windows.

Note

After you have unpacked the Mosaic software, there are several files you should read before installing the software. The file INSTALL.WRI gives important installation information. The file FAQ.WRI answers some common questions about Mosaic, and also contains some installation information. There are several other WRI files, but these two are the most useful for someone just starting out with Mosaic.

Tip
When you create the Mosaic program item, the Program Manager uses the icon that is built into Mosaic, unless you specify a different icon.

Mosaic Basics

Installing Viewers

You can run Mosaic without installing any additional viewers or configuring Mosaic to use them. But you may want to install these so you can view images, watch movies, and listen to sounds that you download through Mosaic. In general, to install a viewer for Mosaic, you only need to load the viewer program onto your local disk, then tell Mosaic where it is located, and what type of files you can view with it. To set up Mosaic to use a viewer, follow these steps:

1. If you haven't already downloaded the files for the viewers you need, consult the section "Multimedia Viewers" earlier in this chapter, to find the viewer you need, then use FTP to transfer it.

Note

If you are using a program you already have installed as a viewer, skip to step 6.

2. Create a directory for the viewer.

3. If the viewer files are compressed with PKZIP, unzip them into this directory.

4. Start Windows (if it isn't running).

5. If the viewer has an install or setup program, run it from Program Manager or File Manager by opening the **F**ile menu and choosing **R**un. Then enter the drive, directory, and install or setup like this:

   `c:\viewer\install.exe`

   To install the viewer, follow on-screen directions.

6. After the viewer is installed, edit the MOSAIC.INI file in your c:\WINDOWS directory. (Use Notepad or any other text editor to open and edit this file.) Scroll down until you see the [Viewers] section, as pictured in figure 3.4.

Fig. 3.4
Your MOSAIC.INI file contains statements that tell Mosaic where it can find viewers for the different file types.

```
[Viewers]
TYPE0="audio/wav"
TYPE1="application/postscript"
TYPE2="image/gif"
TYPE3="image/jpeg"
TYPE4="video/mpeg"
TYPE5="video/quicktime"
TYPE6="video/msvideo"
TYPE7="application/x-rtf"
TYPE8="audio/x-midi"
TYPE9="application/zip"
rem TYPE9="audio/basic"
application/postscript="ghostview %ls"
image/gif="c:\windows\apps\lview\lview31 %ls"
image/jpeg="c:\windows\apps\lview\lview31 %ls"
video/mpeg="c:\winapps\mpegplay\mpegplay %ls"
video/quicktime="C:\WINAPPS\QTW\bin\player.exe %ls"
video/msvideo="mplayer %ls"
audio/wav="mplayer %ls"
audio/x-midi="mplayer %ls"
application/x-rtf="write %ls"
application/zip="C:\WINDOWS\APPS\ZIPMGR\ZM400.EXE %ls"
rem audio/basic="notepad %ls"
telnet="c:\netmanag\telnet.exe"
```

7. Find the lines for the file types for the viewer you are installing. (For example, GIF and JPEG for an image viewer, AU and WAV for a sound player, and so on.)

8. Change the path and program name in these lines to the path and program name of the viewer you installed. The line should look like this:

```
image/gif="c:\mosaic\lview\lview31 %ls"
```

where `image/gif` is the type of file and file extension,
`c:\mosaic\lview\lview31` is the path and file name for your viewer,
and `%ls` ends every entry.

> **Note**
>
> If there isn't a line for the file type you need, you can add it anywhere in the
> viewer section using this syntax.

9. Save the file and exit the text editor. (If you are using an editor other
than Notepad, be sure to save as text only.)

You can make additional changes to installed viewers in this section at any
time.

> **Note**
>
> One of the nice features of Mosaic is that you can define "viewers" for things like
> Excel or Word files so that if Mosaic loads one of these file types, it automatically
> starts up the correct application to display the file. If you would like to define "view-
> ers" for specific application files, check out items 11 and 12 in the FAQ.WRI file
> included with the Mosaic release. These items discuss in more detail how to modify
> the MOSAIC.INI file to define viewers for various file types, and specify new file types.

Using the Mosaic Interface

After you have installed all of the software that you need to run Mosaic, you
can connect to your Internet provider and start Mosaic. Mosaic is a very powerful application, but it is graphically oriented and not difficult to use after
you are familiar with all of its features.

Starting Mosaic

Before starting Mosaic, you should first be connected to the Internet. If your
Internet connection is via your LAN, be sure you are logged onto your network. If you are connected to the Internet by a modem, start your TCP/IP
software and login to your account.

After you have established your Internet connection, open the Mosaic program group (or whatever program group you put Mosaic in), and double-click
the Mosaic icon. You are now ready to explore the Internet with Mosaic.

II

Mosaic Basics

The Mosaic Window

When Mosaic starts up, it loads the document that is specified as the home page in your MOSAIC.INI file. Your window should look like the one shown in figure 3.5.

The full URL for the default home page (which is the Windows Mosaic home page, not the Mosaic home page) is: **http://www.ncsa.uiuc.edu/SDG/ Software/Mosaic/NCSAMosaicHome.html**

Fig. 3.5
The different parts of the Mosaic window.

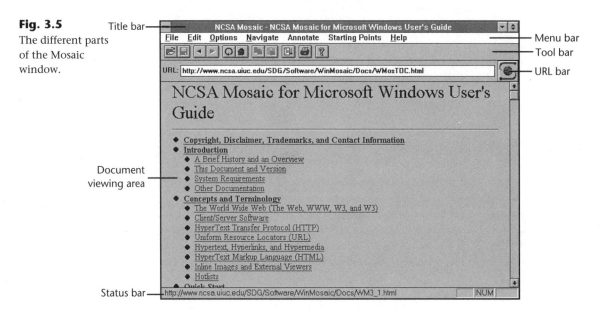

A brief description of each window part is given in the remainder of this chapter. Each window function is discussed in more depth in Chapter 5, "Navigating with Mosaic," and Chapter 6, "Shortcuts to Favorite Places."

Caution

Although the current version of Mosaic is very powerful, it is an application that is still under development. Some of the features shown in the menus and tool bar are not yet implemented. Features (words or icons that you would select) that are not available are dimmed. The developers intend to implement these features as soon as possible.

■ The title bar contains the usual window function buttons (control menu box, and maximize and minimize buttons). In addition, it has the name of the application (NCSA Mosaic) and the name of the WWW document that you are viewing.

■ The menu bar gives access to all of the functions you need to use Mosaic. You can retrieve documents to view, print documents, customize the look of your Mosaic window, navigate between documents, annotate documents, save files, and access Mosaic's on-line help.

■ The URL bar shows the URL of the current document. When you open a document, its URL is displayed, and the Mosaic logo on the right side of the URL bar spins while the document is being retrieved.

■ The document viewing area is the area of the window where you see the text of a document and any inline images it may contain.

■ The status bar serves two functions. While Mosaic is loading your document, it shows the progress of the different files that are being loaded. When you are viewing a document, it shows the URL of the hyperlink that is under your cursor. The three boxes at the right of the status bar show the state of your Caps Lock, Num Lock, and Scroll Lock keys on your keyboard.

■ The tool bar gives you quick access to some of the most used features in Mosaic (see fig. 3.6).

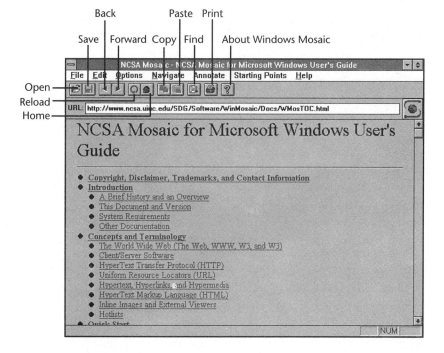

Fig. 3.6
The buttons on the toolbar.

The following list gives basic descriptions of these buttons:

■ **Open.** Opens a URL

■ **Save.** Saves the current document to disk (not yet implemented)

■ **Back**. Displays the previous document in the history list

■ **Next**. Displays the next document in the history list

■ **Reload**. Reloads the current document

■ **Home**. Goes to the default home page

■ **Copy**. Copies the current selection to the Clipboard

■ **Paste**. Pastes the contents of the Clipboard to the active window (not yet implemented)

■ **Find.** Finds a text string in the current document

■ **Print**. Prints the current document

■ **About Windows Mosaic.** Shows the About Windows Mosaic window

From Here...

To learn more about using Mosaic and to find interesting WWW documents, refer to these chapters:

■ Chapter 5, "Navigating with Mosaic," tells you how to use Mosaic to find and view documents on the WWW.

■ Chapter 6, "Shortcuts to Favorite Places," tells you how to become an expert WWW Navigator.

■ Chapter 13, "Hot Home Pages," discusses where to find some of the most interesting collections of WWW documents.

Chapter 4

Getting Mosaic for Mac Running

Before you can surf the net with Mosaic on your Macintosh, your Mac must be connected to the Internet and have the relevant software loaded.

In this chapter, you learn to do the following:

- Assess your computer to see if it can handle Mosaic for Macintosh

- Obtain a copy of Mosaic for Macintosh and its auxiliary viewers

- Install and configure Mosaic and its viewers

- Recognize the Mosaic for Macintosh interface and interact with it

Can Your Computer System Run Mosaic for Macintosh?

Before you attempt to load and run Mosaic for Macintosh, you must determine whether your personal computer has adequate resources for the job. Mosaic is a fairly hefty application; it will test your system's capabilities.

Basic System Requirements

The Macintosh product line is quite consistent across all models, so in general Mosaic will run on any Mac with System 7. You may, however, experience dilemmas with a Mac Plus keyboard, as it lacks a Control key.

To run Mosaic, your computer needs adequate main memory (RAM). Most Macintoshes have at least 4M RAM. Most systems are usually 1M-3M and because Mosaic needs 3M and also transparently launches auxiliary programs on the fly that take up to 1M, things get tight quickly. 6M of RAM is recommend. If you are short on memory, you might try an alternative to Mosaic, the less resource-intensive MacWeb (discussed in chapter 12), or the commercial RAM Doubler product. In a pinch, Mosaic will run somewhat crippled, without graphics or sounds, in 4M RAM.

Minimum disk space required is 3M, not counting room to download and install the basic Mosaic configuration. Mosaic needs some space for temporary files as it's running. If you collect all the auxiliary viewers, you'll need about 3M more. To be comfortable, plan on 10M total.

Because a big part of Mosaic's appeal is its multimedia offerings, having the right peripherals to fully enjoy them is a big win. A color monitor is a must. All Macs have sound capabilities and new models sometimes feature stereo speaker jacks.

Mosaic performance is primarily limited by the link speed, not by your system speed, but of course more processor speed is always nice.

Network Requirements

Mosaic is a TCP/IP-based client application that requires TCP/IP Internet access. You have to be on a LAN that has a high speed dedicated connection, or you need to set up a SLIP or PPP link using a modem and a regular phone line. The second option is discussed in books such as Adam Engst's *Internet Starter Kit for Macintosh* (published by Hayden Books). Note that System 7 requires only MacTCP 1.1.1, but Mosaic requires a newer version, 2.0.2; the latest is 2.0.4 (patches are available on-line).

Other Software Requirements

You also need a utility to download the files to your Mac. If you are UNIX-literate and you have a shell account on your access provider's host, it is possible to obtain the files that way. An easier route is to have Fetch, the best Macintosh FTP client application, ahead of time so that you can FTP files directly to your computer.

All files that you download from the Internet come archived and compressed, indicated by file extensions such as SEA, HQX, CPT, and SIT. You need a utility to uncompress and unarchive them. Fortunately, a freeware product from Aladdin Systems, Stuffit Expander, can handle all common formats. You may very well already have a copy of this product, as it is often included with commercial software.

Where to Get Mosaic for Macintosh and Associated Software

All the software necessary to run Mosaic is public domain, freeware, or shareware written by universities, companies, or individuals. The following sections discuss where you can find and download this software.

Obtaining Network Software

If you are on an Ethernet LAN, you probably already have a TCP/IP stack and a system administrator. If you are not on an Ethernet LAN, you have to set up your standalone Mac with a SLIP or PPP connection. Though it is assumed in this book that you have already solved this issue, here is a recap of the elements you need:

- SLIP or PPP software, which can be obtained by downloading from the net, by buying an Internet beginner's book that includes a disk, or by buying a commercial communications package (such as Symantec's VersaTilities).

- MacTCP, the only TCP/IP stack for the Mac, available from Apple (separately and now bundled, starting with System 7.5) or included with the books or commercial packages mentioned previously.

- A high speed modem—V.32 9600 bps or above.

- A provider, such as Netcom or Panix.

The next sections discuss where on the Internet you can find Mosaic and its helper applications, exactly which helper applications to look for, and what versions are the latest.

Where to Get Mosaic Software

You can download Mosaic software from the Internet. If you haven't downloaded from the Internet, don't panic—there's a first time for everything. The process is painless. Use the Internet's File Transfer Protocol, or FTP, to access public access sites (called anonymous because that's the guest login name) where public domain, freeware, or shareware archives of Macintosh software reside.

Be aware that the software in these archives is work in progress, and unlike infrequent upgrades of commercial software, new versions come out weekly or monthly rather than yearly. The current versions at the time of writing this book will undoubtedly not be the current versions when you read this book. Usually it isn't critical to have the latest and greatest version of an application; in fact, it can be considered wise to lag behind a bit, to avoid new bugs. Update your versions quarterly if you want to, and keep your ear to the Net with respect to bug reports and major version updates. Otherwise, don't worry.

Major FTP sites are usually run by universities on a voluntary basis. The number of people on the Internet is growing by about 20 percent per month. It should be no surprise that traditional Mac archives are overloaded; you may experience slow response, refused connections, or policy changes.

Another difficulty you may run into is that naming conventions for directories and file names are inconsistent across FTP sites, as are archive/compression methods. Thus, it is difficult to definitively and concisely document how to obtain these applications.

Now, here's some good news. There is a subset of all the Mac software archive sites, the Info-Mac sites, numbering about 30 worldwide, that follow standard directory and file naming conventions. You may hear these sites referred to as Info-Mac *mirrors*, because they mirror or duplicate each other exactly. Restrict your searches to these sites; if one is busy, just move on to the next one. Also, use Anarchie (available at any of the Info-Mac sites, in the directory Communications/tcp/anarchie-130.hqx). It's more than just a Mac implementation of Archie, a global FTP-space search tool; it's that plus FTP. Even if you are competent with Fetch, the most popular Mac FTP client, changing to Anarchie is a good move.

Anarchie plus the Info-Mac sites greatly simplify an otherwise frustrating downloading task. However, in case you choose to go it alone, a few of the Info-Mac FTP sites are **ftp.hawaii.edu**, **grind.isca.uiowa.edu**, and **mrcnext.cso.uiuc.edu**.

The next step is to move from Fetch, Anarchie, and StuffIt Expander, to Mosaic and its helper applications. A little extra work on the front end can save you enormous amounts of effort and grief later.

Use Fetch to retrieve a copy of StuffIt Expander (see fig. 4.1).

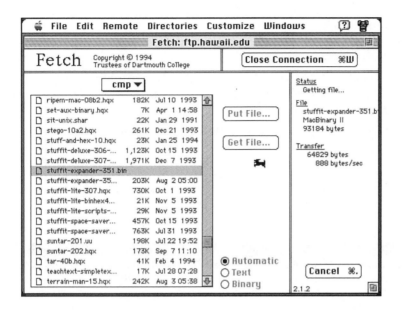

Fig. 4.1
You can use Fetch to retrieve the binary of StuffIt Expander from an Info-Mac site like **ftp.hawaii.edu**.

Next, use Anarchie to select and download Mosaic from an Info-Mac mirror (see fig. 4.2).

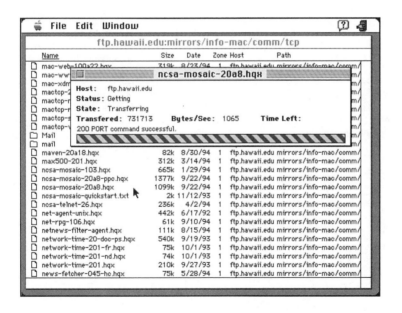

Fig. 4.2
The Info-Mac site **ftp.hawaii.edu**, using Anarchie to download Mosaic.

II

Mosaic Basics

Multimedia Viewers

To add some pizzazz to your exploration of the Internet with its multimedia capabilities, Mosaic must be able to interpret graphics and sound files. Because graphics and sound files can be large, they are usually compressed to save server disk space and transmission time. Mosaic can interpret the majority of files it accesses by itself. To view some images, watch movies, and listen to sounds, however, Mosaic needs help from additional utilities or auxiliary viewers.

Table 4.1 lists the external viewers Mosaic is initially configured to use, the latest version number, their size in kilobytes, and their location on any Info-Mac server.

Table 4.1 Mosaic Viewers and Their Info-Mac locations		
Application	**K**	**Directory**
Anarchie 1.3	461	Communications/tcp/anarchie-131.hqx
GhostScript 2.5.2b3	3058	Graphic/util/mac-ghostscript-242b3.hqx
GIFConverter 2.3.7	475	Graphic/util/gif-converter-237.hqx
JPEGView 3.3	776	Graphic/util/jpeg-view-33.hqx
NCSA Mosaic 2.0A8	1099	Communications/tcp/ncsa-mosaic-20a8.hqx
Sound Machine 2.1	75	Sound/util/sound-machine-21.hqx
Sparkle 2.14b	344	Graphic/util/sparkle-214b.hqx
StuffIt Expander 3.5.1	93	Compress-Translate/stuffit-expander-351.bin

Some notes on the applications in Table 4.1:

■ StuffIt Expander not only is used during Mosaic installation, but also is used while Mosaic is running to uncompress downloaded information. Note that Info-Mac files nearly all have HQX endings.

- GhostScript is a PostScript on-line viewer. Because GhostScript is so large and used infrequently, feel free to come back for it later.

- JPEGView, Sparkle, and GIFConverter handle graphics. GIFConverter is shareware, for which the author requests voluntary payment.

- Sound Machine handles sound files.

- You'll see a PowerPC version of Mosaic next to the one mentioned in table 4.1, named **ncsa-mosaic-20a8-ppc.hqx**.

- An upgrade patch from earlier versions of MacTCP to the latest, 2.0.4, is also available as **Communications/tcp/mactcp-20x-to-204-updt.hqx**.

Mosaic also uses some programs you probably already have local to your Macintosh as helper applications, such as TeachText, Microsoft Word, and Simple Player (the latter bundled with QuickTime from Apple).

Setting Up Mosaic for Macintosh on Your System

Mosaic and its viewers install in the normal Macintosh fashion; if you are familiar with this process, you can safely skim or skip this section.

First, here are some general Macintosh housekeeping procedures we like to follow:

- Place the application(s) you are installing in a top-level folder called Applications.

- For any application that you launch often, consider making it an Apple menu item. Consult your Mac manual for the specifics, but here's a quick lesson: click the application once, open the File menu and choose Make Alias, and place the resulting alias in System:Apple Menu Items.

If you followed these suggestions and if you used Anarchie and Info-Mac sites to retrieve the files, you can now install Mosaic and its helper applications.

For each application you downloaded, Anarchie has left three files on your Desktop. The first file is the actual downloaded file, ending with the file name extension HQX. This is an ASCII-encoded or BinHexed file; it just means 8-bit ASCII was encoded into 7-bit ASCII because some transmissions will lose the eighth bit. Throw this file away. Anarchie automatically unencoded it already to produce the second file, a compressed archive, usually ending with the file name extension SIT. Throw this file away too. Lastly, Anarchie automatically uncompressed and unarchived the second file to produce the third file, a Macintosh folder (usually) containing the program you were after and any associated files such as documentation. Keep this file and move it into your top-level folder named Applications.

In case you didn't use Anarchie, you may have to manually and perhaps repeatedly use StuffIt Expander for this unpacking. Note that the file to be unpacked has to be dragged on top of the StuffIt Expander icon; it doesn't work to double-click on either the packed file or StuffIt Expander.

Optionally, throw away all documentation and samples to save disk space. If an application is left alone in a folder, move it up a level and delete its folder.

JPEGView and GhostScript are unusual in that they have system extensions. Drag and drop JPEGView, JFIF Preview and MacGS Menu INIT to the System Folder icon. This triggers Finder to ask if you want to put them in the Control Panels folder; you do. Reboot so the extensions take effect.

Make an Apple menu alias for the Mosaic application and rename it Mosaic. There is no need to do this for Mosaic's helper applications as Mosaic launches them as needed automatically.

Using the Mosaic Interface

For all the complexity required to make WWW work, Mosaic is incredibly easy to use, which is exactly why it was created. In this section you bring up your Internet link, launch Mosaic, and familiarize yourself with Mosaic's look and feel.

Starting Mosaic

First, you must have your link to the Internet up and running. On a LAN with a dedicated link to the world, that's no problem—it's always up. If you are using InterSLIP or MacPPP as your connection software there is also no problem—they can detect when a TCP/IP application such as Mosaic attempts to access the Net, and they bring up the link transparently. Otherwise, you have to manually launch your SLIP link.

Now double-click the Mosaic icon to launch it (or, if you have created an Apple menu item for it, select the Mosaic icon).

The Mosaic Interface

This section explains the basics of Mosaic's user interface—what it looks like and what you can do with it.

The Document Window

The first screen you see is the NCSA Mosaic Home Page (see fig. 4.3). This section explains the document window first, and then explains the menus and buttons.

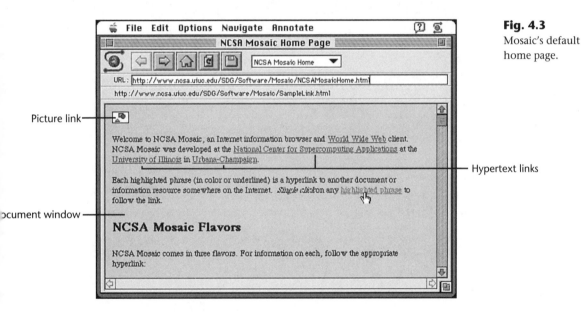

Fig. 4.3
Mosaic's default home page.

Notice that some text is highlighted; if you have a color monitor, this text also is blue. These highlighted phrases are the hyperlinks; click one and it branches to another page or screen. If you choose to backtrack to a previous screen, you will see that any branches already explored are red.

Also, notice the little square icons. These are links to either graphics or sound files, the multimedia part of Mosaic. Click them and a picture expands or sounds play. Compare figures 4.3 and 4.4; figure 4.4 shows the expanded graphic from figure 4.3.

Mosaic Basics

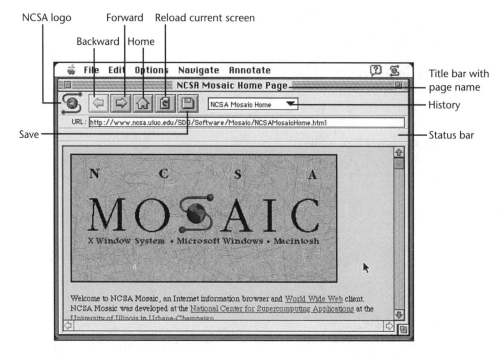

Fig. 4.4
Picture icon
expanded and
several links
already explored.

NCSA logo   Forward   Reload current screen

Backward | Home

Title bar with
page name

History

Save

Status bar

Mosaic's Interface

This section covers Mosaic's menus, buttons, and status windows (refer to fig. 4.4).

You immediately see many familiar elements. The usual elements of Macintosh's user interface are present, including the window close box, window zoom box, window resize box, and scroll bars. Mosaic uses the Macintosh title bar to display the name of the current web page.

With Mosaic's pull-down menus you can type a URL name to jump to. You can set your personal preferences such as colors and fonts. You also can choose to start your journey from one of a half dozen recommended starting points. You can control whether images are automatically expanded, which is especially useful if you are on a slow link. Lastly, you might create your own hot list of nifty URLs (or bookmarks) you find on your explorations, so you can find them easily again.

Next, find the NCSA logo (an icon that resembles an uppercase S); it spins to show downloading activity. To the right of the S are five tool icons that provide shortcuts for moving forward or for moving backward a page, for returning to the home page, for reloading the current screen, and for saving a screen to a local file.

To the right of the five icons is the history list. If you click and hold the down arrow, a stack of the pages you've visited displays; you can use the mouse to select one and jump back to it immediately.

Open the Options pull-down menu and choose the first item, Show URLs. A new window appears below the line of items. It's called the URL bar, and shows the URL of the web page you are currently viewing. It's up to you whether to leave the URL bar showing (you can hide it by toggling Show URLs), though typing in new URL descriptions here is a bit faster than using Open URL in the File menu.

Look at the last display item, the status bar, located below the URL bar. Informative messages (good and bad) are displayed here. As you pass the mouse arrow over highlighted text, the hyperlink of that text is displayed. When you choose to explore a hyperlink by clicking it, the status window either says the link is being downloaded or that an error occurred.

From Here...

Now you're ready to explore. Use the following chapters as your guide:

- Chapter 5, "Navigating with Mosaic," teaches you more about manipulating Mosaic.

- Chapter 6, "Shortcuts to Favorite Places," shows you advanced Mosaic tricks.

- Chapter 13, "Hot Home Pages," points you to the best of WWW home pages.

II

Mosaic Basics

Chapter 5

Navigating with Mosaic

The World Wide Web is one of the best examples of *cyberspace*. This system of linking documents together so that you can move between them with little effort lets you travel to many different places, literally, around the world, learning about any topic you can imagine. But, like any traveler in a new place, you can easily get lost.

Mosaic is an easy-to-use interface that lets you travel the WWW. It has many convenient features to allow you to keep track of where you've been and get to places quickly. This chapter assumes that you have read the section, "Using the Mosaic Interface" at the end of chapter 3, "Getting Mosaic for Windows Running," and are familiar with the Mosaic concepts discussed in chapter 2, "Introduction to the World Wide Web."

In this chapter, you learn to do the following:

- Start up Mosaic

- Use Mosaic's basic features

- Navigate between documents

- Handle errors you may encounter

What Is a Home Page?

The designers of Mosaic define a *home page* (or home document) as the document that you tell Mosaic to display when it starts up. This document should contain links to the documents and WWW sites that you use most frequently. Many people mistakenly use the term home page for the welcome page that you get when you connect to a WWW site. A home page provides you with access to the WWW sites or documents that you use most. Your project or company may have its own home page to give members easy access to needed information. You can load someone else's home page or design your own.

When you start the Mosaic software, it comes with the home page predefined as the NCSA Mosaic welcome page for your particular computer type (Windows or Macintosh). You probably want to change this, because, for one thing, the NCSA Mosaic page is probably not very useful to you, unless you are involved in the installation and maintenance of Mosaic at your site, and you want to keep up with the latest information from NCSA. Retrieving a document causes a load on the machine where the document is located. If everyone used the NCSA Mosaic home page as their home page, the NCSA WWW machine would become very slow.

Telling Mosaic What Home Page to Load

Mosaic finds the URL for your home page in the Main section of your MOSAIC.INI file. Replace the default URL (everything after the equal sign) in the line

```
Home Page=http://www.ncsa.uiuc.edu/SDG/Software/WinMosaic/HomePage.html
```

with the URL for the document you want to display as your home page. Your home page can be any document that you can access at a WWW site. (See "Working with Local Files" later in this chapter for details on how to make your own home page or on how to make a file saved on your computer into a home page.)

When Mosaic starts up, it displays the document that was specified in your MOSAIC.INI file. After the home page loads, the URL for your home page appears in the URL bar (if you have it enabled). From here, you can click on any of the links in your home page document to load the documents you use frequently.

If you want to return to your home page at any time, open the **N**avigate menu and choose **H**ome. This reloads your home page document.

If you have a Mac, it's easy to change the home page. Open the Options menu, choose Use this URL for Home. This makes the currently open document your new home page. You can also change this by opening the Options menu and choosing Preferences. Click Misc (miscellaneous) and type the URL in the Home Page text box in the Preferences dialog box (see fig. 5.1).

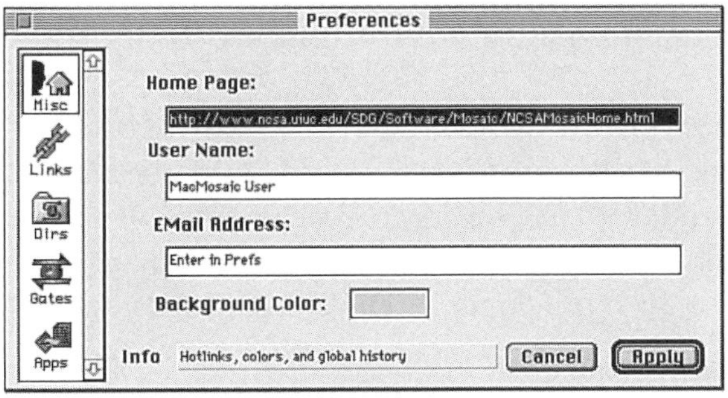

Fig. 5.1
Changing the home page on a Mac in the Preferences dialog box.

You can also tell Mosaic not to load any page when it starts up. To do this, edit your MOSAIC.INI file. In the Main section of the file, set the following:

```
Autoload Home Page=no
```

Mosaic starts up with a blank display, and you can begin your navigation of the WWW from there.

To set Mac Mosaic so that it doesn't open a home page automatically, open the Options menu and choose Preferences. Click Misc and then delete the home page from the Home Page text box. A better strategy is to have a local .html document as your home page so it starts up immediately. See "Creating Your Personal Home Page" later in this chapter.

II

Mosaic Basics

Moving between Documents

After you start Mosaic, you can move between WWW documents in two ways—you can click on links in the document you are viewing or you can use Mosaic's Open URL dialog box to enter a URL. If you have loaded a document, it will probably include links to other documents. After all, the purpose of the WWW is to let you move quickly between related documents without having to enter long path names. If there are no links in the document, it's not a very useful WWW document. But, even if your current document has no links, you can still move between documents.

Moving between Documents Using Links

Tip

A third way to move between documents is to use hotlists that contain items with predefined URLs. Creating and using hotlists is covered in chapter 6, "Shortcuts to Favorite Places."

Hypertext links in a document are indicated in the document viewing area. They may be indicated in a number of different ways. If your monitor is color, the links can be displayed in a different color than other text. If you have a black-and-white monitor, the links can be underlined. On all displays, when you move your cursor over an area of the screen that has an active link, your cursor changes from an arrow to a pointing hand.

> **Note**
>
> On the Macintosh, Mosaic can distinguish links to documents that you have viewed previously from links to documents that you have never viewed (or viewed long ago). By default, blue links are those that you have not travelled, and red links are those you have seen.

A *link* can be a word, a group of words, or an image. Look at the Windows Mosaic home page in figure 5.2. When you run Mosaic on a color display, you see a number of blue items. The words *University of Illinois*, *Last Update*, *alpha 6*, *GrowStub*, *Second International WWW Conference '94: Mosaic and the Web*, and *NEW* are all in blue (the default hyperlink color, which you can change). In addition, the large graphic at the top of the window is outlined in blue.

If you move your cursor over any of these words or over the graphic, the cursor changes to a pointing hand. The URL associated with each of the links that you pass over appears in the status bar (if it is enabled). To activate a link, place your cursor over the link and click. Mosaic loads that document and displays the URL for the document in the URL bar (if it is enabled).

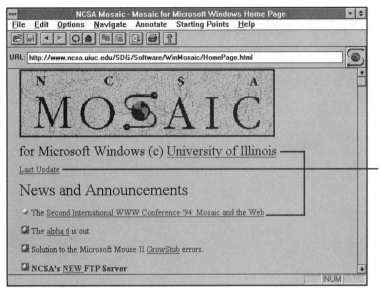

Fig. 5.2
The Windows
Mosaic home page,
with hyperlinks
identified.

Hyperlinks

Moving Backward and Forward

Typing long URLs and scrolling through documents to look for the links you want gets rather tedious. If you're jumping between a number of documents, take advantage of three helpful navigating commands: **B**ack, **F**orward, and **R**eload.

Mosaic keeps information about what documents you have loaded (see a discussion of the history list in chapter 6), and lets you move quickly between these documents using the **B**ack and **F**orward commands. The **B**ack command takes you to the previous document that you had open. To go back, open the **N**avigate menu and choose **B**ack.

The next of these commands is **F**orward. The thing you have to remember about **F**orward is that you can only move forward after moving back. (This concept is rather confusing, but makes more sense when you have read about history lists in chapter 6). To move forward, open the **N**avigate menu and choose **F**orward.

The last command is **R**eload. This command again displays the document that you are currently viewing. To reload the current document, open the **N**avigate menu and choose **R**eload.

> **Note**
>
> Sometimes documents have forward and backward link buttons at the top or bottom of the document. This is especially true for a series of documents that is meant to be read in order, or where the documents are closely related. These link buttons usually take you to the next or to the preceding document in the series. There is often an "up" button that takes you back to the point from which you entered the series, also. To use these buttons, click them just as you would any other link in a document.

Tip

On the Macintosh, you can get rid of all the documents in your cache (causing Mosaic to reload them the next time you jump to them). Open Options and choose Flush Cache.

When you are reading documents, often you move back and forth between one document and others which are linked to that document. To keep from having to load the main document from its URL every time you view it, Mosaic keeps copies of the last few documents you viewed on your local computer. This is called *caching*.

Caching is good because it keeps Mosaic from making unnecessary demands on Internet resources. It does take up resources on your own computer, though, so you can only cache a limited number of documents. In Windows Mosaic, you can edit your MOSAIC.INI file and set the number of documents you want to cache by setting the Number= line in the [Document Caching] section of the file (the default is 2).

Moving between Documents Using URLs

If you don't want to go to any of the documents whose links are displayed in the current document, or if you did not load a home page or for some other reason currently have no document displayed, you can load a new document by specifying its URL to Mosaic. Refer to the "URLs" section in chapter 2 for information about how to correctly format a URL. To enter a URL directly:

1. Open the **F**ile menu and choose **O**pen URL.

2. The Open URL dialog box appears (see fig. 5.3). Click the box next to URL. The contents of the box (set to the first item in your current hotlist) are highlighted.

Fig. 5.3

The Open URL window enables you to enter directly the URL for the next document that you want to view.

Open URL		
URL: http://www.ncsa.uiuc.edu/SDG/Software/Mosaic	Starting Points Document	
Current Hotlist: Starting Points	OK	Cancel

Note

This dialog box looks slightly different on a Mac (see fig. 5.4). As you can see, there is simply a blank text box in which to enter the URL. When you open this dialog box again, the last URL you typed is there.

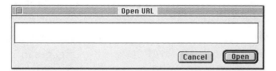

Fig. 5.4
The Open URL dialog box on a Mac.

3. If you want to enter a completely new URL, just begin typing the URL in the box and the old contents are deleted. If you want to modify the URL that is shown, click the box again and your cursor is inserted in the text, where you can edit the current URL.

4. Choose OK (Open on the Mac) to load the URL that you entered, or choose Cancel if you do not want to load that document. If you choose OK, Mosaic loads that document and displays the URL for the document in the URL bar (if you have it enabled).

Note

When you load a new document, Mosaic usually erases the document that was in the document viewing area and displays the new document there. On the Macintosh, you have the option of opening a new document window, which displays more than one document at a time. To open a new document window, open the File menu and choose New Window: a new window appears with your home page displayed. If you choose Clone Window, the new window displays the same document as the first window. To close any of your Mosaic document windows, open the File menu and choose Close.

What You See When a Document Is Loaded

When you load a document, Mosaic gives you a lot of information about what is happening. The globe in the URL bar rotates, with its beacon flashing. A number of different messages appear in the status bar. These messages can include:

- `Doing nameserver lookup on:<hostname>`

- `Connecting to HTTP server` (If it is another type of server, such as Gopher or FTP, that protocol is indicated rather than HTTP.)

II

Mosaic Basics

■ `Reading response`

■ `Transferring:<counter> bytes`

■ `Transferring inline image <filename.gif>:<counter> bytes`

Loading documents can take a few minutes, especially if the document has a lot of large graphics and your computer has a relatively slow (less than 9600 bps) connection to the Internet. There is one thing you can do to speed up the loading of the document: tell Mosaic not to load the in-line graphics from the document. To stop the loading of in-line images in Windows Mosaic, open **O**ptions and choose Display Inline Images. This feature is turned off if there is no check mark next to it. On the Macintosh, open Options and select Auto-Load Images.

If you turn off the loading of in-line graphics, Mosaic displays placeholder icons in the document instead of the graphics. If you want to see one of the graphics that was not loaded, click the graphic icon and Mosaic will load that graphic.

It is nice to be able to follow the status of the document load because this can be the first (or sometimes the only) indication that there is a problem. For example, if you try to load a document that is of a type Mosaic does not recognize, Mosaic makes the connection to the server, but simply aborts the load because it does not recognize the document type. If Mosaic aborts a load in this way, it shows an initial connecting message, but then doesn't show a transferring message in the status bar. Another indication of a transfer error is that the globe in the URL bar stops spinning. Mosaic gives no other indication that it aborted the document load.

It is also nice to be able to watch the counter increase as the document is loaded. If you know the file size of the document you are loading, you have an idea of how far along you are and how much longer you can expect it to be before the document is loaded.

> ### Note
>
> If you don't know the size of the file you are loading, the counter isn't very useful. There is another Web browser from EINet (they have Windows and Mac versions) that adds a visual progress meter to show how much of the page has loaded. This shareware program is covered in chapter 12, "Other Ways to Access the World Wide Web."

Looking for Information in a Document

If the WWW document you are reading is short, it is easy to scroll through the document (or use Page Up and Page Down) to find information of interest to you. If you have loaded a very long document, though, Mosaic does provide a way to look for information. Follow these steps:

1. Open the **E**dit menu and choose **F**ind to bring up the Find window.

2. Click the box next to Find What: and enter the word for which you want to search.

3. Click Match Case if you want Mosaic to match exactly the capitalization of the word you entered.

4. Choose Find Next to begin the search. If a match is found, Mosaic scrolls the window to the section where the match is. An alert box informs you if no match is found.

Caution

The Find feature does not work properly in the Windows version of Mosaic. It does not always find matching words when they do exist, and does not always notify you when no matches are found. Sometimes, the find feature causes your PC to lock up, requiring you to reboot your computer. This is a known bug.

Saving and Printing Documents

In general, the purpose of the WWW is to be able to have one copy of a document that many people can view, although there are times when you might want to save a copy of a document to your local computer. Mosaic gives you several options for saving files.

On both the Macintosh and Windows versions of Mosaic, you can open the File menu and choose Save As (this feature did not work in the 2.0a6 Windows version, but is working in the 2.0a7 version). This brings up a Save As dialog box that lets you browse through your directories and store the file wherever you like.

II

Mosaic Basics

> **Note**
>
> In the Windows version of Mosaic, the documents are stored as HTML documents and can be loaded and viewed. On the Macintosh, there is an option to save the document as unformatted text or HTML. Only the unformatted text option is working. If you try to save the document as HTML, it does not save properly and crashes the Macintosh if you try to save it repeatedly.

Tip

If you want to load a single file to disk, in Windows Mosaic you can Shift-click on the hyperlink rather than selecting Load to Disk from the Options menu. This loads only that one file to disk, and you won't have to worry about forgetting to turn off Load to Disk.

Tip

If you want to save the file you are currently viewing to disk, click Load to Disk from the **O**ptions menu, then click Reload from the **N**avigate menu. This brings up the Save As dialog box.

There is another way to save files in both the Windows and Macintosh version of Mosaic. Open the **O**ptions menu and choose **L**oad to Disk. A check mark appears next to the item, and the feature is enabled. The next time you click a hyperlink, rather than Mosaic loading the document for viewing, it brings up a Save As dialog box, letting you specify a file on your local disk where the document can be saved. You can save any format document in this manner—HTML file, image file, sound file, or unformatted text.

Remember to turn off the option if you want to go back to viewing files with Mosaic (open the **O**ptions menu and select **L**oad to Disk again to turn it off).

When you save an HTML document to your local disk, remember that the document probably contains hyperlinks in it. These links can be relative or absolute. An absolute reference contains the complete address of the document that is being referenced, including the host name, directory path, and file name. A relative reference assumes that the previous machine and directory path are being used, and just the file name (or possibly a subdirectory and file name) is specified.

If the document references other documents with relative addresses, you can not view those documents unless you copy them to your local disk and set them up with the same directory structure they had at the original site. You might want to set up a document and its linked documents on your local disk if you want to view the document without connecting to the Internet. The problem with this is that if the original document changes, you are not aware of it and are viewing an outdated version of the document.

Absolute references always work unless your Internet connection fails or the referenced documents are moved.

In addition to being able to save documents, both the Windows and Macintosh versions of Mosaic allow you to print documents. Open the **F**ile menu and choose **P**rint to send a copy of the current document to your printer.

Customizing Your Mosaic Window

This chapter has covered some of the features of Mosaic that let you move between documents. You can customize a number of these features; you can set up Mosaic to behave in a way that is most comfortable for you. This section discusses how to set up Mosaic to your preferences.

Customizing the Hyperlink Indicators in Windows

You can change the default appearance and color of the hyperlinks in the documents Mosaic loads. To do so, edit the MOSAIC.INI file and set the following lines:

```
[Main]
Anchor Underline=no
Anchor Cursor=yes
[Settings]
Anchor Color=0,0,255
```

Setting Anchor Underline to No turns off the anchor underlining in documents (this feature does not work and is a reported bug in the 2.0 alpha 6 release of Mosaic, and does not appear to have been fixed in the 2.0 alpha 8 release). Setting Anchor Cursor to Yes enables the Anchor Color variable. The Anchor Color variable takes values from 0 to 255 for red, green, and blue components to create the hyperlink identifying color (this feature also appears to be broken, although it is not a listed bug).

You can set your cursor so that it does not change shape when you are over a hyperlink. Open the **O**ptions menu, and select Change Cursor Over Anchors (it's off when the check mark disappears). If this option is on, your cursor will change (by default, to a pointing hand) when it is over a link.

Customizing the Hyperlink Indicators and Background Colors on a Mac

Changing the colors used for explored and unexplored links is quite straightforward on the Macintosh.

1. Open the Options menu and choose Preferences.

2. In the Preferences dialog box, choose Links from the strip of buttons on the left side. You see a variety of possible link items: the top right are the explored and unexplored color choices (see fig. 5.5).

3. If you click one of the color boxes, you get a color wheel from which you can choose your favorite colors (see fig. 5.6).

Fig. 5.5
Among other
things, the
Macintosh
Preferences dialog
box lets you
change the color
of your explored
and unexplored
hotlinks.

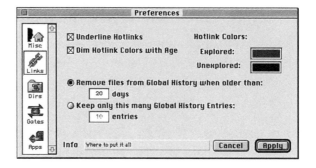

Fig. 5.6
The color wheel
dialog box gives
you a wide range
of colors to choose
from for your
hotlink colors.

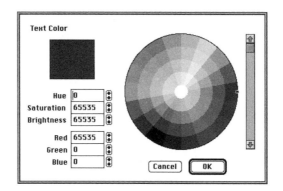

4. Click the color you want. The color in the box on the left of the dialog box should reflect your choice.

5. Click OK and then Apply and you're finished.

You can also change the color used for the background of the Mosaic window.

1. Open the Options menu and choose Preferences.

2. In the Preferences dialog box, choose Misc from the strip of buttons on the left side. At the bottom of the dialog box, you see the words Background Color with a color box next to them (see fig. 5.7).

3. If you click the color box, you get a color wheel from which you can choose your favorite colors (see fig. 5.8).

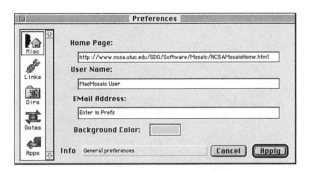

Fig. 5.7
You can also set
the color of your
Mosaic window
background in the
Preferences dialog
box.

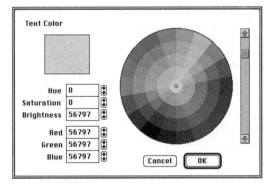

Fig. 5.8
The color wheel
dialog box gives
you a wide range
of colors to choose
from for your
background color.

4. Click on the color you want. The color in the box on the left of the dialog box should reflect your choice.

5. Click OK and then Apply and you're finished.

Customizing the Displayed Fonts in Windows

You can customize the fonts that Mosaic uses when displaying documents. HTML documents use standard paragraph tags to describe each paragraph in the document. Mosaic lets you specify the font family, size, and style for each of the standard HTML paragraph tags.

1. Open the **O**ptions menu, and choose Font. A walking menu appears that lists the different HTML paragraph tags.

2. From this walking menu, select the paragraph tag of the font you want to change. Even if you aren't familiar with HTML, you can guess what the different paragraph types are. For example, Normal is the regular text font, Heading1 is usually the large heading at the top of a document, and so on.

II

Mosaic Basics

3. When you select a paragraph tag, the Font window appears, as shown in figure 5.9.

Fig. 5.9
The Style Window dialog box lets you define the font displayed for the paragraph type you selected.

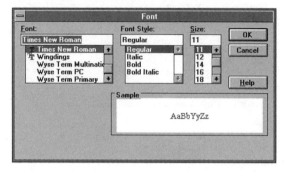

4. Scroll down through the Font list until you find the font you want and select it. You can also set the Font Style (bold, italic, and so on) and the Size.

5. Choose OK to make the selections take effect, or Cancel if you decide not to change the fonts.

The changes that you make take effect immediately, and are used by Mosaic in future sessions.

Customizing the Displayed Fonts on a Mac

You can customize the fonts that Mosaic uses when displaying documents. HTML documents use standard paragraph tags to describe each paragraph in the document. Macintosh Mosaic lets you specify the font family, size, style, color, and spacing for each of the standard HTML paragraph tags.

To change fonts on the Macintosh, you first have to decide whether your changes are global to all formats or specific to an individual format.

On the Options menu, choose Styles. You see the Style Window dialog box, as shown in figure 5.10. Running along the left side of this dialog box are four icons: document (Doc), paragraph (Para), character (Char) and Table.

To make global changes, click the Doc icon. To change the respective size of all typefaces used in Mosaic, you can either click the up arrow once (to increment the size of each typeface) or down arrow once (to decrement the size of each typeface) next to the label (Change Respective Size of ALL Tags). To set ALL of the fonts in the document to the same value, click the font, color, or size buttons on the lower right under Check Attribute to Set for ALL Tags and fill in the appropriate fields. If you want to these changes to apply to every font in the document, click Apply. If you change your mind, click Cancel.

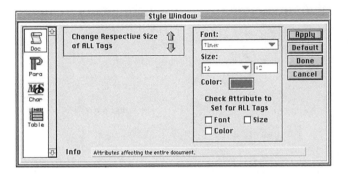

Fig. 5.10
The Style Window dialog box lets you change the font attributes of entire documents, paragraphs types, characters types, or tables.

More likely than not, however, you want to modify specific paragraph tags, not an entire document. To modify individual tags, follow these steps:

1. Click the paragraph icon on the left side of the Style Window dialog box. Now you see the possible settings have changed to those shown in figure 5.11. The key item here is the top left box called HTML style.

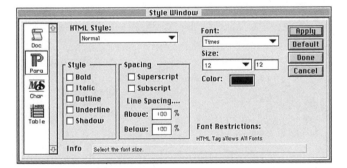

Fig. 5.11
The Paragraph option in the Style Window dialog box lets you change the font characteristics of each HTML paragraph tag.

2. Click any of about a dozen different paragraph tags in a document, then modify it to your preferences (see fig. 5.12). To modify a paragraph tag, choose it from the HTML style box.

3. After you select the paragraph tag to modify, set the parameters to your liking for any of the characteristics (font family, size, style, color or spacing), and choose Apply. If you decide that you don't want to modify the paragraph tag, choose Cancel.

II

Mosaic Basics

Fig. 5.12
The HTML Style pop-up menu allows you to select individual HTML paragraph tags to modify.

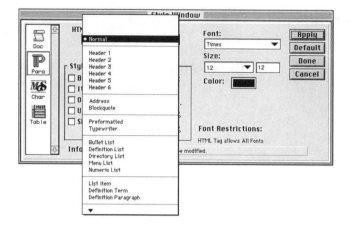

HTML also has a number of built-in character tags that you can modify. To modify individual tags, follow these steps:

1. Click the character icon on the left side of the Style Window dialog box. The HTML style box still appears in the dialog box, but if you click it now, it shows you the HTML character tags available, not the paragraph tags (see fig. 5.13).

Fig. 5.13
The Character option in the Style Window dialog box lets you change the font styles of the available HTML character tags.

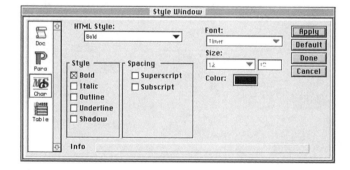

2. After you select the character tag to modify, set the parameters to your liking. You can only modify the style and spacing of the character tags. When you have set everything, choose Apply. If you decide that you don't want to modify the paragraph tag, choose Cancel.

You can also set the font styles for HTML table tags. To do this, click the Table icon in the Style Window dialog box. The list of HTML styles is shorter, but other than that, parameters are very similar to those for the regular HTML paragraph tags (see fig. 5.14). Choose the table tag you want to modify from the list of HTML Styles, change the parameters to your specifications, and choose Apply (or Cancel if you change your mind).

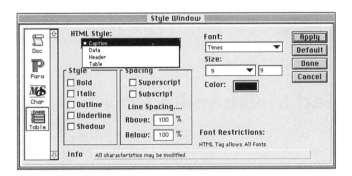

Fig. 5.14
The Styles Window dialog box lets you modify the font characteristics of HTML table tags.

Customizing the Window Areas

◀ See "Using the Mosaic Inter-face," p. 63

Many of the different window areas in Mosaic are optional (not, however, the document viewing area—Mosaic wouldn't be very useful without that!). The title bar and menu bar cannot be removed, but the tool bar, URL bar, and status bar can all be turned off. Turning these window areas off gives you a bigger viewing area, but removes some timesaving and informational features.

- To turn off the tool bar, open the **O**ptions menu and click Show **T**oolbar. The check mark next to the menu item disappears and the tool bar is removed from the window. (This option isn't available on a Mac.)

- To turn off the URL bar, open the **O**ptions menu and click Show Current URL. The check mark next to the menu item disappears and the URL bar is removed from the window. (Note that this also removes the globe; you can no longer click the globe to interrupt a command.)

> **Note**
>
> On the Mac, open the Options menu. The top item on the menu is Show URLs or Hide URLs. If the URL bar is showing and you want to hide it, choose Hide URLs.

- To turn off the status bar, open the **O**ptions menu and click Show **S**tatus Bar. The check mark next to the menu item disappears and the status bar is removed from the window.

Mosaic Basics

> **Note**
>
> On the Mac, open the Options menu. The second item on the menu is Show Status Messages or Hide Status Messages. If the messages are showing and you want to hide them, choose Hide Status Messages.

Viewing Multimedia Files

◀ See "Can Your Computer System Run Mosaic for Windows," p. 48

◀ See "Can Your Computer System Run Mosaic for Macintosh," p. 67

One of Mosaic's best features is that it enables you to view documents of many different types. If you remember from the introductory chapters, Mosaic is a *multimedia application,* which means that you can view files containing a number of different types of media—pictures, sound, and animation. Mosaic can display text and inline graphics directly, but to display other types of files, you must have viewers for these files installed on your machine.

After you have a viewer installed and Mosaic knows where to find it and what type of files it displays, you can load files of that type and Mosaic automatically starts the viewer to display them. Mosaic can recognize any of a number of standard image, sound, and animation formats. Some of the more common ones are shown in table 5.1.

Table 5.1 Multimedia File Types Recognized By Mosaic	
Media	**File Type**
Audio	WAV, MIDI
Image	JPEG, GIF, TIFF
Video	MPEG, AVI, MOV
Formatted text	PS, RTF, DOC

When you find a file on a WWW server that is one of the types in table 5.1, and you set up an external viewer for that file type to work with Mosaic, you only need to click the hyperlink for the file and Mosaic launches the viewer application with the file loaded. You now can use any of the features of the viewer application to examine, modify, or save the file you loaded (see fig. 5.15).

Fig. 5.15
When Mosaic loads a file type that it recognizes, the viewer you specify for that file type displays the image, sound, animation, and so on.

Notice that because the image is loaded in an external application, you can use Mosaic at the same time you view the image.

Temporary Files on the Mac

The Mac version of Mosaic uses temporary files to store downloaded multimedia files while the download is in progress and while you are viewing the files. Several commands and options relate to these temporary files.

When Mosaic loads files that need an external viewer, it temporarily stores the files in the System Folder before launching the viewer. Although Mosaic deletes these files when you exit the application, you may want to set up a separate temporary file to keep your System Folder from becoming cluttered.

To tell Mosaic to use a temporary folder instead of storing temporary files in the System Folder, open the Options menu and select Use Mac Temporary Folder. When this option is selected, by default, Mosaic stores the temporary files in an invisible folder called Temporary Items on the top level of your system disk.

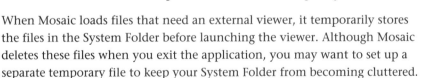

Caution

At one time, the invisible Temporary Items file occasionally disappeared and caused an error when an external viewer attempted to access this file. The authors could not verify whether this bug was fixed in the latest release of Mac Mosaic.

You can specify a different file for Mosaic to use for temporary storage by opening the Options menu and selecting Preferences. In the Preferences dialog box, click the Dirs (directories) icon. The current temporary directory is shown at the top of the dialog box (see fig. 5.16). Click Set Temp Directory and use the File Browser dialog box that appears to navigate to the directory where you want Mosaic to store its temporary files. Click Select for your changes to take effect, or Cancel to leave the directory as is.

Fig. 5.16
The Preferences dialog box lets you specify a directory for Mosaic to use for temporary file storage.

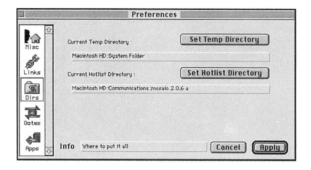

Working with Local Files

When you think of using Mosaic, you think of retrieving documents from WWW servers on the Internet to view. Mosaic can read documents from your local file system as well as it can read documents from halfway around the world. If you are sharing documents among members of your organization, many of the documents you view may be on a local file server, or possibly on your local computer.

Mosaic provides an option to make it easy to load a local file. If you want to load a local file, open the **F**ile menu and click Open **L**ocal File. This brings up the Open dialog box shown in figure 5.17; this window lets you browse through all your local disks to find a file.

You can also load a local file in the same manner that you load any URL. Open the **F**ile menu and choose **O**pen URL. To specify a local file in the URL box, precede the directory path of the file with **file:///c¦** (you can substitute any of your local disk drives for c). The three slashes tell Mosaic that you are looking for a local file, and the bar is used instead of a colon because the colon has a specific purpose in a URL. Use slashes in the directory path you enter, even if you are describing a directory on a PC where the backslash is usually used. Mosaic properly translates the slashes when it retrieves the file.

◀ See "URLs," p. 38

Local URLs can be used just as all URLs are used—as items in hotlists, links in documents, and so on.

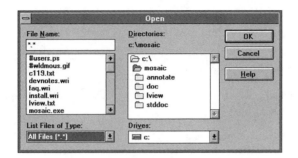

Fig. 5.17
The Open dialog box enables you to enter a local file name or to browse your local file system to find the next document that you want to view.

Creating Your Personal Home Page

Creating your own home page is simple. HTML comprises special codes, placed between < > symbols, that tell a Web browser what each piece of text is.

To create a home page, first open a text editor, or a word processor that lets you save your work in ASCII format. At the top of the page, type the document title. The title doesn't appear in the document when it is displayed in a browser, but is used as an identifier. Mosaic displays the title in the window's title bar.

Below the title, type the first heading you want to appear in the document. This heading appears at the top of the page. Then type a line or two of text. Below those lines, type another header then type the name of a document to which you want to link your home page. For example:

```
Personal Home Page
Personal Home Page
This is my very own home page.
Very Important Links
The Simpsons
```

In this example, Personal Home Page is the document title and the first heading. Next is a line of normal text (This is my very own home page), followed by another heading (Very Important Links). The Simpsons is the first link.

Next enter the HTML codes. The codes for the title are <TITLE> and </TITLE>, and placed as in this example:

```
<TITLE>Personal Home Page</TITLE>
```

The codes for a first heading are <H1> and </H1>. These codes are before and after the text in the same way as the preceding example. The body text doesn't need any code preceding it; browsers assume that if text has no code in front of it, it must be normal text. But it does need a paragraph marker. At the end of each paragraph you must add <P>. Putting blank lines between lines of text will not separate them—Web browser joins the text together, unless the lines are separated by <P>.

Now, the second heading. A second-level heading uses the codes <H2> and </H2>. Here is an example:

```
<TITLE>Personal Home Page</TITLE>
<H1>Personal Home Page</H1>
This is my very own home page.<P>
<H2>Very Important Links</H2>
The Simpsons
```

The last part of this example is the link to The Simpsons. The text you want to act as a link must be preceded by the URL. So, to go to The Simpsons Web page, precede the text with this: **<A HREF="http://cc.lut.fi/~mega/ simpsons.html">**. Place the URL between the <A HREF=" and the ">. After the text place the </A> code. The link looks like the following:

```
<A HREF="http://cc.lut.fi/[td]mega/simpsons.html">The Simpsons</A>
```

Now save the file. Remember, save it in ASCII format (use the HTM extension in DOS, .html on the Mac). You've created your own home page.

Open this file in Mosaic by opening the File menu and choosing Open Local File . When you open it you can click your link to travel to the referenced document.

If you want to learn more about working with HTML files see *Using the WWW* (Que), *WWW Unleashed* (Sams Publishing), or *The Complete Idiot's Guide to the World Wide Web* (Alpha Books).

You can also find extensive online documentation: start at **http:// www.ncsa.uiuc.edu/General/Internet/WWW/ HTMLPrimer.html**. This document gives a very thorough overview of the HTML commands that enable you to create WWW documents. It also gives you some document design advice, and gives you pointers to other HTML references.

Viewing Source Documents

Another way to learn HTML is to look at some HTML source files. Open the File menu and choose **D**ocument Source when you have a document loaded in Mosaic. This command opens a window that shows the HTML source for the current document. It shows you what the HTML document looks like, with all the hypertext codes still inside it (when Mosaic loads a document it strips all the codes out before it displays it). To close this window, select the

OK button at the bottom of the window, or open the **F**ile menu and choose E**x**it. Figure 5.18 shows a document loaded into Mosaic and its corresponding HTML code.

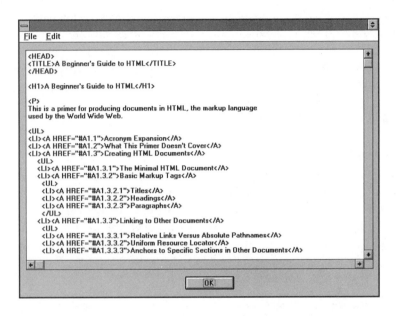

Fig. 5.18
The Document Source window enables you to scroll through the source file for the current document and see what HTML commands were used to create the document.

In the Document Source window, you can highlight and copy text to the Clipboard. Open the **E**dit menu and choose **C**opy. To save the entire source for this document to your local disk, open the **F**ile menu in the Document Source window and choose **S**ave. The Save As dialog box appears, letting you save the HTML source in a file anywhere on your local file system.

To close this window, click the OK button at the bottom of the window, or open the **F**ile menu and choose E**x**it.

Another way to save the HTML source of a document is to open the **O**ptions menu and choose **L**oad to Disk, then click on a link to the document. This brings up the Save As dialog box, which lets you save the HTML source for the document anywhere on your local file system.

Problems That Occur While Navigating the WWW

The World Wide Web is really a concept still under development, and Mosaic is definitely an application still under development. For an alpha release, it works pretty well. But, with a complex application like Mosaic and a conceptually young Internet service like the WWW, there are bound to be problems occasionally.

Some problems that occur are related to limited resources on any particular Internet host (for example, the number of people who can connect to the host at one time may be limited). Traffic over the Internet is steadily growing and communications may be slow. Other problems may be actual bugs in Mosaic. Throughout the book, related problems are discussed when a topic is being discussed. This section discusses problems that are common to many different Mosaic functions that are not mentioned elsewhere in the book.

Mosaic Bugs

Mosaic admittedly has its flaws. After all, it is an alpha release, not yet to the point of a beta release. The designers realize this is somewhat of an inconvenience, and have tried to provide some help by publishing a list of known bugs. To see a list of bugs for Windows Mosaic, open the **H**elp menu and click **B**ug List. Mosaic loads a document that describes all known Windows Mosaic bugs, and tells you how to get in touch with the developers if you find a bug that they don't know about.

 To see a list of bugs for Mac Mosaic, load the MacMosaic home page at the NCSA **http://www.ncsa.uiuc.edu/SDG/Software/MacMosaic**. In this document, there's a link to an HTML document that lists known bugs (**Bugs-mac.html**).

Most Mosaic bugs are discussed in the sections of this book that are related to the functions that cause the bugs. In the Windows version, the only Mosaic bug that currently is common enough to be mentioned is that Help buttons in some windows fail. Sometimes a window that Mosaic brings up has a Help button that brings up a blank Windows Help window. One such window is the Save As window that you get when you are loading files to disk. Also, sometimes you see the message For Help, Press F1 in the status bar while you are using Mosaic. Pressing F1 also brings up a blank Windows Help window.

User Errors

Sometimes you can inadvertently ask Mosaic to do something it can't do. You can make a mistake when typing in the URL, or try to fetch the right document from the wrong machine. Here are a few of the more common user errors and Mosaic's reaction to them.

- **Enter an invalid protocol**. Windows Mosaic gives you an `Access not available` error alert like the one shown in figure 5.19. Choose OK to make the alert disappear, and then try to load a valid URL. (Mac Mosaic gives an `Unable to Access Document` error.)

Fig. 5.19
When Mosaic encounters an error, it usually brings up an alert box like this one to let you know what happened.

- **Try to load a document that doesn't exist**. You get a `File/directory does not exist` error alert. Choose OK to make the alert disappear, and then try to load a valid URL. (Mac Mosaic gives you a `Not Found` error.)

- **Try to load from a site that doesn't exist**. You get a `Failed DNS Lookup` error alert. Choose OK to make the alert disappear, and then try to load a valid URL. (Mac Mosaic gives you an `Unable to connect to remote host` error.)

Network Errors

A number of network-related errors can be caused by a machine being down, too much traffic on the network, too many people using a host's resources, or any number of other problems. These types of problems are associated with having a large number of different types of machines and services on a large network.

The following list of error alerts is by no means exhaustive, but shows some of the most common errors. If you load the Bug List document from the Windows Mosaic Help menu and scroll down to the bottom, you see the link `Common Error Messages` in a section entitled "Bug Like Features." This link loads a document (**http://www.ncsa.uiuc.edu/SDG/Software/ WinMosaic/errors.html**) that lists most of the errors that you can see (but it doesn't tell you what caused them or how to avoid them). These errors can occur with Macintosh Mosaic, also, but they are reported slightly differently.

- `SOCKET:Connection has been refused`. This error usually occurs because the maximum number of people allowed to use the host's resources are currently on-line. Try again later.

Mosaic Basics

- `SOCKET:Connection timed out`. This message comes up if Mosaic tries to communicate with a host and receives no answer within a specific time period. The host is too busy to answer or the machine is hung up.

- `SOCKET:Host is down`. The host that you tried to reach is down. Try to reach another host that provides the same service or try this one again later.

- `Failed DNS Lookup`. The host that you tried to reach does not exist. This may or may not be a real error. If you typed the name of the host incorrectly, it is an error. This error also seems to occur if Mosaic tries to look up the host and doesn't get a response from the name server in a specific period of time.

- `Transfer canceled`. This error is not common, but seems to occur when there are communications problems. For example, if you are connected to your Internet provider using the SL/IP protocol, and the phone line that you are using to dial in becomes noisy for some reason, it will cause a transfer to abort.

From Here...

To learn more about using the WWW and Mosaic, refer to these chapters:

- Chapter 2, "Introduction to the World Wide Web," Gives you background information about the WWW.

- Chapter 6, "Shortcuts to Favorite Places," gives you some tips on effective browsing and how to get where you want to go quickly.

- Chapter 13, "Hot Home Pages," gives you some pointers on where to go to find interesting documents on the WWW.

Chapter 6

Shortcuts to Favorite Places

The WWW lets you move easily between documents. Although this is convenient, it also can be a curse. While moving back and forth, you easily can get lost—and URLs can be long, complicated, and difficult to remember.

Mosaic has many features that allow you to keep track of where you were and allow you to get to places quickly. This chapter assumes you have read chapter 5, "Navigating with Mosaic."

In this chapter, you learn to do the following:

- Navigate the WWW efficiently

- Keep track of sites that interest you

- Quickly access the sites you use the most

Effective Browsing Techniques

Navigating between WWW documents can be confusing. Documents often connect back to documents you already read. You don't know you're going to a document you've already seen because different words or pictures are used for the hyperlink than the ones you used originally.

Sometimes you can't tell from the hyperlink whether the document is of interest to you—loading documents uses valuable time. Often, you waste time loading documents that you dismiss immediately. This section helps you learn to reduce unnecessary document loading and circular navigating.

How to Keep Track of Where You've Been

Keeping track of where you are and where you were is one of the biggest challenges of using Mosaic. For example, assume you're reading a document that deals with agriculture and you click a hyperlink to take you to Hay Field Seeding Suggestions. The document turns out to be one you loaded earlier—when you found a hyperlink for Pasture Management Techniques. How can you avoid this frustrating repetition?

One suggestion is to have a home page that provides links to your most-visited WWW pages. This home page is useful, for example, if you are working on a group project and frequently use documents with known locations. You can either create your own home page or someone can create a project home page for your group. In this scenario, you are probably already familiar with the servers, if not the exact documents.

But what if you're navigating in uncharted waters on the WWW? Although it sounds difficult, you probably can learn to recognize the URLs of the sites that keep information of interest to you. If the URL bar is displayed, the URL for the current document is shown there. If you have the status bar displayed, open the **O**ptions menu and choose Show Anchor URLs (on the Mac, open Options and deselect Hide URLs). The status bar shows the URL of a hyperlink when you move the cursor over it (see fig. 6.1). As you move between documents, you begin to remember some of the URLs you see frequently—when you put your cursor over a hyperlink, you recognize documents you know.

Fig. 6.1

The status bar displays the URLs of hyperlinks. (Remember, the status bar is near the top of the screen on the Mac.)

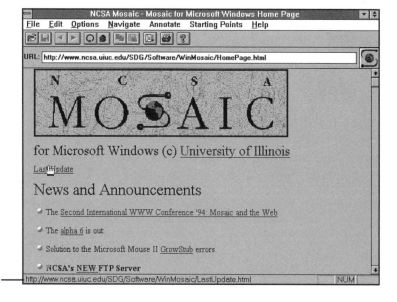

Status bar

How to Get Where You Were

Trying to navigate back to a document you viewed in the current Mosaic session also can be challenging. In general, to go to the document you viewed prior to the current document, open the **N**avigate menu and choose the **B**ack command (or the left arrow in the toolbar). Choosing the **F**orward command (or the right arrow) takes you to the last document you viewed after this document. This sounds rather confusing, but is understandable if you look at how Mosaic determines these links.

The **N**avigate menu has an item called History that brings up a window, similar to the one shown in figure 6.2. Notice, there is a list of URLs in this window—the URL for the current document is highlighted.

Fig. 6.2
The NCSA Mosaic History window shows a linear list of URLs you visit.

II

Mosaic Basics

> **Note**
>
> The history list is different on the Mac. It is a drop-down list to the right of the toolbar buttons (see fig. 6.3). To open the history list, click the arrow (which you can't see in this figure because the list is open) and select an item.

The history list shows you the URLs of the document chain that led you to this point and any documents that you visited after the current document. If you use the **B**ack navigation command, you move up the list. If you use the **F**orward navigation command, you move down the list. Click any URL in the list and choose Load to jump to that document (and that point in the list).

Fig. 6.3
The history list is always available on the Mac.

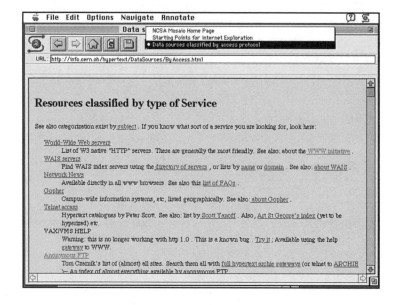

Tip
If the History window is open when you use the **F**orward and **B**ack commands, you can see the highlighted item move in the list of URLs.

If you move up to one of the higher level links and then jump to a new URL from that document it wipes out all the URLs past the current document. So, while you can use the **B**ack and **F**orward navigation commands to move between documents you already visited, if you jump to a new document while in the middle of the list, you erase the links at the end of the list.

To move quickly between documents that you load, use the history list. If you want to add a new document to the list of ones you're viewing, make sure you're at the end of the list before you jump to that document. You don't have to use hyperlinks to add the document you load to the history list. Load the document from the **F**ile menu's **O**pen URL menu item or the URL toolbar button, and it is added to the list.

Global History and Explored Hotlinks on the Mac

The Mac version of Mosaic has another useful history feature that isn't available in the Windows version yet. This feature is *global history*. In addition to keeping a history list of all pages you open in a session, the Mac keeps a global history of all sites you visit, even in earlier sessions. You cannot jump back to previous documents, but the hyperlinks for the sites you visited (explore) are shown in a different color than unexplored sites. This feature is very useful if you can't remember all the sites and don't want to waste time reloading a document that you already saw.

By default, the sites in the global history list are shown in red (as opposed to blue for unexplored sites). You can change the color for these previously explored sites. The global history list doesn't extend back in time indefinitely. By default, Mosaic keeps an item on the list for only 20 days. After that, it is removed from the list and appears in blue as an unexplored site. You can change this default, too, to suit your needs. You can also set a limit on the number of items tracked on the global hotlist. (Use this option or remove items after a given number of days.)

To change the color of explored sites, to change the length of time an item remains on the global history list, or to set a limit on the number of items on the list, follow these steps:

◀ See "Customizing the Hyperlink Indicators on a Mac," p. 89

To change colors, open the Options menu and choose Preferences. In the Preferences dialog box, choose the Links item from the strip of buttons on the left side. You'll see a variety of possible link items (see fig. 6.4): the top right are the explored and unexplored color choices. If you click one of the color boxes, you get a color wheel from which you can choose your favorite colors (see fig. 6.5). Click OK and then click Apply.

The Links Preference dialog box also lets you change the length of time an item can remain on the global history list or how long the list can be (see fig. 6.4). Click the small radio button to the left of the explanatory phrase for the item that you want to set. After you've done that, the radio button will darken, and you can now click the entry field for that item and type in any value. The default values are 20 days for global history, and a maximum list size of 10 entries.

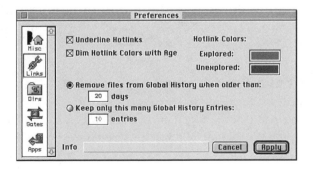

Fig. 6.4
The Links Preferences dialog box lets you set up how long an item remains in your global history list and the maximum length of the list.

Fig. 6.5
The color wheel allows you to easily set your explored and unexplored link colors by clicking the color you want.

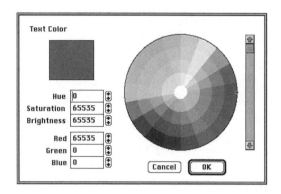

> **Note**
>
> The global history is kept in a file called Mosaic Global History. You can open this file and edit it in a text editor if you want to remove or change individual items.

Create Lists of Your Favorite URLs

If you don't want to learn to use HTML commands to create a home page with all your favorite WWW documents, Mosaic has an alternative. To quickly access your favorite URLs, Mosaic enables you to create up to 20 personal menus and submenus. In addition, you can have a QUICKLIST that lets you access your favorite documents.

> **Note**
>
> The Macintosh doesn't have a QUICKLIST, but you can have an unlimited number of hotlists and the per list limit of items is 99. The 2.0 alpha 8 release of Macintosh Mosaic also lets you have user-configurable menus similar to Windows Mosaic.

Creating Your Own Menus

You can create up to 20 menus in Mosaic. As it is distributed, Mosaic has one preconfigured menu. The Starting Points menu lets you access a number of documents on the WWW that help you learn about the World Wide Web and the Internet, and gives you quick access to Internet Services and information repositories. You may want to create your own menus, though, to gain access to documents and services you use most. For example, you might want to have a menu for each project you work on, with each menu giving you access to the documents and services you need for that project.

The Personal Menus dialog box allows you to add, delete, and edit Mosaic menus. To open the Personal Menus dialog box, open the **N**avigate menu and choose **M**enu Editor (see fig. 6.6).

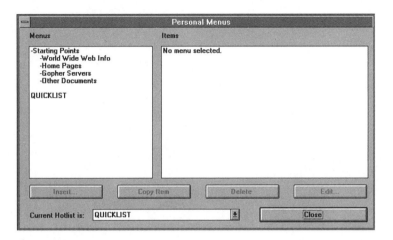

Fig. 6.6
The Mosaic Personal Menus dialog box shows current menus and items on those menus, and lets you create, delete, and edit these menus.

The existing user-configurable menus are shown in the Menus section of the dialog box. If you click a menu in this list, the items from that menu are displayed in the Items section. When you're finished modifying your personal menus, click Close to close the dialog box.

Note

As of release 2.0.a6, the Mac version of Mosaic does not have a functional menu editing feature. Open the Navigate menu and choose Custom Menu to see what the feature may look like when it does work (see fig. 6.7). The 2.0.a8 version that was released just as this book went to press has implemented the Custom Menu feature. The Edit and Delete buttons work in essentially the same way they do in the Windows version; the New Menu button adds a new menu as described for Windows in the next section, and the New Doc button adds a new document to a menu as described for Windows later in this chapter. The Menu Hierarchy box shows the current menus and their structure and where new menus are added, as described for Windows later in this chapter. Click the menus in the Menu Hierarchy box to expand them in the Mac version because there is no Items box like in the Windows version.

Fig. 6.7
The Custom Menu dialog box in the Mac version is inoperative in version 2.0.a6, but functional in 2.0.a8.

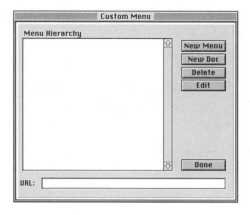

Creating a New Menu

Personal menus let you group WWW documents that you use frequently. For example, you may want to have a menu for each project you work on. The top-level menus you add are displayed in the menu bar, between the Starting Points menu and the Help menu (see fig. 6.8 for an example of a user-configured menu). You can click the menu and select items from it, just as you can with the other menus built into Mosaic. Mosaic has a limit of 20 user-configurable menus and submenus.

Fig. 6.8
The menu Internet Resources has been added to the menu bar.

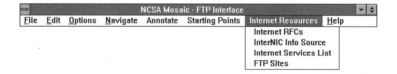

To create a new menu, follow these steps:

1. Open the **N**avigate menu and choose **M**enu Editor to open the Personal Menus dialog box.

2. Click the blank line above the word QUICKLIST in the Menus section of the dialog box. The Add Item dialog box appears (see fig. 6.9).

Fig. 6.9
Enter the title of the menu you are adding in the Add Item dialog box.

3. Click the box next to Title and enter the name of the menu you want to add. Notice that the Menu radio button is checked automatically—you can't deselect it or select another radio button.

4. Click Close. The new menu appears highlighted in the Menus section of the Personal Menus dialog box. You are now ready to add items to the menu.

Note

Choose descriptive, yet short names for your menus. Mosaic displays these names in the menu bar; there isn't much room! If the menu list becomes longer than one line, Mosaic expands the size of the menu bar as many lines as it needs to display all menu names.

Tip

If you have a SuperVGA monitor, use Windows setup to choose a driver for a higher screen resolution (800 × 600) to get more menu items on-screen.

II

Mosaic Basics

Adding Items to a Menu

After you create a new menu, you can add the items you want to appear in the menu—you can also add items to any existing menu. Mosaic currently has a limit of 40 items per menu.

To add items to a menu, follow these steps:

1. Open the **N**avigate menu and choose **M**enu Editor to open the Personal Menus dialog box.

2. In the Menus section of the dialog box, click the name of the menu to which you want to add items.

3. If there are existing items in that menu, you can place the new item anywhere in the list. If you click the name of an item in the Items section, the new item is added before the selected one. If you do not select one of the current items, the new item is added to the end of the list.

4. When you have selected the menu and item position, choose Insert. The Add Item dialog box appears (see fig. 6.10).

Fig. 6.10

In the Add Item dialog box, enter the name of the menu item you are adding and the URL associated with it, if there is one. You can also identify the type of the item.

You can now add items to the menu. The items can be of three types: a Document (with its associated URL), a Menu (submenu), or a Separator (to let you visually group items in a menu).

> ### Note
>
> On the Macintosh, you add a document with the New Doc button in the Custom Menu dialog box, and you add a submenu with the New Menu button (make sure the New Menu Bar Item checkbox is not checked if you want the new menu to be a submenu).

Adding a Document. You will probably add documents most often to your menus. In this case, "document" indicates any valid WWW URL; you can actually access more than just documents. Your URL can use any Internet protocol that Mosaic recognizes, including Gopher, FTP, and Telnet.

To add a document item to a menu, follow these steps:

1. Select the Document Item radio button in the Add Item dialog box. The fields pertaining to this item type become active (see fig. 6.11).

Fig. 6.11
When you select the Document Item radio button, the URL and Title fields become active.

2. Click the box next to Title and enter the name you want to appear in the menu. By default, the title and URL of the current document appear in the fields.

3. Click the box next to URL and enter the complete URL used to access this document—if it isn't already in the field.

Tip
A quick way to add a document to the end of the menu you've selected as your current hotlist is to open the **Navi**gate menu and choose **A**dd Current To Hotlist.

4. Choose OK. The item appears in the Items section of the Personal Menus window.

> ### Note
>
> If you want to have a menu item that is the same or similar to an existing menu item, you can copy that menu item to the Add Items buffer. Select the menu that contains the desired item in the Personal Menus dialog box. Click the desired item in the Items section (it is highlighted), and then choose Copy Item. The title and URL of the selected item appear in the Add Item dialog box the next time it is opened.

Adding a Submenu. Another way to group related items in your menus is to create a submenu that contains the related items. Remember, Mosaic has a limit of 20 user-configurable menus and submenus.

To create a submenu, follow these steps:

1. In the Add Item dialog box, select the Menu radio button. The fields that pertain to this item type become active, as shown in figure 6.12.

2. Click the box next to Title and enter the name you want to appear in the menu.

3. Choose OK. The item appears in the Items section of the Personal Menu dialog box. Note that it has a right angle bracket next to it to indicate that it's a menu.

Adding a Separator. If you don't want to add any submenus, but still want to group some of your menu entries, you can visually group items in a menu by putting a thin line called a *separator* between groups of related items.

To add a separator, follow these steps:

1. In the Add Item dialog box, select the Separator radio button. No active entry fields are in the Add Item dialog box (see fig. 6.13).

Fig. 6.13
When you click the Separator radio button, all entry fields become inactive; you do not need to enter any information for this type of item.

2. Choose OK. A line appears in the Items section of the Personal Menu dialog box.

Editing a Menu Item

After you create a menu, you may want to change the name or URLs of some of the items in the menu. You can do this with the Edit button in the Personal Menus dialog box.

To edit menu items, follow these steps:

1. Open the **N**avigate menu and choose **M**enu Editor. The Personal Menus dialog box appears.

2. Click the name of the menu that has the item you want to change.

3. Select the item in the Items list you want to change and choose Edit. The Edit Item dialog box appears (see fig. 6.14).

Fig. 6.14
The Edit Item dialog box lets you change the title or URL of an existing menu item.

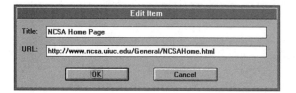

4. Edit the title and/or URL for that item, and then choose OK.

Your menu item is now changed as you specified. You can also edit a menu to change its name (the URL field doesn't appear).

Tip
Double-clicking either a menu or an item in the Personal Menus dialog box brings up the Edit Item dialog box for that item.

Deleting a Menu Item

Mosaic also lets you delete a menu item or an entire menu. To delete menus or menu items, follow these steps:

1. Open the **N**avigate menu and choose **M**enu Editor. The Personal Menus dialog box appears.

2. Click the name of the menu or menu item you want to delete, and choose Delete. You see a Menu Editor alert box asking you to confirm the deletion (see fig. 6.15).

Fig. 6.15
This Menu Editor alert box makes sure you want to delete the item or menu.

3. Choose OK to delete the menu or item.

If you are deleting an item, it is removed. If you are deleting a menu, you are asked if you want to recursively delete the menu—meaning it deletes everything under the menu. Choose OK; it is confusing to delete a menu, but not to delete items on that menu.

> **Caution**
>
> One of the problems with the 2.0 alpha 6 release of Mosaic involves deleting submenus. Mosaic asks if you are sure you want to delete the submenu, but if you try to cancel the request, the submenu is still deleted. Parts of the deleted submenu may show up when you look at a list of menus in the Current Hotlist field in the Open URL window.

Creating Your Own QUICKLIST

The QUICKLIST is a permanent hotlist that you cannot delete—or change the title. The QUICKLIST does not show up as a menu in the menu bar: the only way to access it is to make it the Current Hotlist and select an item from it in the Open URL window (this procedure is explained in more detail in the section, "Setting and Using the Current Hotlist," later in this chapter).

You can insert, edit, and delete items in the QUICKLIST the same way you do for any of the other user-configurable menus—using the Personal Menus dialog box. Unlike the other user-configurable menus, which have a limit of 40 items, there is no limit to the number of items in the QUICKLIST.

> **Note**
>
> There is not a Mac QUICKLIST feature. Because the Mac version allows for unlimited hotlists, each with as many as 99 items, there isn't a need for a QUICKLIST on the Mac.

Quick Access to Your Favorite URLs

Now that you have all these hotlists set up, how do you use them? You can select items directly from the user-configurable menus, or you can select them from the Open URL window. This saves you the trouble of having to remember and type in long URLs.

Accessing Items in a Hotlist

The user-configurable menus and QUICKLIST comprise the hotlists. You can access items from the user-configurable menus either directly or from the Open URL window. The QUICKLIST items can only be accessed from the Open URL window.

Setting and Using the Current Hotlist

One way to use a hotlist is to make it the Current Hotlist in the Open URL dialog box. There are two ways to do this. The first way is as follows:

1. Open the **F**ile menu and choose **O**pen URL (or click the Open URL button on the toolbar). The Open URL dialog box appears. The Current Hotlist field shows the current hotlist (see fig. 6.16).

Fig. 6.16

You can change the Current Hotlist in the Open URL dialog box.

2. Click the Current Hotlist field to display a drop-down list of available hotlists (see fig. 6.17).

Fig. 6.17

You can select any of the user-configurable menus to be the Current Hotlist.

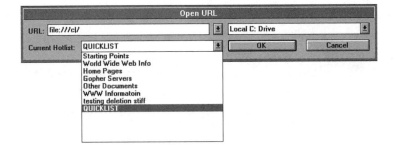

3. Click the hotlist you want to be designated the Current Hotlist.

4. You can now click Cancel (which will keep the hotlist you selected), or select a URL to open from this dialog box.

The other way to set the Current Hotlist is from the Personal Menus dialog box. To do this, follow these steps:

1. Open the **N**avigate menu and choose **M**enu Editor. The Personal Menus dialog box appears (see fig. 6.18).

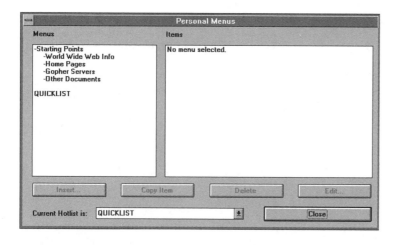

Fig. 6.18
You can set the Current Hotlist from the Personal Menus window.

2. Click in the Current Hotlist field to display a drop-down list of available hotlists (see fig. 6.19).

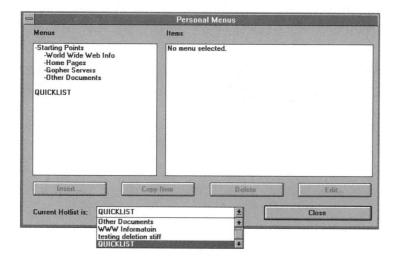

Fig. 6.19
You can select any of the user-configurable menus to be the Current Hotlist.

3. Click the hotlist you want to designate as the Current Hotlist.

4. Click Close to dismiss this dialog box.

Note

The only way to set the current hotlist on the Mac is to open the Navigate Menu and choose Hotlist. Select the Hotlist from the drop-down list at the top of the dialog box. (See fig. 6.20.)

II

Mosaic Basics

Fig. 6.20
Choose a hotlist
from the drop-
down list at the
top of the dialog
box.

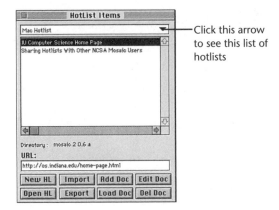

Click this arrow
to see this list of
hotlists

Now that you have the Current Hotlist set, how do you use it? The Open URL
dialog box gives you quick access to the items in the Current Hotlist. The
URL field and the field to its right contain information from the current
hotlist. If you click the URL field, you can select any of the URLs from the
items in the Current Hotlist. If you click the field to its right, you can select
any of the items in the Current Hotlist by title. To load the item you select,
choose OK.

> ### Note
>
> To load a hotlist document on the Mac, select the item in the list and then click Load
> Doc.

Tip
To add the current
document to the
Current Hotlist,
open the **N**avigate
menu and choose
Add Current to
Hotlist. The docu-
ment is added to
the end of the
Current Hotlist.

Remember, the only way to access items in the QUICKLIST is to make it
the Current Hotlist and to load the items it contains from the Open URL
window.

Loading a Document from a Menu

All documents in your hotlists (except for those in the QUICKLIST) are accessible from the menus you create. These menus appear between the Annotate
and Help menu items in the menu bar. To access a document in one of these
menus, simply follow these steps:

> ### Note
>
> Remember, as of this writing, you can't customize the menus in the 2.0.a6 Mac
> version—your hotlist entries aren't available there. They are available in the 2.0.a8
> version, though, and can be accessed in the same way as the Windows menus.

1. Click the menu.

2. Choose an item from the menu. If the item you choose is also a menu, a submenu pops up, and from it you can choose an item (see fig. 6.21).

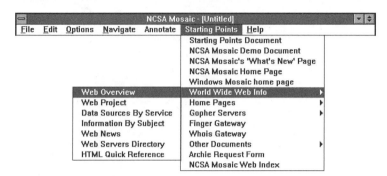

Fig. 6.21
The personal menus you create allow you to quickly load URLs from the menu bar.

When you release the mouse button after selecting an item, Mosaic loads the URL for that item.

Sharing Hotlists

Sharing hotlists is a good way to make coworkers and colleagues aware of information resources they would otherwise not know. At this time, Mosaic does not have an automated way of exporting and importing hotlists. However, if you edit your MOSAIC.INI file, you find the hotlists defined after the Annotations section in the file and at the end of the file. Entries have headings, such as User Menu1, followed by the name and URL for each item in the menu. You can copy these menu definitions from your MOSAIC.INI file into an e-mail message, or file and distribute them to people you think might be interested in them. They can then edit their MOSAIC.INI file and insert these menus in the file.

Note

You can share a hotlist with someone else in the Mac version by giving them a copy of the file for that Hotlist. These files are stored in the folder determined by the Current Hotlist Directory setting in the Preferences dialog box. By default, this is in the same folder as Mosaic. To change the folder, click the Set Hotlist Directory and choose a directory in the dialog box.

Using Built-In Hotlists

Mosaic, as distributed from NCSA, comes with two built-in hotlists: the Starting Points hotlist and the QUICKLIST. You can edit both lists to suit your particular needs, and you can delete the Starting Points hotlist just as you can delete any other user-configurable menu.

> ### Note
>
> The current version of Mosaic for the Mac does not come with a built-in Starting Points menu. Because the Mac does not need a QUICKLIST feature, it is also not predefined. At the bottom of the Navigate menu, however, are six predefined, useful Web sites that Mac Mosaic users may want to explore. One of these menu items, Network Starting Points, links to a Web document (`http://www.ncsa.uiuc.edu` `/SDG/Software/Mosaic/StaringPoints/NetworkStartingPoints.html`) that contains all the same sites that are in the predefined Starting Points menu in Windows. So, by opening this document, you easily can access all sites in the Windows Starting Points menu. And, you can save this file and copy the URLs to create Hotlists.

The Starting Points Hotlist

If you are new to the Internet and the World Wide Web, you may want to use the Starting Points hotlist to do some exploring and familiarize yourself with some of the most common Internet and WWW resources available. Some items in the Starting Points hotlist are:

- *The Starting Points Documents.* These contain links to many documents that provide introductory information to the Internet and the World Wide Web.

- *The NCSA Mosaic 'What's New' Page.* This gives an overview of new WWW resources. There are links to previous months' announcements at the end of this document.

- *World Wide Web Info menu.* A menu containing links to documents that give background information about the WWW and have links to interesting WWW sites.

- *Home Pages.* A menu that links you to some of the more interesting home pages on the WWW.

- *Gopher Servers.* A connection to a number of different Gopher servers that also gives you access to Veronica searches.

- *Other Documents.* These contain links to some interesting WWW and Internet services, such as a Beginners Guide to HTML and a summary report from the 1990 census.

The QUICKLIST Hotlist

The built-in QUICKLIST hotlist gives you access to some of the same places as the Starting Points hotlist. In addition, the QUICKLIST gives you:

- Quick access to your local hard disk.

- Access to on-line weather forecast information.

You may want to explore the items included with this list when you first start using Mosaic. If they are not of any use to you, replace the items with ones you use frequently.

Editing Mac Hotlists

You need a way to edit Hotlists on the Mac. This is done in the Hotlist Items dialog box, the same place you select a current hotlist or open a hotlist item (see fig. 6.22) To open this dialog box, open the Navigate menu and choose Hotlist.

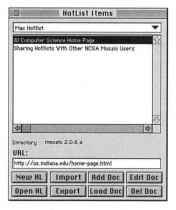

Fig. 6.22
Any change to any hotlist can be made in the Hotlist Items dialog box.

To create a new Hotlist, open the Hotlist Items dialog box and click New HL. This creates a new Hotlist called Untitled Hotlist.1. There aren't any items in it when you create it.

To add the open document to the current hotlist, open the Navigate menu and choose Add This Document.

To add any document to any hotlist follow these steps:

1. Open the Hotlist Items dialog box.

2. From the drop-down list, select the hotlist to which you want to add the item.

3. Click Add Doc. The dialog box shown in figure 6.23 appears.

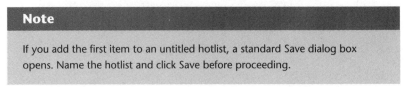

Note

If you add the first item to an untitled hotlist, a standard Save dialog box opens. Name the hotlist and click Save before proceeding.

Fig. 6.23
In the Hotlist Item dialog box, you can add new items to a hotlist.

4. Enter the name of the item and the URL (or you can click Add Current to add the current document), and then click OK.

To edit a hotlist item, select the item and then choose Edit Doc. You see a dialog box similar to the Hotlist Item dialog box. You can edit the title or URL. When you're finished, click OK.

To delete an item, select the item, and then click Del Doc. The item is deleted immediately! There isn't a dialog box asking you to confirm the deletion.

To open a hotlist in a different folder than the default, click Open HL, and then choose the hotlist in the Open dialog box.

Using Annotations

Sometimes when you are exploring the WWW, you might find a document that has lots of information, but only a small amount of it is important to you. It would be nice if you could somehow mark the information of importance so that you could find it quickly. Mosaic has a feature that lets you make notes in a document to remind you of why this document is important to you and where the important information is.

Setting Up Mosaic to Use Annotations

Mosaic stores any annotations that you make as files. The first thing that you need to do is set up Mosaic so that it knows where to store these files. You can also specify a default title for your annotations.

To set up the annotation information in your MOSAIC.INI file follow these steps:

1. Edit the MOSAIC.INI with a text editor like Notepad.

2. Find the [Annotations] section of the file.

3. Change the Directory= entry to point to the directory where you want the annotation files to be stored.

4. Change the Default Title= entry to the default title for your annotations.

5. Set Group Annotations=no.

6. Although Mosaic does not support an e-mail protocol at this time, it lets you define a default e-mail address, and uses this address as the default value for the Author field in the Annotations Window. To set your e-mail address, scroll up to the top of your MOSAIC.INI file and under the [Main] section, change the E-mail= entry to your e-mail address,

You should now be ready to use Mosaic's annotation feature.

Using Mosaic's Annotation Feature

To add an annotation to a document, follow these steps:

1. Open the **A**nnotate menu and choose **A**nnotate. The Annotate Window dialog box shown in figure 6.24 appears.

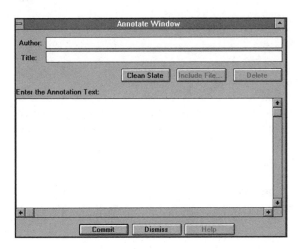

Fig. 6.24
The Annotate Window dialog box lets you create annotations for Mosaic documents.

Mosaic Basics

2. Enter the Author information. It will default to the e-mail address in your MOSAIC.INI file, if you have specified one.

3. Enter the Title of this annotation.

4. Enter the text of the annotation where indicated (see fig. 6.24). You can make notes here about anything—interesting links in this document, a note of why this document is useful to you, and so on. If you would like to erase all of the annotation text you have entered, choose Clean Slate and reenter the annotation text.

5. If you are satisfied with this annotation, choose Commit. This will save the annotation in a file in the annotation directory that you specified in your MOSAIC.INI file. If you decide that you don't want to add this annotation, choose Dismiss.

Note

The Annotations feature was not working in the 2.0.a6 Macintosh version that was used while writing this book, but has been implemented in the 2.0.a8 version that was released just as this book went to print. To add a text annotation in 2.0.a8, open the Annotate menu and choose Text. The procedure is essentially the same as in Windows as described earlier in "Using Mosaic's Annotation Feature." (You can change the default user name in the Mac version by opening the Options menu and choosing Preferences. Click the Misc button and enter your name in the User Name text box.) You can delete an annotation by selecting it, then opening the Annotate menu and choosing Delete Annotation. However, the edit feature on the Mac version was still buggy enough to be of no use.

Note that in Windows Mosaic, the Delete, Include File, and Help buttons are not yet working. Also, the Edit this annotation and Delete this annotation items on the Annotations menu do not seem to work in the 2.0a6 or 2.0a7 versions of Windows Mosaic.

The next time you load this document, the title of your annotation and the date it was entered will show up as a link at the end of the document. Click the link to read your annotation (to return to the document, open the **N**avigate menu and choose **B**ack).

You can have more than one annotation in a document. Click the title of the one that you want to read.

Adding an Audio Annotation on the Mac

The Macintosh version of Mosaic also offers audio annotations, a feature we haven't seen yet in the Windows version. Like the text annotations, this just became functional in the 2.0a8 release. To add an audio annotation to the current document:

1. Be sure the microphone on your Mac is plugged in and working.

2. Open the Annotate menu and choose Audio. A dialog box opens in which you can enter your name and a title for the annotation.

3. Click record. This will open the dialog box shown in figure 6.25.

Fig. 6.25
This dialog box is used to record an audio annotation.

4. Click the record button then speak into the microphone.

5. Click the Stop button when finished.

6. Click Save to save the annotation.

To listen to the annotation, click the link for it in the document. A new document opens, like the one in figure 6.26, indicating that this is an audio annotation. Click where it says To hear the annotation.

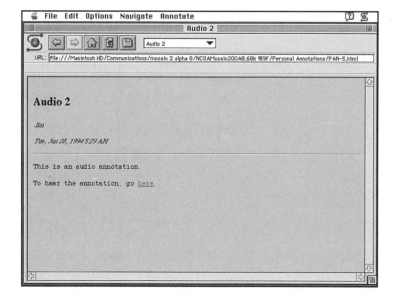

Fig. 6.26
A document containing an audio annotation.

Searching Indexes and Using Forms

Some Web documents are special *index documents*, documents that are connected to *index servers*. These documents let you search for information. For example, choose the Starting Points, Starting Points Document menu option, then, when the Starting Points document appears, find the NCSA Doc Finder link and click it. When you see the WAIS Search on NCSA's HTML Documents document, click the `click here to begin search` link. You see the document in fig. 6.27. (Or go straight to **http://docfinder.ncsa.uiuc.edu:7999/bin/finder** by typing the URL into the URL text box and pressing Enter.)

Fig. 6.27

Type your search word into the text box and press Enter.

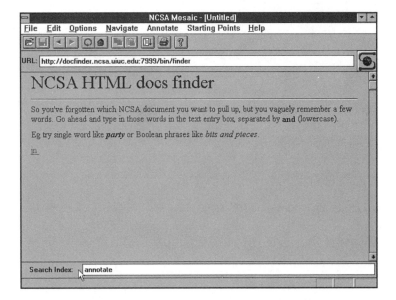

Now, type the word for which you want to search. For example, if you are looking for documents related to annotations, type **annotate** and press Enter. The search begins, and if something is found, you'll see a document containing links to each document, as shown in figure 6.28. (If nothing is found, you may just see a blank page. Use the Back toolbar button to return to the search document.) You can click these links to go to the document.

You have just used a Web *form*, a sort of interactive document. Not all Web browsers have *forms support*—luckily, Mosaic does.

Other forms are more complicated than the one you just looked at. Sometimes you will see option buttons and check boxes, multiple text boxes, and even command buttons that you click. Using these forms is just like using a program's dialog box.

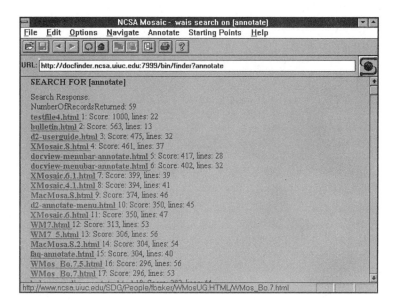

Fig. 6.28
The search results are placed in a Web document, with links to the items found.

There are several other very useful Web Pages that use forms to help you search the Web for relevant documents. While none of these searches are perfect, using one of them is better than randomly jumping from page to page looking for information you might need. Here is a list with the names and URL addresses of some of the better search pages:

■ EINet Galaxy - Search the World Wide Web

http://galaxy.einet.net/www/www.html

■ Webcrawler Searcher

http://www.biotech.washington.edu

or

**http://www.biotech.washington.edu/WebCrawler
/WebQuery.html**

■ WWWW - the World Wide Web Worm

**http://www.cs.colorado.edu/home/mcbryan
/WWWW.html**

Note

For more information on other Web searchers and indexes, refer to chapter 5 in Que's *Using the World Wide Web.*

From Here...

To learn more about using the WWW and Mosaic, refer to:

■ Chapter 5, "Navigating with Mosaic," which discusses how to use Mosaic's basic navigation features.

■ Part III "Advanced Mosaic Features," which talks about other Internet services you can access through Mosaic.

■ Chapter 13, "Hot Home Pages," which gives you some pointers on where to find interesting documents on the WWW.

Part III

Advanced Mosaic Features

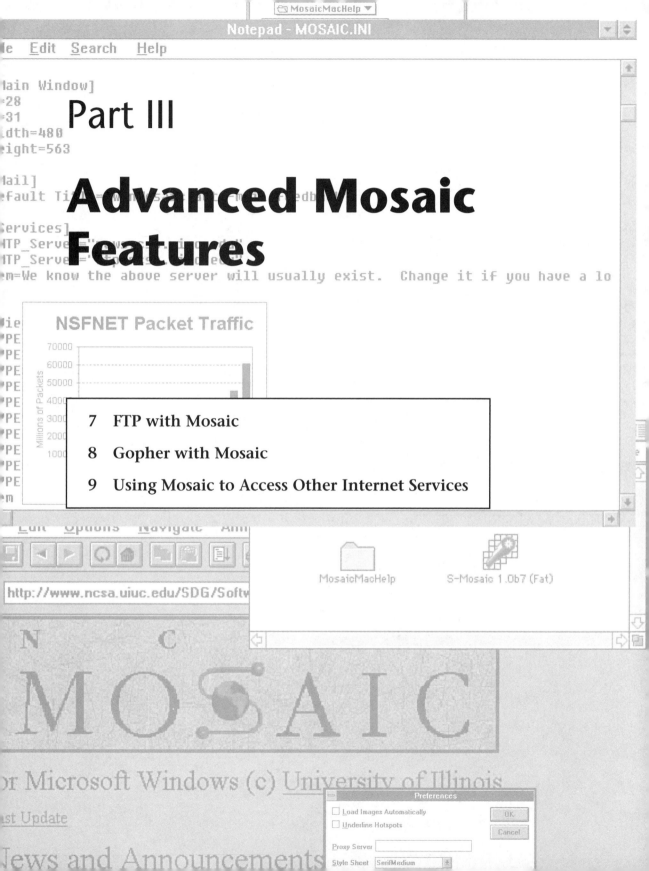

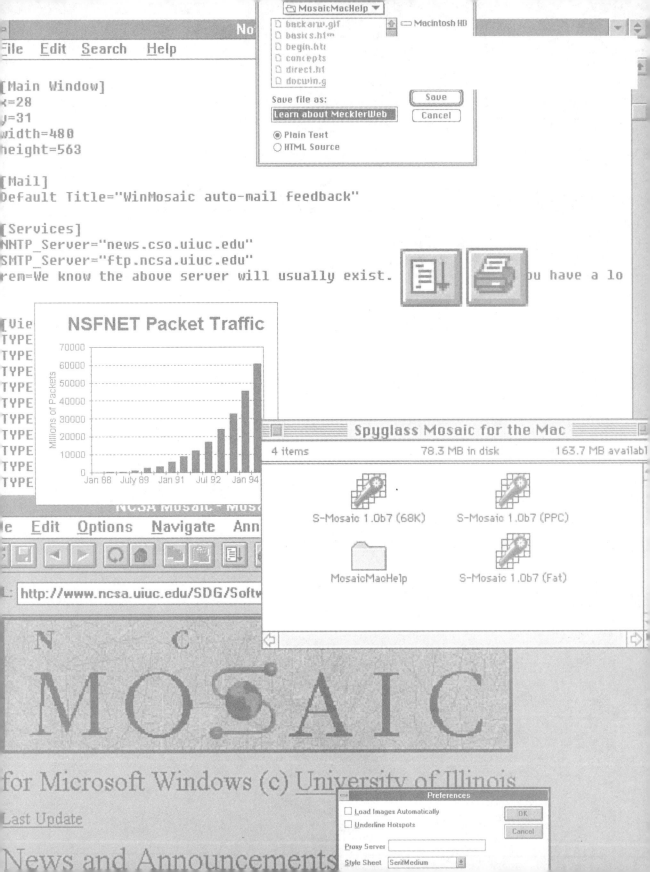

Chapter 7

FTP with Mosaic

Although the initial intent of the WWW was to have a system that allowed easy retrieval of hypermedia documents for viewing, the designers of Mosaic saw the potential of having an interface that accessed not only WWW documents, but other Internet services as well. One of the oldest Internet services in existence is FTP, the File Transfer Protocol, which allows a person to transfer files from one Internet site to another. Mosaic's GUI (Graphical User Interface) allows easy FTP browsing and file retrieval without the need to learn the cryptic FTP commands.

Although the Internet FTP service can be used to transfer files from any account on the Internet, Mosaic supports only anonymous FTP service. Anonymous FTP sites are set up so that anyone on the Internet can access that site, browse the files there, and download any files of interest.

In this chapter, you learn to do the following:

- Find information on anonymous FTP servers

- Connect to anonymous FTP servers

- Retrieve files

Locating the FTP Information You Want

One of the big problems with the Internet is that there is no central source where you can go to find out where the information you want is located. One Internet service that is specifically designed to locate information on anonymous FTP servers is *Archie*.

Using Archie to Find Information on FTP Servers

Archie is an Internet service that allows you to search a database of FTP information for a particular program or file. Sites that provide anonymous FTP servers can register with the maintainers of the Archie database so that the information about their server is in the database. The Archie servers periodically check the computers that are registered with them and update the Archie databases to reflect the current directory structure of the registered FTP sites. Archie is a good way to look for the source of a program or particular document that you are interested in, but is not too useful for finding out information about particular topics.

▶ See "Using Mosaic to Access Telnet," p. 163

Mosaic does not provide direct Archie access, but there are a few different ways to do an Archie search from Mosaic. One way is to connect to an Archie server using Telnet. The other way is to use the Archie search form that is available from the Starting Points menu. The steps that follow show you how to do an Archie search using this form.

> **Note**
>
> Another Archie WWW page can be found at **http://www.lerc.nasa.gov/Doc/ archieplex.html**.

1. Open the **S**tarting Points menu and choose **A**rchie Request Form. The Archie Request Form, shown in figure 7.1, is displayed.

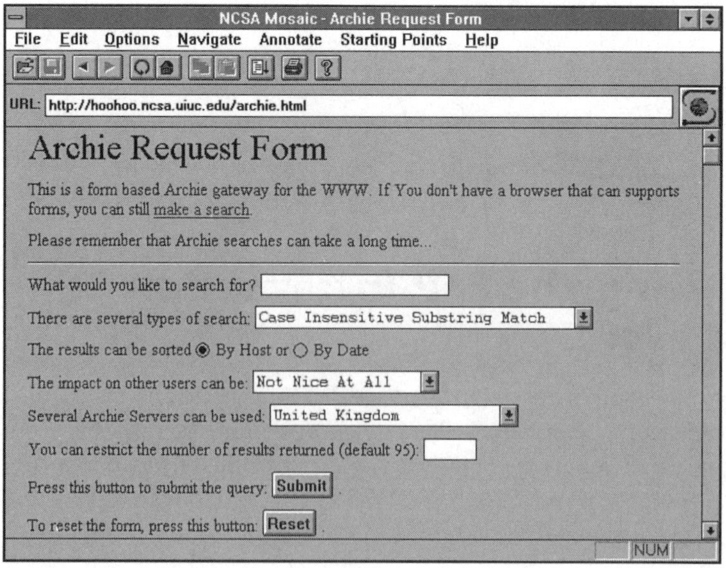

Fig. 7.1
The Archie Request Form is available from Mosaic's Starting Points menu.

2. Enter the file name (or part of the file name) you would like to search for in the box next to What would you like to search for?

3. Click on the box below There are several types of search: if you want to change the default value. Archie can do any of the searches shown in table 7.1.

Tip
Because Macintosh users do not have a Starting Points menu they (and those Windows users whose Starting Points menu is missing or altered) can access this form by opening the URL **http://hoohoo.ncsa.uiuc.edu/archie.html**.

Table 7.1	**Archie Search Types**
Type	**Description**
Exact	File name must match the search string you enter exactly, including the case of all letters.
Case-insensitive substring	File names that contain the string of characters you enter will match, regardless of the capitalization of the letters.
Case-sensitive substring	File names that contain the string of characters you enter with the exact capitalization that you enter will match.
Regular expressions	Files names that contain the complicated character patterns that you specify will match.

4. In the line The results can be sorted click the radio button for the sorting method that you prefer. Archie can return the results of the search sorted by hostname (sorted alphabetically by domain, then by organization), or by date of update of the file's information in the database (with more recent files shown first).

5. Choose the priority at which your search is done in the line that begins The impact on other users can be:. You have five options, from Not Nice At All to Extremely Nice. The middle choice (Nicer) is probably a good compromise between making unnecessary demands on network resources and waiting a long time to get your search results.

6. The box under Several Archie Servers allows you to select the Archie server you want to use to do the search. You might want to select an Archie server that is geographically close to you because it is likely to be physically close to you on the network, giving you a faster response time. Of course, your response time also depends on how busy the host running the server is and the number of people making requests to the server.

III

Advanced Mosaic Features

The servers in the U.S. are listed by the organization that provides them, and other servers are listed by country. Some of the servers that are available to use are:

- **Internic** (New Jersey)

- **University of Nebraska** (Nebraska)

- **ANS archie server** (New York)

- **Rutgers University** (New Jersey)

- **SURAnet** (Maryland)

- Australia

- Canada

- Germany

- Japan

- Sweden

- United Kingdom

7. If you want to limit the number of matching files that are returned to you, you can enter a number in the box next to You can restrict the number of results returned (default 95):.

8. When you have all of the fields filled, choose Submit. Your search is sent to the Archie server that you requested. When the search is finished, the results are returned to you, as shown in figure 7.2.

9. After you have the results of your search, you can connect to an FTP server that has the file in which you are interested. Click one of the links in the list of results to connect to a directory that contains the file in which you are interested. You can now load the file for viewing or save it to your local disk. (This is discussed in more detail in the section "Retrieving a File," later in this chapter.)

Note

Archie servers work by queuing the requests that they get, and processing the requests in the order they were received. If you connect to an Archie server using Telnet, the Archie server notifies you what number you are in the queue and the estimated amount of time until your request is processed. When you use the Archie Request Form, you do not get any of this queue information. So, if the Archie server you've selected is busy, you may find yourself sitting for a number of minutes waiting for the results of your search. (And, if the Archie server you've chosen is not responding, you are not notified of this error; the form continues to indicate that it is attempting to do the search.)

If the search is taking a long time and you want to cancel it, click the Mosaic icon (spinning globe). You can now select a new server and choose Submit, or you can set all of the fields in the window back to their default values by choosing Reset, and set up another search.

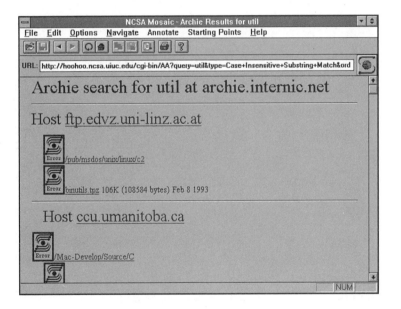

Fig. 7.2
The results of an Archie search done from the Archie Request Form.

III

Advanced Mosaic Features

Tip
Mac Mosaic users
can access the
Monster FTP List
document by
opening the Navi-
gate menu and
selecting Network
Starting Points.
Scroll down
through this docu-
ment until you
find the entry FTP
Sites. Click this
entry to load the
Monster FTP List.

Browsing FTP Servers

One way of finding information available at anonymous FTP servers is to browse through the directories on the server. At a server that is set up correctly, there should be a lot of informational files that tell you exactly what is on the server. The section "Exploring the FTP Servers," later in this chapter, discusses how to approach browsing on a server.

Other Ways to Find Information on FTP Servers

Although Archie is the primary means of locating files on FTP servers, there are a few other ways that you can find servers that may be of interest to you.

A summary of anonymous FTP servers can be found at the URL **http://hoohoo.ncsa.uiuc.edu:80/ftp-interface.html**. A quick way to access this list is to open the Starting Points menu and choose Other Documents. From the drop-down menu that appears, choose FTP Sites. This brings up the document shown in figure 7.3.

Fig. 7.3
The Monster FTP
List document,
with pointers to
the alphabetically
organized files that
make up the list.

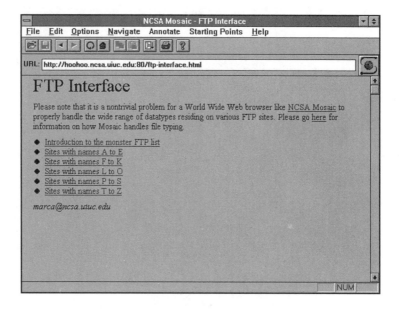

This document allows you to view a series of documents that contains an alphabetical listing of a large number of anonymous FTP servers. A description of the documents is found in the first document in the list, Introduction to the monster FTP list. The remaining documents contain a synopsis of anonymous FTP servers, including the server's address (which is a hypertext link to that site), the e-mail address of its administrator, the organization that manages the server, and a brief summary of what can be found on the server.

You can use WAIS to find the address of documents that may be of interest to you. Using WAIS to find information is discussed in chapter 9, "Using Mosaic to Access Other Internet Services."

▶ See "Using Mosaic to Access WAIS," p. 172

Connecting to an Anonymous FTP Server

When you want to connect to an anonymous FTP server on the Internet, you do it the same way that you do anything in Mosaic—you use a URL. However, because you are not retrieving a WWW document, you do not use the HTTP protocol in the URL. Instead, you specify the FTP protocol. An example of a URL that you might use to connect to an anonymous FTP server is **ftp:// ds.internic.net**.

When you use **ftp:** in a URL, you tell Mosaic to communicate with the Internet host that you specify using FTP. If you have ever used FTP, you know that the normal sequence of events is to open a connection to an Internet host, do a directory of the host after you are connected, change directories if necessary, get any files that you are interested in, and disconnect from the host.

Mosaic gives you a graphical interface that hides these FTP commands. A graphical representation of the file structure appears on the Internet host, and you can point and click to open files just like you do in File Manager. In reality, Mosaic is interpreting your pointing and clicking and sending the corresponding FTP commands to the Internet host. It then takes the information that the host sends back and changes it to a picture instead of printing the information as text.

After you are connected to an anonymous FTP server, you can easily navigate around the server using Mosaic's navigation commands. Navigating at an FTP server is not that different from navigating between WWW hypertext documents—but, with an FTP server you are viewing directories and their contents. The contents may be text, image, sound, or even HTML files. Mosaic shows you the directories, but to see the contents of the files, you have to have the correct viewers installed and set up for Mosaic to use (text and HTML files can be displayed by Mosaic itself).

Retrieving Information Using FTP

After you have found an anonymous FTP server that has information of interest to you, you can use Mosaic to connect to the server, explore its holdings, and retrieve any files you may want. This section explains how to do this.

III

Advanced Mosaic Features

Exploring an Anonymous FTP Server

When you connect to an anonymous FTP server, Mosaic shows you the directory structure of the server. You start at the top directory level, and can move down into any subdirectories in the server.

1. Open the **F**ile menu and choose **O**pen URL. In the Open URL window, enter the URL of the FTP server you want to connect to and choose OK. Figures 7.4 and 7.5 show an example of what you see when you connect to an anonymous FTP server.

Fig. 7.4

The top level directory of the **nic.merit.edu** FTP server, showing two text files and a number of subdirectories (folders).

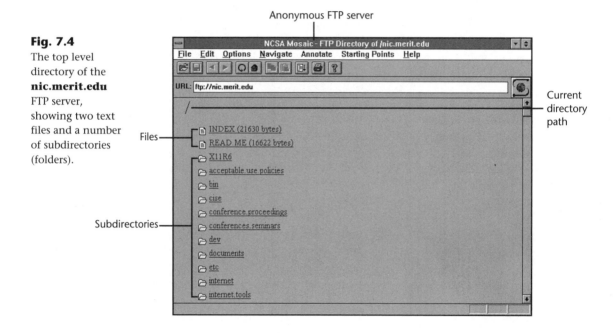

In figure 7.4, notice that the title bar tells you that you are in the FTP directory of the Internet host **/nic.merit.edu**. In the document viewing area, you see a / (slash) that tells you that you are in the root directory for that host.

You also see a list with icons next to the entries. The first two items in the list are INDEX and READ.ME. Notice that the icons look like a sheet of paper, and that they have a size (in bytes) to the right of them. The icons indicate that these two files are text files that Mosaic knows how to display. The items that follow these two files all have folder icons next to them. These files are subdirectories that you can browse by clicking the subdirectory names.

Anonymous ftp server

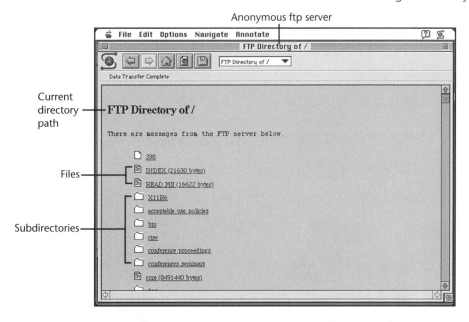

Current directory path

Files

Subdirectories

Fig. 7.5
The FTP server
nic.merit.edu in
Mosaic for the
Macintosh.

Note

Under the Options menu, there is an item labeled Extended FTP Directory Parsing. If this option is turned on (there is a check mark next to it), FTP directories are shown as described in this section (icons next to the file and directory names, sizes next to files, etc.). If this option is turned off, all directories and files are shown only with a dot to the left of the name, and no sizes are given for files (although not all sites are set up to show file sizes, even if extended directory parsing is enabled).

Caution

The 2.0 alpha 6 version has some bugs in the FTP section of the application. After you have moved around a few directory levels at an FTP server, the icons that tell you what you're looking at (text file, directory, image, and so on) may disappear. The only way to make them come back is to quit Mosaic and restart it. You can still navigate around the FTP server without having the icons, as long as you don't mind accidentally loading a file that you may not be able to view (if, for example, you try to load an MPEG file thinking that it's a directory, and you don't have a viewer for it installed on your PC).

2. If you can find a document called README, READ.ME, or readme.txt., click it and Mosaic displays it. It is common to place a file with a name

III

Advanced Mosaic Features

like this on FTP servers. The file is used to describe what is on the server, list any restrictions on the use of the server, or other administrative-type messages. You should always look for one of these files when you connect to an unfamiliar FTP server. Figure 7.6 shows the contents of a typical READ.ME document.

Fig. 7.6
The READ.ME document from the **nic.merit.edu** FTP server, describing the server and what you can find there.

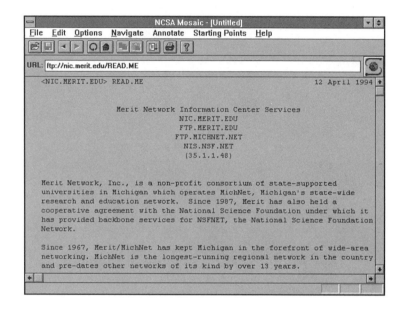

Tip
FTP servers often show you the size of the files in each directory so that you have some idea of how long the file transfer will take when you load the file for viewing in Mosaic or when you save it to your local disk.

3. After you have finished reading about the FTP server to which you are connected, Open the **N**avigate menu and choose **B**ack to return to the top level directory of the server. From there, you can click on some of the subdirectories that look interesting to you. When you click a subdirectory, the contents of that directory is displayed, with the directory path shown at the top of Mosaic's document viewing area (see fig. 7.7).

4. The first item underneath the directory path in figure 7.7 is labeled Up to Parent Directory. Click this item to return to the directory level above the current one. This is a quick way to get to the directory above you when you have been browsing through directories at a server. You might think that the Navigate/Back command in Mosaic would take you to the directory above you, but this command just takes you to the previous link, which may be in the directory under you!

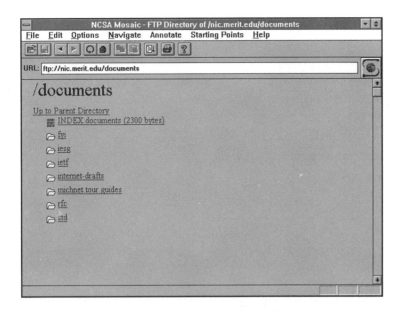

Fig. 7.7
The
/nic.merit.edu/
documents
directory.

Note

Near the top of the directory list in figure 7.7 is the INDEX.documents file. Notice
that the icon next to this file is not recognizable as anything. That's because Mosaic
does not recognize the file-type of this file. If Mosaic retrieved this file, it would not
know how to display it. If you click this file, Mosaic attempts to retrieve it, but when
it realizes that it doesn't know what to do with the file, Mosaic simply aborts the
transfer.

Mosaic is an application under development. The developers may eventually offer
you an option for displaying a file of unknown type. When Mosaic aborts a transfer, it
usually does not inform you. You just notice that there is no activity in the Status bar
and your document view area has not changed (and the globe in the Mosaic icon
button is no longer spinning).

Retrieving a File from an Anonymous FTP Server

After you have found a file that you are interested in (either through an
Archie search or by browsing through an FTP server), you can retrieve the file
and view it from Mosaic, or you can save it to your local disk.

III

Advanced Mosaic Features

Viewing a File

1. To view a file on an anonymous FTP server, place the cursor on the document name and click it. After Mosaic has finished loading a document, you should see something like figure 7.8.

> ### Note
>
> Many of the files you find on an anonymous FTP server are text files without any HTML commands in them. These files are displayed like the one in figure 7.8, without any formatting. If you click a file that needs an external viewer and you have set up Mosaic to work with that viewer, Mosaic launches the viewer with the selected file loaded into it. You can then use any of the viewer's features (including saving the file to your local disk). If do not have a viewer for the file type that you are loading, Mosaic loads the file, and then gives you an error saying that it can't find the viewer for that file type.

Fig. 7.8
The fyi_05 document from the /nic.merit.edu/ documents/fyi directory. This document is about naming conventions for computers.

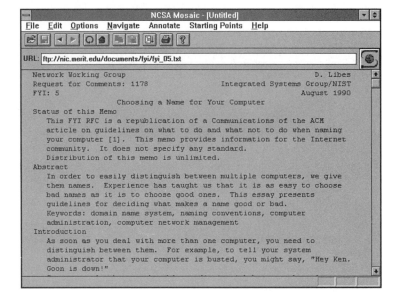

2. When you are done viewing a document at an FTP server, open the **N**avigate menu and choose **B**ack to return to the directory the file came from. The files viewed at FTP servers are likely to be plain text files (if they were hypertext files, they would be on a WWW server), image files, or sound files. Because these documents have no hyperlinks in them, they don't link you to other documents or other WWW servers. To navigate around at an FTP server, you simply move through the directory structure (folders).

Saving a File to Your Local Computer

If you would like to save the document you are reading, there are **S**ave and Save **A**s options under the **F**ile menu. These features were not yet working in the 2.0 Alpha 6 version of Mosaic that was used to write this book. However, these features are implemented in the 2.0 Alpha 8 version of Mosaic that was released just as this book was going to press.

The steps for saving a file using the Save As command are as follows:

1. While you are viewing a document that you want to save, open the **F**ile menu and choose Save **A**s. You see a Save As window, like the one shown in figure 7.9, that asks you where you want to save the file.

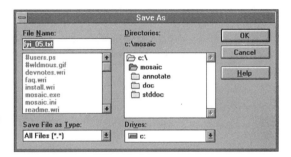

Fig. 7.9
When you save a file to disk, you can put it anywhere on your local directory system.

2. Fill in the information in the window and choose OK. Mosaic attempts to save the file to your local disk.

There is another way that you can save files from Mosaic. The following procedure saves the file associated with a URL to a file on your local disk.

> **Caution**
>
> In the 2.06a release of Mosaic that was used to write this book, trying to save a file to disk on a Macintosh did not work and sometimes caused the Macintosh to crash. Currently, the only Macintosh Mosaic-based software that allows you to successfully save a file to disk (as either HTML or text) is Spry S-Mosaic. This bug has been fixed in 2.08a release for Macintosh, but I have not extensively tested this version to see how well it works. See chapter 5, "Navigating with Mosaic," for a discussion of the Save feature in version 2.08a for Mac.

1. Open the **O**ptions menu and choose **L**oad to Disk.

2. Click on the hyperlink for the document that you want to save. You see a Save As window, such as the one shown in figure 7.9 (or figure 7.10 for the Macintosh), that asks you where you want to save the file.

Fig. 7.10
Loading a file to
disk uses the
familiar Save
dialog box on a
Mac.

Tip
If you want to
load a single file to
disk, you can
Shift-click on the
hyperlink rather
than selecting
Load to Disk from
the Options menu.

3. Fill in the information in the window and choose OK. Mosaic attempts
   to load that URL to disk instead of displaying it in the document viewing area.

If you forget to turn off Load to Disk, Mosaic tries to load the URL of the next
hyperlink you click to disk instead of loading it to view. If this happens, you
have to select Cancel in the Save As window, then turn off Load to Disk before you can view another document.

From Here...

To learn more about using the WWW and Mosaic, refer to these chapters:

Tip
If you want to save
the file you are
currently viewing
to disk, click Load
to Disk from the
Options menu,
then click Reload
from the **N**avigate
menu. This brings
up the Save As
dialog box.

■ Chapter 2, "Introduction to the World Wide Web," gives you background information about the WWW.

■ Chapter 5, "Navigating with Mosaic," familiarizes you with the Mosaic
   features that help you find and view documents on the WWW.

■ Chapter 9, "Using Mosaic to Access Other Internet Services," gives you
   information on using WAIS to find information on the WWW, besides
   telling you how to use Telnet and access Usenet news groups with Mosaic.

■ Chapter 14, "Hot FTP and Gopher Sites," gives you some pointers on
   where to find interesting files you can view and retrieve.

Chapter 8

Gopher with Mosaic

Like Mosaic, the intent of the Gopher designers is to give you access to multiple Internet services from a single interface. Mosaic, however, is a GUI application, while Gopher is text-based and can be used from any terminal. Just as Mosaic can give you a graphical interface to anonymous FTP servers, it can also give you the same type of interface to Gopher servers.

Gopher servers are similar to anonymous FTP servers in that anyone on the Internet can access the server, browse around it, and download any files of interest. Unlike anonymous FTP servers, which are viewed simply as directory structures with the actual file and directory name displayed, Gopher servers are menu-oriented and let you connect to other Internet services such as Telnet, WAIS, and other Gopher servers, besides letting you view and retrieve files.

In this chapter, you learn how to do the following:

- Find Gopher servers that have information you want

- Navigate through GopherSpace

- Retrieve files from a Gopher site

- Use other Internet services from a Gopher site

Connecting to a Gopher Server

If you want to connect to a Gopher server on the Internet, you do it the same way you do anything in Mosaic—you use a URL. Because you are not retrieving a WWW document, you do not use the HTTP protocol in the URL. You specify the Gopher protocol instead. An example of a URL that you might use to connect to a Gopher server is **gopher://gopher.nsf.gov**.

Understanding the Gopher Protocol

When you begin a URL with **gopher:**, you tell Mosaic to communicate with the Internet host that you specify using the Gopher protocol. Gopher was originally developed to be used from an ASCII terminal, not from a GUI interface. When you use a Gopher program from a terminal, the normal sequence of events is to connect to a Gopher server on an Internet host, select one of the menu items that is presented to you, change directories or connect to other Internet services if necessary, get any files that you are interested in, and exit from the Gopher program.

Mosaic gives you a graphical interface that hides these Gopher commands. You see a graphical representation of each item in the Gopher menu and you can point and click to change directories, open files, and connect to other Internet services. In reality, Mosaic is interpreting your pointing and clicking and sending the corresponding Gopher commands to the Gopher server. Mosaic then takes the information that the server sends back and changes it to a picture instead of printing the information as text.

After you are connected to a Gopher server, you easily can navigate around the server by using Mosaic's navigation commands. Navigating at a Gopher server is not that different than navigating between WWW hypertext documents, except at a Gopher server you are viewing menus, which are represented in a way similar to the FTP servers. The menus are shown as lists of items with icons next to them, marked either as files, directories, or other Internet services.

Caution

The 2.0 alpha 6 version has some bugs in the Gopher section of the application (these are similar to the ones in the FTP section, and may have been fixed in the 2.0 alpha 7 release). After you have moved around a few menus at a Gopher site, the icons that tell you what you're looking at (text file, other menus, Telnet connection, and so on) disappear. The only way to make them come back is to quit Mosaic and start it again. You can still navigate around the Gopher site without having the icons—if you are familiar with the site. But, because the Gopher URLs aren't obvious about what the hyperlink is going to do, it's very hard to try to navigate around an unfamiliar site without the icons.

One of the main differences between the Gopher and FTP servers is that with FTP, you are limited to accessing files and directories on the host where the server resides. With Gopher, a menu item might be on the same host, or it may take you to another host at a very distant site. Menu items may be text, image, sound, HTML files, or connections to other Internet services. To see the contents of the files, you have to have the correct viewers installed for Mosaic (text and HTML files can be displayed by Mosaic itself).

Locating the Gopher Information You Want

A big problem with the Internet is that there is no central information source where you can find the location of items of interest to you. You can always connect to servers that you know exist and just browse around the servers looking for things that might be of interest to you. However, there is an Internet service called Veronica that is specifically designed to locate information on Gopher servers.

Browsing Gopher Servers

One way of finding information available at a Gopher server is simply to browse through the menus on the server. At a server that is set up correctly, there should be lots of informational files that tell you exactly what is on the server. The section, "Exploring the Gopher Servers," later in this chapter, discusses how to approach browsing on a Gopher server.

▶ See "Using Mosaic to Access WAIS," p. 172

Finding Information on Gopher Servers

Although Gopher itself was designed as an information-finding aid, there are some other sources of information about interesting Gopher servers. WAIS is an Internet service that allows you to look through databases of documents to find information. Also, you can use Archie to search for a file on an anonymous FTP server, then see if the Internet site where the file resides has a Gopher server. Internet sites often have a Gopher server that lets you access the information found on the site's anonymous FTP server, as well as additional resources.

◀ See "Using Archie to Find Information on FTP Servers," p. 134

Tip

Many Internet sites precede their server names with the type of service they provide. For example, the fictitious company "Bigcorp" might have the servers **ftp.bigcorp.com**, **gopher.bigcorp. com**, and **www.bigcorp.com**.

Using Veronica to Search GopherSpace

Just as Archie is a service that allows you to search file names and directories on anonymous FTP servers, Veronica allows you to search menu items on Gopher servers. You can limit your Veronica search to directories that contain the word(s) that you are interested in, or you can search through all of GopherSpace, finding files and directories that might be of interest to you.

The first thing that you need to do is figure out what words you want to search for. Your search string should contain enough words to make the

III

Advanced Mosaic Features

search as specific as possible (otherwise, thousands of matches might be found). Once you have built your search string, you can use Veronica to do the search.

Building Your Search String

Veronica allows you to search on just one word, or use multiple word search strings. There are also two options that you can use in your search, one to specify the number of items that are returned, and one to specify the type of items that are returned.

Using Boolean Operators and Wild Cards

If you want to do a simple multiple word search, you can just enter the words you want to search for with spaces between them. This type of search finds items that contain all the search words, although the words will not necessarily be adjacent or in the same order.

You can also use Boolean operators (and, or, not) and wild cards (*) in your searches, and group words with parentheses. Table 8.1 shows you how to use these different operators in your search string.

Table 8.1	Operators for Veronica Search Strings
Operator	**Description**
and	Directs the search to return items that contain the words (or grouped words) before and after the "and"
or	Directs the search to return items that contain either the word (or grouped words) before the "or" or following the "or"
not	Directs the search to return items that do not contain the word specified after "not" (usually grouped with other operators)
*	Used at the end of a word (or part of a word), matches words that begin with the characters that precede the *
( )	Used to group words so that operators work on groups of words rather than individual words

Some examples of search strings that you might use when doing Veronica searches are "women and politics," "chicken and (casseroles or rice)," "financ*," and "education not primary."

Options

You have two options in your Veronica search string (you can place the search string either before or after the search words). The first option is

-m*<number>*, which allows you to limit the items returned by the search to *<number>*. If you search with no limits specified, most Veronica servers will return the first 200 items and will put a note at the end of the list telling you how many additional items were found (some servers have a different default number than 200). By using the -m option without an argument, you can tell Veronica to return all of the matches it finds.

The second option, -t*<type>* allows you to limit the types of the files that Veronica returns from its search. For example, you can limit the files to text, sound, HTML, and so on. Table 8.2 shows the types of files that can be specified.

Table 8.2 Veronica Search File Types	
Type	**Description**
0	Text File
1	Directory
2	CSO name server
4	Mac HQX file
5	PC binary
7	Full Text Index (Gopher menu)
8	Telnet Session
9	Binary File
s	Sound
I	Image (other than GIF)
M	MIME multipart/mixed message
T	TN3270 Session
g	GIF image
h	HTML, HyperText Markup Language

Performing a Search

To use Veronica, you have to be connected to a Gopher server that gives you access to a Veronica server. The following steps show you how to connect to a Gopher that provides Veronica search service and show you how to do a search.

1. Open the Starting Points menu, choose Gopher Servers, and from the drop-down menu that appears, select Veronica Search. Mosaic displays a menu that looks like the one in figure 8.1.

> ### Note
>
> In addition to giving you easy access to a Veronica search menu, the Gopher Servers item on the Starting Points menu lets you quickly connect to some of the more popular Gopher servers (including the one at the University of Minnesota where Gopher was developed).
>
> On the Macintosh, open the Navigate menu and choose Network Starting Points. This loads a document that contains many of the same links that are available from the Windows Starting Points menu. Scroll through the document to the Gopher section and click on Veronica to start the Veronica search.

Notice that the title bar tells you that you are running NCSA Mosaic, but you are in an "Untitled" document. Remember, Mosaic is an application still under development, so some things may not look as you would expect them to. (The Macintosh title bar shown in figure 8.2 is also incorrect, although in a different way.)

Fig. 8.1
The Gopher menu that appears when you select Veronica Search from the Gopher Server/Starting Points menu.

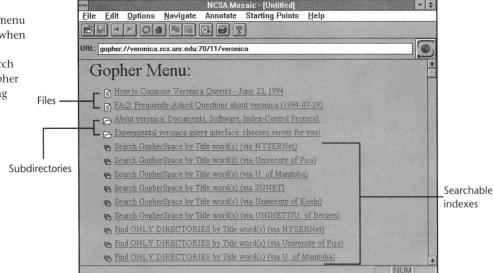

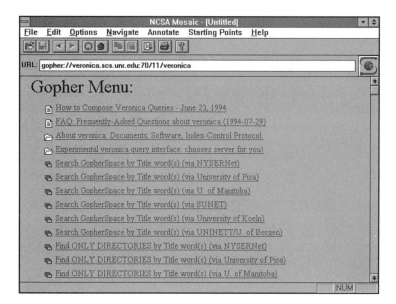

Fig. 8.2
The Mac version of
Mosaic displays
the Gopher site in
essentially the
same format.
(Don't be surprised
if the title bar on
the window
doesn't contain
the name of the
Gopher server, as
is the case here.)

At the top of the document viewing area it says Gopher Menu: which lets
you know that what you are viewing is a Gopher server. What you see
below that heading looks the same as what you see when you use the
FTP protocol—folders that represent directories, and files. (The icon
that looks like a stack of cards. represents a searchable index.) Notice,
however, directory or file names are not next to these folders —instead
there are descriptive phrases.

Note

If you do not have the default Starting Points menu and cannot access the
Gopher Servers/Veronica Search item from this menu, you can directly connect to a gopher that gives you access to Veronica. To do so, Open the **F**ile
menu and select **O**pen URL. Enter the URL **gopher://gopher2.tc.umn.edu**
and select OK. After you are connected to this Gopher server, Click the menu
item Other Gopher and Information Servers. From the menu that
appears, click Search titles in GopherSpace using veronica. You can
continue with step 2 from here to do a Veronica search.

III

Advanced Mosaic Features

2. You can select a specific Veronica server, or let the Veronica search select the server for you. To select a specific server, click one of the entries in the list that has a server name following it in parentheses. Entries that begin with "Search GopherSpace by Title Word(s)" will find files or directories that contain your search word(s). Entries that begin with "Find ONLY DIRECTORIES by Title Word(s)" will find just directories that contain the search word(s).

Click the Experimental veronica query interface item to let Veronica choose the server to use. This brings up the menu shown in figure 8.3.

Fig. 8.3

This menu gives you access to the experimental Veronica query interface, which selects a Gopher server for you, rather than requiring you to choose one.

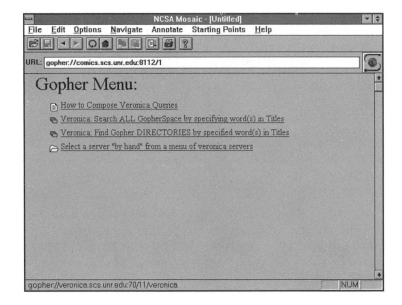

3. Click Veronica: Search ALL GopherSpace by specifying word(s) in Titles to search the titles of all the files on all the Gopher servers. Click Veronica: Find Gopher DIRECTORIES by specified word(s) in Titles to search only directories. (Notice that these two items have the stack of cards icon that indicates a search function.) A search form, like the one shown in figure 8.4, is loaded in the document viewing area.

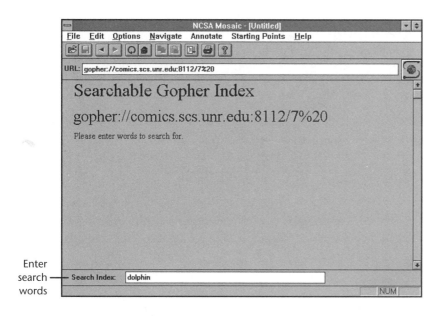

Enter
search —
words

4. Click in the Search Index: box at the bottom of the screen and enter the words for which you want to search.

5. The Veronica search builds the Gopher menu shown in figure 8.5 (the viewing area has been scrolled so that it shows the middle of the list). Notice that the search found both image and text files. Veronica can build a menu that has any type of Gopher item in it—Telnet connections, animations, and so on. You can now click these items and view them.

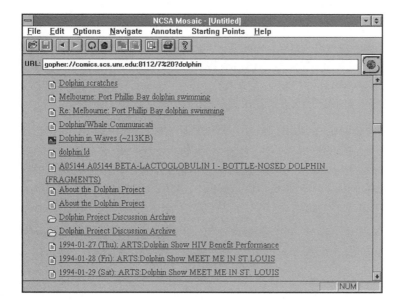

III

Advanced Mosaic Features

Note

If you get an error returned to you as the result of your search (for example, `0***Too many connections  Try again soon.***`) you will need to do your search over again. However, doing a search on the same string is not straightforward. If you just return to the search window and press Enter again, it will return you to the error screen since that was the result of the search for that string (Mosaic cannot tell the difference between a good result and an error). To get Veronica to try another search, you must change the search string—for example, reverse the order of some of the words because order does not matter.

When you are done looking through the menu built by the Veronica search, open the **N**avigate menu and select **B**ack to take you back to the search window. From there, you can navigate back to other menus on this Gopher server or go to a completely new URL.

Exploring Gopher Servers

Veronica can help find items of interest to you at Gopher servers, but it is limited to searching for file and directory names only. It would be nice if you could search the contents of the files, but it would take an enormous amount of time to search every file on every Gopher server that exists.

Some individual Gopher servers have a full-text search service as one of their menu items. These search services search the text of the items (or a subset of the items) found on that particular Gopher. So if you can find a Gopher server that has information that you are interested in, you can use the full-text search to find the particular files that would be of interest to you.

Browsing with a Gopher Server

Just looking around is often an effective way to find things at a Gopher server, especially if it's a well-run server that has a lot of informational documents and descriptive menu item names.

The following steps show you how to browse a Gopher server:

1. Open the File menu and choose Open URL. In the Open URL window, enter the URL of the Gopher server you want to explore and select OK. After Mosaic loads the main menu for this Gopher server, you should see something like what is shown in figure 8.6.

Tip

If you find a Gopher server that you use often, add it to one of your hotlists so that you can access it quickly. See chapter 6, "Shortcuts to Favorite Places," to learn how to do this.

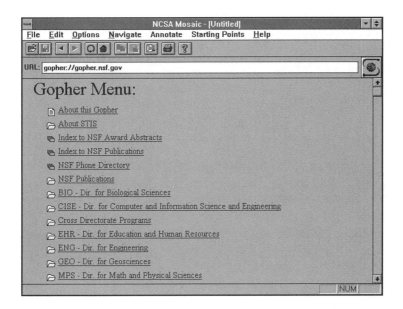

Fig. 8.6
The top-level menu of the **gopher.nsf.gov** Gopher server, showing a text file, a number of subdirectories (folders), and some search indexes.

The first item in the menu in figure 8.6 is About this Gopher, which is shown as a text file (indicated by the sheet of paper icon). If you place your cursor over the hyperlink for this item, you will see the URL for the item in the status bar. What is actually being retrieved when you click this hyperlink is a file called about.

The next item in the menu has a folder icon next to it. This item takes you to another Gopher menu. The three menu items following the folder have icons that look like stacked index cards. These items give you access to a search index that lets you do a full-text search on files at this Gopher. If you scroll down to the very bottom of this menu, you will notice that the icon for the next-to-the-last item (shown in fig. 8.7) looks like a little terminal. This item allows you to use the Telnet service to connect to a bulletin board, which gives you access to the same things that this Gopher server does.

Tip
Notice that a number of messages flash by in the status area when you connect to a Gopher server. Some of these messages include: Doing Name Service Lookup, Parsing Gopher Menu, and Transferring.

Note

If you have the correct viewers installed, you can load any files you find at a Gopher server and view them. One problem, though, is that you don't know the format of the files. Even if you place your cursor over the hyperlinks for the animations and images, the file names that are shown in the status bar have no extensions, so you don't know what type of viewer you need for them.

III

Advanced Mosaic Features

Fig. 8.7
The end of
the top-level
menu of the
gopher.nsf.gov
Gopher server.

Subdirectories——

Telnet connection——

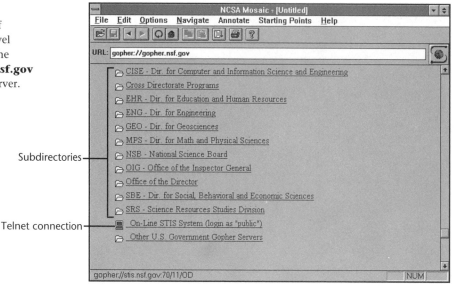

2. To find out information about the Gopher server, look for a file like the
   About this Gopher document shown in figure 8.6. Most Gopher servers
   have a document like this in their top-level menu to give you some idea
   of what you can do from that server. To read this document, just place
   your cursor on the name and click. When Mosaic finishes loading the
   document, you should see something that looks similar to figure 8.8.

Fig. 8.8
The About this
Gopher document
from the
gopher.nsf.gov
Gopher server,
briefly describing
the server and
what you can
find there.

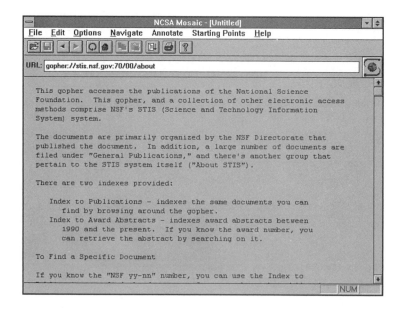

This is a short document that tells you what is on this Gopher server and how to locate the items in which you are interested. You probably want to go back to the main menu now and look for a file that interests you. Although you can browse through a Gopher site like you do an anonymous FTP site, Gopher servers are really structured to help you find information on a particular topic that is of interest to you.

3. Open the **N**avigate menu and select **B**ack to return to the main menu for this Gopher server. Now that you are back at the main menu, there are a number of options. You could keep clicking menu items that sound interesting, looking at files and jumping to different menus (possibly on different Gopher servers) as you go along. Or, because there are three index items that tell you what is available from this Gopher server, try looking up something.

Note

Unlike Mosaic's anonymous FTP screens which give you an `Up to Parent Directory` link, the Back command in the Navigate menu is the only hypertext command available to move you along your link path. There isn't an item in the document viewing area that takes you to the previous menu, because, in most cases, the Gopher server does not know what menu you came from. Unlike a directory structure where every piece of the directory is fixed and can be accessed with complete certainty, a Gopher menu can have a number of different menus that link to it.

Use the navigating tips discussed in chapter 6, "Shortcuts to Favorite Places," to help you figure out how to keep track of where you've been.

Doing a Full-Text Search a Gopher Server

A search index is one of the easiest ways to find something that interests you on the Gopher server. If the Gopher server has a full-text search index available, click that item in the Gopher menu. You will get a search form, and can do a search as described in the section "Using Veronica to Search GopherSpace" earlier in this chapter.

Saving Files from a Gopher Server

If you want to save the document you are reading, there are **S**ave and Save **A**s options under the **F**ile menu. These features were not yet working in the 2.0 alpha 6 version of Mosaic that was used to write this book. However, these features were implemented in the 2.0 alpha 7 version of Mosaic that was released just as this book was going to press. The steps for saving a file using the Save As command are as follows:

1. While you are viewing a document that you want to save, open the **F**ile menu and select Save **A**s. You will get a Save As window like the one shown in figure 8.9 that asks you where you want to save the file.

Fig. 8.9
When you save a file to disk, you can put it any-where on your local directory system.

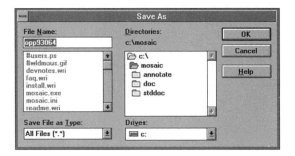

2. Fill in the information in the window and choose OK. Mosaic attempts to save the file to your local disk.

There is another way you can save files from Mosaic. The following procedure saves the file associated with a URL to a file on your computer.

Caution

In the 2.06a release of Mosaic that was used to write this book, trying to save an HTML file to disk on a Macintosh did not save the file correctly and sometimes caused the Macintosh to crash. Currently, the only Macintosh Mosaic-based software that allows you to successfully save a file to disk (as either HTML or text) is Spry S-Mosaic. However, this bug has been fixed in the just released 2.0.8a version of NCSA Mosaic for the Mac. I haven't thoroughly tested this feature though. See chapter 5 for a discussion of Saving files with this version.

Tip
If you want to load a single file to disk, you can Shift-click on the hyperlink rather than selecting Load to Disk from the Options menu.

1. Open the **O**ptions menu and choose **L**oad to Disk.

2. Click the hyperlink for the document you want to save. You get a Save As window as shown in figure 8.9 asking you where you want to save the file.

3. Fill in the information in the window and select OK. Mosaic attempts to load that URL to disk instead of displaying it in the document view-ing area.

If you forget to turn off Load to Disk after saving a document, Mosaic continues trying to load to disk the URL of the next hyperlink you click, instead of loading it to view. If this happens, you have to select Cancel in the Save As window, then turn off Load to Disk before you can view another document.

Connecting to Other Internet Services from a Gopher Server

In addition to items we've already discussed, there are a few other types of items that you might find in a Gopher menu that let you access other Internet services. Some Gopher menu items connect to other Gopher servers (you can do this without realizing it if the menu item label doesn't indicate that it connects to another server).

One other item that you might find in a Gopher menu is a Telnet connection to a service on another Internet host. To do a Gopher Telnet command, Mosaic must use the Telnet program that came with your TCP/IP communications program. It starts up the Telnet program, giving it the host information that is contained in the Gopher menu item. A Telnet window then appears connecting you to the Internet host that was specified in the Gopher menu item.

Tip

If you want to save the file you are currently viewing to disk, click Load to Disk from the **O**ptions menu, and then click Reload from the **N**avigate menu. This will bring up the Save As dialog box.

▶ See "Using Mosaic to Access Telnet," p. 163

From Here...

To learn more about using the WWW and Mosaic, refer to these chapters:

- Chapter 2, "Introduction to the World Wide Web," gives you background information about the WWW.

- Chapter 5, "Navigating with Mosaic," familiarizes you with the Mosaic features that help you find and view documents on the WWW.

- Chapter 9, "Using Mosaic to Access Other Internet Services," gives you information on using WAIS to find information on the WWW, in addition to telling you how to use Telnet and access Usenet news groups with Mosaic.

- Chapter 14, "Hot FTP and Gopher Sites," gives you some pointers on where to find interesting files you can view and retrieve.

III

Advanced Mosaic Features

Chapter 9

Using Mosaic to Access Other Internet Services

Besides Gopher and FTP, which were discussed in previous chapters, Mosaic can also directly access a number of other Internet services.

In this chapter, you learn to do the following:

■ Use Mosaic to access Telnet

■ Use Mosaic to access Usenet newsgroups

■ Use Mosaic to access WAIS

Using Mosaic to Access Telnet

This section discusses using Telnet directly from Mosaic. Telnet can be used to connect to some informational BBS systems on the Internet, or to log in to an account on a remote machine (of course, you have to have an account and know the password, just as you would to log into a machine directly).

◄ See "Connecting to Host Resources Using Telnet," p. 22

Getting Telnet to Work with Mosaic

Mosaic can communicate using the Telnet protocol, but it needs the Telnet program that comes with the TCP/IP software that is installed on your PC. To use the Telnet protocol in a URL, your MOSAIC.INI file must contain a statement at the end of the Viewers section that shows the complete directory path to your Telnet software (see fig. 9.1). (The Macintosh version of Mosaic locates the Telnet program automatically.)

Fig. 9.1

The MOSAIC.INI file, with the Telnet path specified at the end of the Viewers section of the file

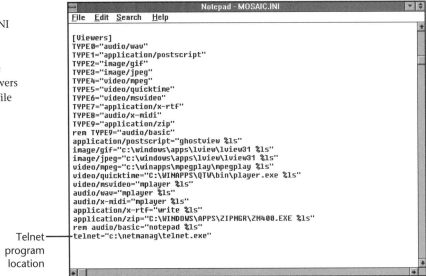

Telnet program location

If your PC is directly connected to the Internet, your MOSAIC.INI file is probably preconfigured with the appropriate address (you can ask your system administrator for help if you have problems making Telnet connections from Mosaic). If you are running over a SL/IP or PPP connection, the TCP/IP communications software that you installed should include a Telnet program.

> **Note**
>
> When you specify a Telnet address in a URL, it sometimes contains a port number in addition to the host name (see the example in the next section, "Using the Telnet Protocol from Mosaic"). When you enter the URL, be sure to separate the host name and the port number with a space. It is a common format to separate the host name and port with a colon (:), but some Telnet programs do not handle this properly, and the connection fails. (This often happens when you are trying to start a Telnet connection from a Gopher menu, where the host name and port number are defined with a colon separating them.)
>
> If the connection fails, it will probably fail with the Telnet window open. If this happens, find the Connect item in the menu bar and select it. This should have the name of the failed connection in it. You can correctly enter the host name and port number here, and complete the connection.

Using the Telnet Protocol from Mosaic

To use the Telnet protocol from Mosaic, you open a URL just as you do to use any of the Internet services. The URL for a Telnet session should specify the Internet host you want to connect to, and any special port number that may be needed. The following steps show you how to use the Telnet protocol:

1. Open the **F**ile menu and choose **O**pen URL.

2. Enter the URL for the Internet host to which you want to connect (for example, **telnet://downwind.sprl.umich.edu 3000**) in the URL field of the Open URL dialog box.

   If you are connecting normally to a host, you will get a login prompt. If you are connecting to an Internet BBS (like the one shown in figure 9.2) you will get the welcome screen for the BBS.

3. When you are finished with your remote connection, be sure to log off or exit from the BBS. The Telnet window remains open when you close the remote connection. Close the Telnet window if you will not be using it any more.

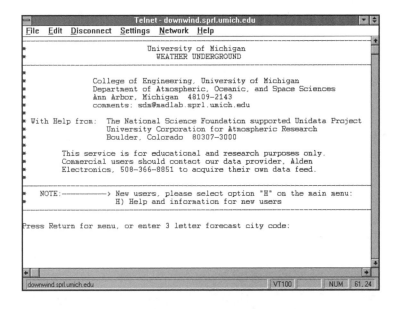

Fig. 9.2
When using Telnet to connect to the Weather Underground System at the University of Michigan, this is the BBS welcome screen you get.

III

Tip
If the Telnet command reports an error, the remote computer may be unavailable, or the network between the two machines may be broken. Wait a while and try again.

Advanced Mosaic Features

Note

Because your Telnet connection is running in a separate window, you can do other things with Mosaic while you are connected to the Telnet service.

Using Archie from Telnet

◄ See "Using Archie to Find Information on FTP Servers," p. 134

Archie is an Internet service that allows you to search a database containing the contents of anonymous FTP servers for a particular program or file. Chapter 7, "FTP with Mosaic," showed you how to do an Archie search using forms. The following steps show you how to connect to an Archie server using the Telnet protocol and perform a search:

1. Open the **F**ile menu and choose **O**pen URL.

2. Enter the URL for the Archie server you want to connect to in the URL field of the Open URL dialog box.

> **Note**
>
> There are a number of Internet Archie servers that you can connect to using Telnet. Some of the ones you might want to try are the following:
>
> | | |
> |---|---|
> | • **archie.internic.net** | New Jersey |
> | • **archie.unl.edu** | Nebraska |
> | • **archie.ans.net** | New York |
> | • **archie.rutgers.edu** | New Jersey |
> | • **archie.sura.net** | Maryland |
> | • **archie.au** | Australia |
> | • **archie.cs.mcgill.ca** | Canada |
> | • **archie.th-darmstadt.de** | Germany |
> | • **archie.wide.ad.jp** | Japan |
> | • **archie.switch.ch** | Switzerland |
> | • **archie.doc.ic.ac.uk** | United Kingdom |

Tip
When picking an Archie server, you should probably pick one that is geographically close to you because it is likely to be physically closer to you on the network, and should give you a faster response time.

3. A welcoming message appears, and the remote computer asks you to log in an account name. Type **archie** as the account name (see fig. 9.3).

4. Enter the command **set pager** to allow you to read what appears on-screen more easily.

5. Enter the command **set search subcase** to tell the Archie program to search for substrings and to let you use upper- and lowercase letters in the search.

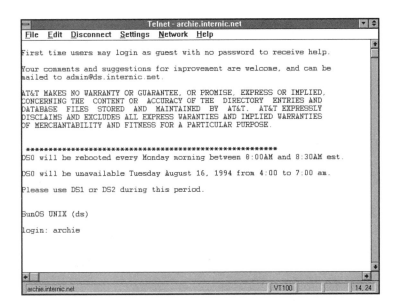

Fig. 9.3
The Telnet window that appears when you connect to **archie.internic.net** through Mosaic, shows the Archie server welcoming message.

6. To search for the file you are interested in, enter **find** followed by the name (or part of the name) of the file you are interested in locating (see figure 9.4). The server will tell you what position you are in the search queue and the estimated time of completion of your search, usually in minutes and seconds.

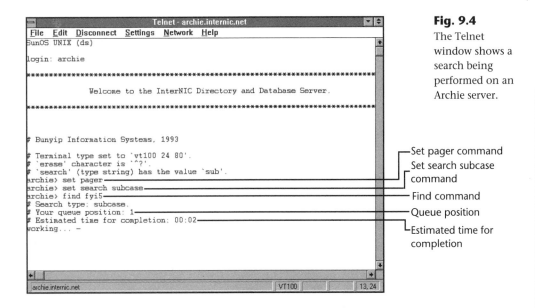

Fig. 9.4
The Telnet window shows a search being performed on an Archie server.

Set pager command

Set search subcase command

Find command

Queue position

Estimated time for completion

III

Advanced Mosaic Features

7. After Archie finishes searching its database for files that match what you are looking for, it displays the results a page at a time (see fig. 9.5). For each matching file, Archie displays several pieces of information that can help you download the file:

- The computer on which the file is located (giving the host name and Internet address numbers for the host).

- The last time that the Archie server connected to this host system to update its database. This date can be important, because the file may have been deleted from the displayed computer system after the Archie server updated its database. If the date displayed for the last update is more than a few weeks old, you may want to choose a different matching file.

- The location of the matching file (generally a directory on the host machine) and information about the matching file, such as the full name, the size of the file, and when the file was created.

Fig. 9.5
The Telnet window shows the result of the Archie search.

Host that has the file

Last time host information was updated

Location of the file

Information about the file

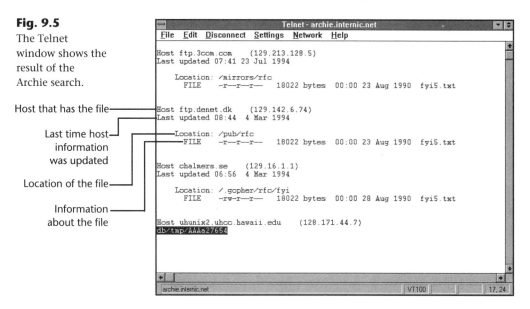

8. Press the spacebar to move to the next page of output. You should note the names of the servers that have a recent copy of the file you are looking for so that you can try to connect to one of these servers using anonymous FTP to retrieve the file.

9. Type **q** to get back to the main Archie prompt. You may do this at any time while viewing the search results.

10. When you are finished searching the Archie database, type `quit` at the
    `archie>` prompt. This disconnects you from the Archie server, but leaves
    your Telnet window open. If you are not going to be making any other
    Telnet connections, you can close the Telnet window.

Using Mosaic to Access Usenet Newsgroups

One of the Internet protocols that Mosaic can use directly is the Usenet news
protocol (properly called the NNTP protocol). This protocol allows Mosaic to
browse and load Usenet newsgroups. These newsgroups are discussion groups
that cover thousands of different topics.

◀ See "Internet Newsgroups (Usenet)," p. 24

Setting Up Mosaic to Read Usenet Newsgroups

To read newsgroups, you must be able to specify a news server to which Mosaic can connect. If you are directly connected to the Internet and have a
local news server at your site, your system administrator probably has
preconfigured your MOSAIC.INI file to use this server. If you have dialed-up
an SL/IP or PPP connection, ask your Internet provider if they have a new
server to which you can connect, or if they know of one. You must then add
a line that specifies the name of the news server in your MOSAIC.INI file in
the Services section, as shown in figure 9.6.

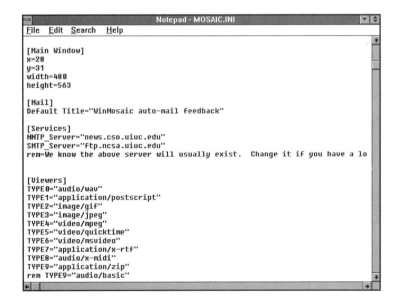

Fig. 9.6
The Usenet news
server path is
specified in the
Services section of
the MOSAIC.INI
file.

On the Macintosh, the process of specifying your news server is a little easier. To set your news server, follow these steps:

1. Open the Options/Preferences dialog box.

2. Choose the Gates options from the left strip of buttons.

3. You'll see a couple of different values to set, the topmost of which is "newshost." Simply specify the name of your local NNTP (network news) host and click Apply.

Reading Usenet Newsgroups

Mosaic is actually not an elegant interface to Usenet. To understand why, you must understand something about the structure of Usenet. Usenet is a collection of thousands of different discussion groups. Each group has a main topic that, hopefully, the participants stick to; but under that main topic there may be dozens of subtopics, with hundreds or even thousands of messages in a single group.

There are many different news readers, but there are a number of features that are common to most news readers. One basic feature shared by most news readers is some method of telling you the names of the newsgroups that exist on your news server so that you can choose which groups you want to read from that list. Some news readers group all of the articles related to a particular topic so that you can glance over the headers and skip to the next topic in which you're interested. Many news readers allow you to post follow-up messages (reply to a post with a post of your own), and messages on a new subtopic. And, a useful feature found in a number of news readers allows you to automatically exclude posts on topics in which you are not interested, or from people you dislike. Unfortunately, the Mosaic Usenet interface lacks all of these features.

From the Mosaic Usenet interface, there is no way of finding the names of any of the newsgroups that exist. Messages are shown in the order that the news server received them, with the newest messages displayed first. No topic grouping of any kind is possible. You cannot post messages from Mosaic, only read them. And there is no way of excluding messages in advance (by topic or author). Mosaic's only advantages are that news articles read with Mosaic are nicely formatted, and Mosaic does provide direct links to related articles when there is quoted material within an article.

An Example of Reading News with Mosaic

The following is an example of reading the newsgroup
news.announce.newusers, You should read this newsgroup to
familiarize yourself with Usenet before you dive in.

1. Open the **F**ile menu and choose **O**pen URL.

2. Enter the URL for the newsgroup you want to read in the URL field
    of the Open URL dialog box (for example, **news:
    news.announce.newusers**). A list of article titles preceded
    by bullets appears, as shown in figure 9.7.

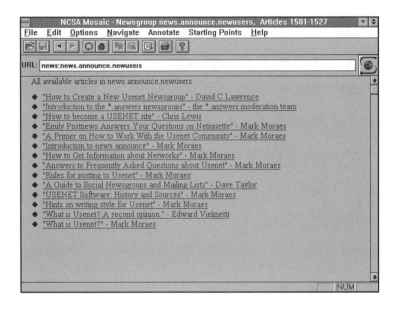

Fig. 9.7
The list of current
articles in the news
group
**news.announce.
newusers**.

3. Click a title that interests you. The body of that article appears in the
    document viewing area. For example, figure 9.8 shows the body of the
    article "Introduction to news.announce."

    The top of the window contains the date of the posting, followed by
    the author's name on the next line. The title of the article appears next.
    After that is a list of other newsgroups where the article is posted (post-
    ing to multiple groups is called *cross-posting*). Next is some historical
    information about the article, followed by the actual text of the article.

4. You now can click one of the newsgroup names to read that newsgroup,
    or select Back from the **N**avigate menu to return to the list of articles.

III

Advanced Mosaic Features

Fig 9.8
The date of posting, author, and title appear at the top of the display, with the cross-posted newsgroups and text of the article following the header information.

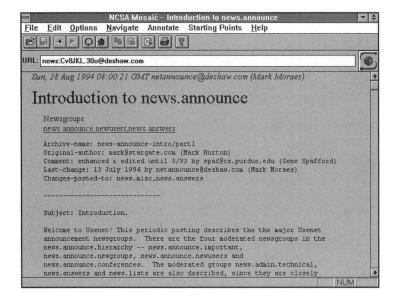

If the article shown in figure 9.8 was a follow-up article, there would be references to the original articles before the article text. These references are hyperlinks to the original articles. If you click these hyperlinks, the original articles are loaded.

If you read a newsgroup that has more than one page of articles, there are hyperlinks at the top ("Earlier Articles") and bottom ("Later Articles") of each page that will move you backward and forward in the list of articles.

Using Mosaic to Access WAIS

One of the big problems with the Internet is that there is no central information source where you can find the location of items of interest to you. You can always connect to servers that you know exist and just browse around them looking for things that might be of interest to you. However, there is an Internet service called WAIS that is specifically designed to locate information sources on the Internet. WAIS allows you to search a set of databases that have been indexed with keywords, and returns addresses where you can locate documents that would be of interest to you.

If you want to do a WAIS search, you first have to connect to a WAIS server. Although Mosaic does directly support WAIS protocol, it does so only on UNIX at this time. So, if you want to use WAIS from Windows Mosaic, you have to Telnet to a WAIS server or find a Gopher server that has a WAIS connection and do your search from there. The Windows and Mac versions of Mosaic currently support WAIS through a gateway. However, using WAIS this way is much more complicated than the Telnet method discussed in the next section.

Using WAIS to Search for Information

One way to do a WAIS search is to Telnet to a public WAIS server. This type of search requires you to use a text-based interface, which is not as convenient as a GUI. Another way to do a WAIS search is to connect to a Gopher server that offers WAIS as one of its menu items. Examples of both types of searches are given here.

Using WAIS from Telnet

There are a number of public sites that allow you to log in to WAIS servers—including **sunsite.unc.edu** (log in as `swais`) and **quake.think.com** (log in as `wais`). The following steps show you how to use the server at **sunsite.unc.edu**:

1. Open **F**ile menu and choose **O**pen URL.

2. Enter the URL **telnet://sunsite.unc.edu** in the URL field of the Open URL dialog box.

   Assuming that you have Telnet set up properly on your PC, a Telnet window opens with the greeting message shown in figure 9.9. (For more information about setting up Telnet to work with Mosaic, see the section "Using Mosaic to Access Telnet" earlier in this chapter.)

3. After the informational messages, you are asked to provide an account to log in to. Type `swais` to log in and use a simple WAIS client program, as explained on-screen.

4. More informational messages appear telling you about the SunSITE computer system. Then the system prompts for the kind of terminal you are using. Type `vt100` (see fig. 9.10).

   Now the remote computer system starts up the WAIS program. After a minute or so, you see the main screen shown in figure 9.11.

   Rather than look through all the databases available (there are hundreds of them), you can use a directory of databases, called the directory-of-servers, to find ones containing the information you want.

Fig. 9.9
Connecting to
the public WAIS
server at
sunsite.unc.edu.

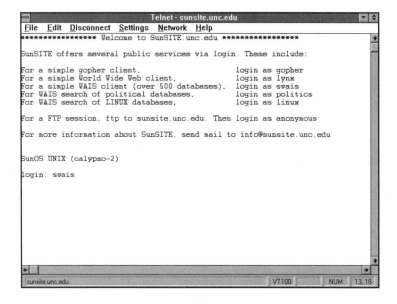

Fig. 9.10
Most computer
systems and
communications
programs let you
use the terminal
type vt100. If you
use a different
terminal type, you
can enter that type
here instead.

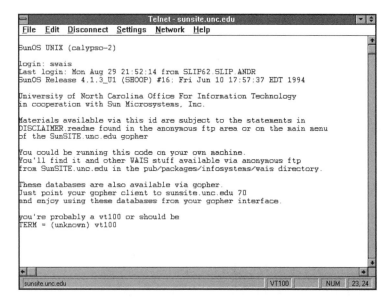

> **Note**
>
> If you use the WAIS server at **quake.think.com**, you automatically start your
> search in the directory-of-servers database and do not have to search for it as
> shown in the next two steps.

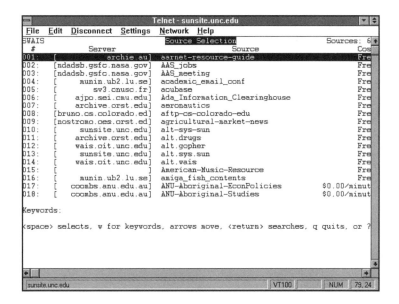

Fig. 9.11
The WAIS main screen shows the different databases of information that are available for you to search.

5. The WAIS program on the **sunsite.unc.edu** machine lets you look for a particular database by typing a slash (/) and the name of the database, and then pressing Enter. Because you want to find the directory-of-servers database, type /**directory-of-servers** (your screen should look like figure 9.12), then press Enter. Other WAIS programs may use a different command.

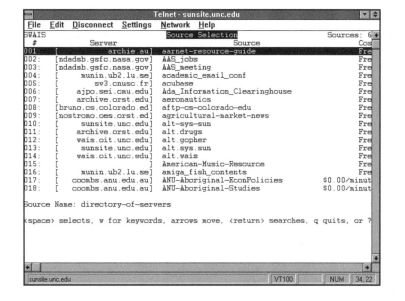

Fig. 9.12
Note that the slash you typed doesn't show up, but causes the program to prompt for the Source Name (the database you want to search).

III

Advanced Mosaic Features

6. Press the spacebar to tell the program that you want to use this database. An asterisk appears next to the line containing the database name.

7. To look for the information you want within the selected database, do a keyword search (by using the w command), Enter w followed by your keywords. Figure 9.13 shows a search for the word "clinton."

Fig. 9.13
The WAIS search screen has the directory-of-servers starred and the word "clinton" entered in the command line.

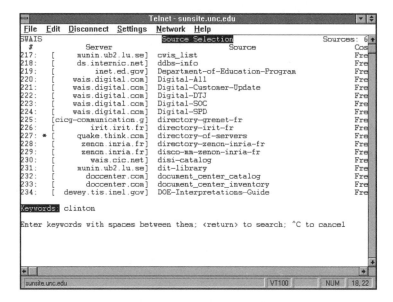

When you press Enter to start the search, the system goes through the directory-of-servers database looking for all the databases that have information about the keywords you entered. You see a list of any matches it finds on a new screen, as shown in figure 9.14.

8. Go back to the list of databases by typing **s**.

9. Press the spacebar to tell WAIS that you won't be searching through the directory-of-servers database any more (the asterisk next to the entry disappears).

10. You should now use one of the databases returned from your search of the directory-of-servers to try to find the information that you are interested in. Type / followed by the name of the database.

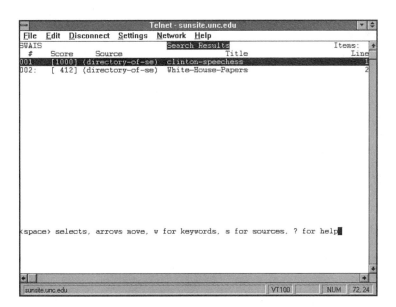

Fig. 9.14
In this example,
the search finds
two databases:
clinton-speechess
and White-House-
Papers.

> **Note**
>
> You can use just a part of the database name when searching, if the part is unique.

11. Press the spacebar to tell WAIS to use this database for searching. An asterisk appears next to the database listing.

12. Now search the database for keywords related to the information you are looking for. You can enter multiple words to make the search more specific to your topic.

The WAIS program looks through the database for documents with these words in them, and assigns a score to each one. The better the match with the search words, the higher the score is. So, if documents with all of your search words in them are available, they will have a high score and will appear near the top of the results list. See figure 9.15 for an example of a search result.

13. To display a document, move to the document and press the spacebar (see fig. 9.16). Press the down-arrow key to move down one document in the list. Press the up-arrow key to move up one document in the list.

III

Advanced Mosaic Features

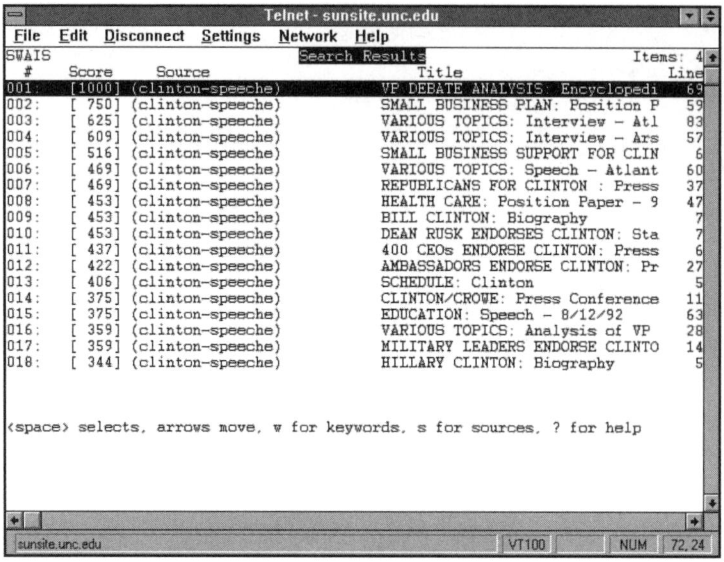

Fig. 9.15
The system finds a number of documents that matched at least some of the keywords, and the ones at the top of the list probably have all of the keywords in them.

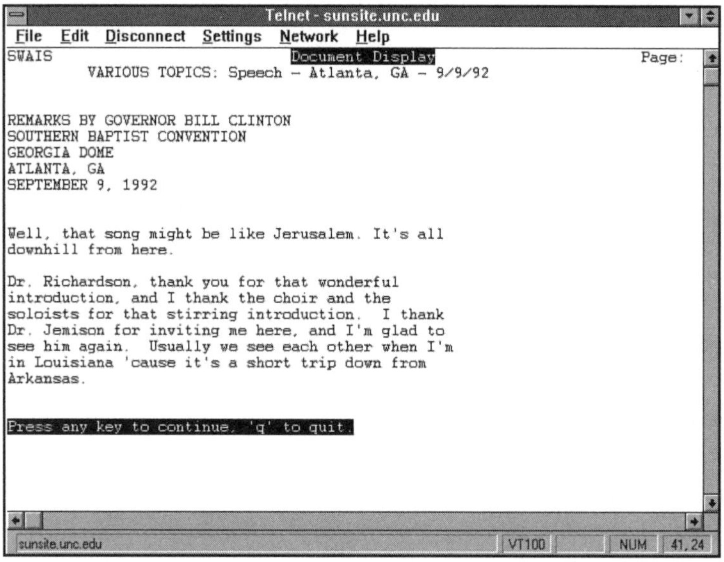

```
┌─┐                    Telnet - sunsite.unc.edu                    ▼│▲
 File  Edit  Disconnect  Settings  Network  Help
SWAIS                            Search Results            Items:  4▲
    #   Score    Source                  Title              Line
 001:  [1000] (clinton-speeche)     VP DEBATE ANALYSIS: Encyclopedi  69
 002:  [ 750] (clinton-speeche)     SMALL BUSINESS PLAN: Position P  59
 003:  [ 625] (clinton-speeche)     VARIOUS TOPICS: Interview - Atl  83
 004:  [ 609] (clinton-speeche)     VARIOUS TOPICS: Interview - Ars  57
 005:  [ 516] (clinton-speeche)     SMALL BUSINESS SUPPORT FOR CLIN   6
 006:  [ 469] (clinton-speeche)     VARIOUS TOPICS: Speech - Atlant  60
 007:  [ 469] (clinton-speeche)     REPUBLICANS FOR CLINTON : Press  37
 008:  [ 453] (clinton-speeche)     HEALTH CARE: Position Paper - 9  47
 009:  [ 453] (clinton-speeche)     BILL CLINTON: Biography           7
 010:  [ 453] (clinton-speeche)     DEAN RUSK ENDORSES CLINTON: Sta   7
 011:  [ 437] (clinton-speeche)     400 CEOs ENDORSE CLINTON: Press   6
 012:  [ 422] (clinton-speeche)     AMBASSADORS ENDORSE CLINTON: Pr  27
 013:  [ 406] (clinton-speeche)     SCHEDULE: Clinton                 5
 014:  [ 375] (clinton-speeche)     CLINTON/CROWE: Press Conference  11
 015:  [ 375] (clinton-speeche)     EDUCATION: Speech - 8/12/92      63
 016:  [ 359] (clinton-speeche)     VARIOUS TOPICS: Analysis of VP   28
 017:  [ 359] (clinton-speeche)     MILITARY LEADERS ENDORSE CLINTO  14
 018:  [ 344] (clinton-speeche)     HILLARY CLINTON: Biography        5



 <space> selects, arrows move, w for keywords, s for sources, ? for help

                                                                    ▼
 ◄                                                                  ►
 sunsite.unc.edu                              VT100       NUM   72, 24
```

Fig. 9.16
The WAIS program displays the document, a copy of a speech given by President Clinton in Atlanta, Georgia.

```
┌─┐                    Telnet - sunsite.unc.edu                    ▼│▲
 File  Edit  Disconnect  Settings  Network  Help
SWAIS                            Document Display          Page:   ▲
          VARIOUS TOPICS: Speech - Atlanta, GA - 9/9/92

 REMARKS BY GOVERNOR BILL CLINTON
 SOUTHERN BAPTIST CONVENTION
 GEORGIA DOME
 ATLANTA, GA
 SEPTEMBER 9, 1992

 Well, that song might be like Jerusalem. It's all
 downhill from here.

 Dr. Richardson, thank you for that wonderful
 introduction, and I thank the choir and the
 soloists for that stirring introduction.  I thank
 Dr. Jemison for inviting me here, and I'm glad to
 see him again.  Usually we see each other when I'm
 in Louisiana 'cause it's a short trip down from
 Arkansas.

 Press any key to continue, 'q' to quit.



 ◄                                                                  ►
 sunsite.unc.edu                              VT100       NUM   41, 24
```

Tip
You can get more information about the WAIS commands by typing **h** or **?** in the WAIS program.

You can quit the WAIS program by typing **q**. This terminates the connection to **sunsite.unc.edu**, but leaves the Telnet window open. If you are not going to make any other Telnet connections, close the Telnet window.

Using WAIS from a Gopher Server

There are a number of public Gopher servers that give you access to WAIS servers—including **launchpad.unc.edu** and **gopher-gw.micro. umn.edu**. The following steps show you how to use the Gopher server at **launchpad.unc.edu** to do a WAIS search:

1. Open **F**ile menu and choose **O**pen URL.

2. Enter the URL **gopher://launchpad.unc.edu** in the URL field of the Open URL dialog box. You get a short Gopher menu.

3. Click the menu item Surfing the Net! This loads a menu that contains, among other things, the item Search WAIS Based Information.

4. Click Search WAIS Based Information. This brings up a list of WAIS search directories.

5. Scroll down through the list of servers until you find the entry directory-of-servers.src—it should be a little over half-way through the list (see fig. 9.17).

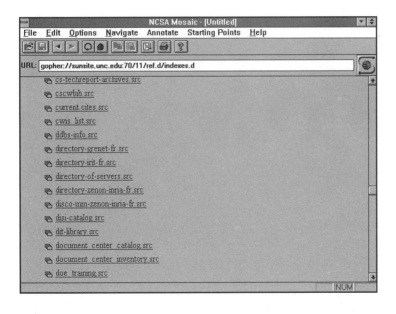

Fig. 9.17
When you click the directory-of-servers.src menu item, a list of databases that you can search using a WAIS server appears.

6. Clicking this menu item loads a search form in the document viewing area that interfaces to a WAIS server to allow you to do a keyword search. You should see something like what is shown in figure 9.18.

Fig. 9.18
The WAIS search form allows you to search for keywords in the selected database.

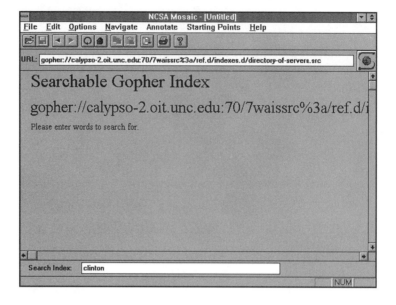

7. Click in the area next to the Search Index at the bottom of the screen, type in a keyword describing the information you want to search for, then press Enter. The result of the search will be displayed as shown in figure 9.19.

Fig. 9.19
The result of the WAIS search for the word "clinton," shows the clinton-speechess and White-House-Papers databases.

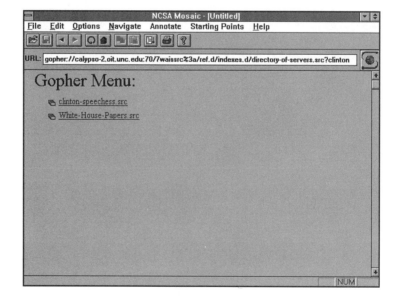

8. You can now search these databases for documents that contain the information you are interested in. Use the Back command from the **N**avigate menu twice to return to the list of WAIS databases. Scroll through the list until you find one of the databases that was returned from your initial search.

> **Note**
>
> You would think that you should be able to click these databases and continue the search from that point, but the Gopher server returns an error when you try to do this. Instead, return to the master list of databases and search from there. (If you use a WAIS server from a Telnet connection, you also have to return to the main list of servers to continue the search.)

9. Click the database that you want to search through and another search form appears. Enter the keywords that you would like to search on in the Search Index box, and press Enter (you can enter multiple words separated by a space to narrow the search). A list of documents appears in the document viewing area (see fig. 9.20).

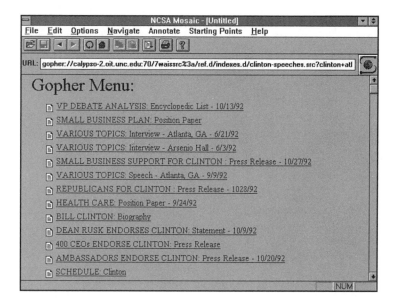

Fig. 9.20
The list of documents is the result from doing a search on the words "clinton atlanta georgia."

III

Advanced Mosaic Features

You now can click the documents to view them. When you are finished, use the Back command from the **N**avigate menu to return to the search window. From here you can navigate back to other menus on this Gopher or go to a completely new URL.

Retrieving a WAIS Document

WAIS servers were designed for viewing documents, not for retrieving them. So, if you are using WAIS via Telnet, there is really no way of retrieving the document that you are viewing (unless the WAIS server shows you the actual address of the file you are viewing—then you can use anonymous FTP to retrieve the file). When you are using WAIS from a Gopher server, however, you can use Mosaic's file saving features to store the file on your local disk.

If you would like to save the document you are reading, there are **S**ave and Save **A**s options under the **F**ile menu. These features were not yet working in the 2.0 alpha 6 version of Mosaic that was used to write this book. However, these features were implemented in the 2.0 alpha 7 version of Mosaic that was released just as this book was going to press. The steps for saving a file using the Save As command are as follows:

1. While you are viewing a document that you want to save, open the **F**ile menu and select Save **A**s. You will get a Save As window like the one shown in figure 9.21 asking you where you want to save the file.

Fig. 9.21
When you save a file, you can put it anywhere on your local directory system.

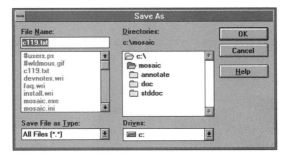

2. Fill in the information in the window and select OK. Mosaic attempts to save the file to your local disk.

There is another way you can save files from Mosaic. The following procedure saves the file associated with a URL to a file on your PC.

1. Open the **O**ptions menu and select **L**oad to Disk.

2. Click the hyperlink for the document that you want to save. You will get a Save As window like the one shown in figure 9.21 asking you where you want to save the file.

3. Fill in the information in the window and select OK. Mosaic attempts to load that URL to disk instead of displaying it in the document viewing area.

Tip
If you want to load a single file to disk, you can Shift-click on the hyperlink rather than selecting **L**oad to Disk from the **O**ptions menu. This loads only that one file to disk.

If you forget to turn off Load to Disk after saving a document, Mosaic tries to load the URL of the next hyperlink you click to disk instead of loading it to view. If this happens, you have to select Cancel in the Save As window, then turn off Load to Disk before you can view another document.

From Here...

To learn more about using the WWW and Mosaic, refer to the following chapters:

- Chapter 2, "Introduction to the World Wide Web," gives you background information about the WWW.

- Chapter 5, "Navigating with Mosaic," familiarizes you with the Mosaic features that help you find and view documents on the WWW.

- Chapter 8, "Gopher with Mosaic," gives you general information on using Gopher servers.

Tip
If you want to save the file you are currently viewing to disk, click **L**oad to Disk from the **O**ptions menu, then click Reload from the **N**avigate menu. This will bring up the Save As dialog box.

III

Advanced Mosaic Features

Part IV

Other WWW Clients

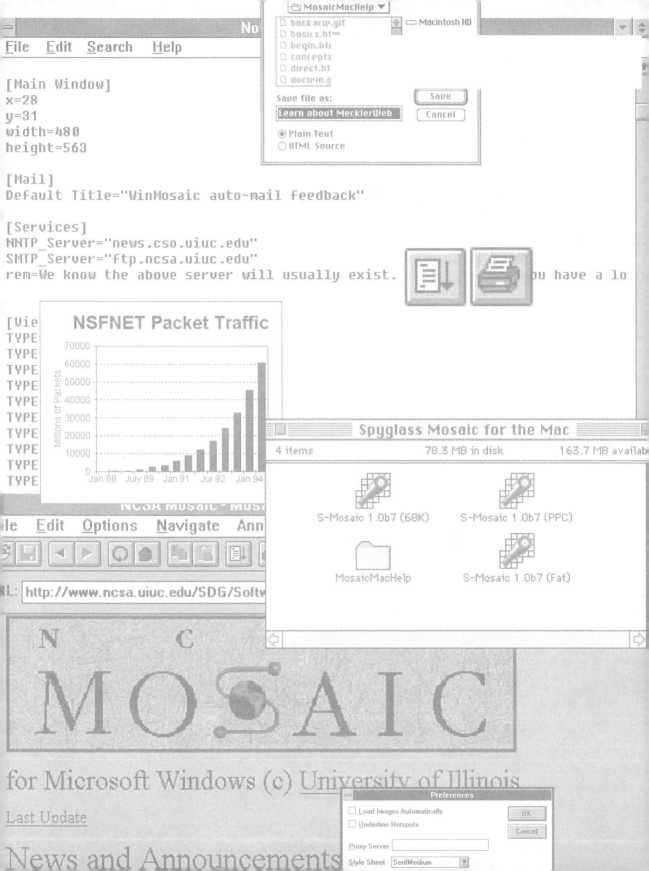

Chapter 10

Other Versions of Mosaic for Windows

The first part of this book describes the features available in the Mosaic program developed by NCSA. While this is an impressive program, NCSA saw the need for Mosaic to be further developed and commercialized. To make this possible, NCSA licensed the program to several commercial software companies. These companies developed their own versions of Mosaic based on the NCSA version.

So why would anyone be interested in purchasing one of these commercial versions when the NCSA version is available for free use? In the NCSA version, many features you expect to work do not. The commercial products—in some cases—polished most of the rough edges and added some features that weren't finished in the NCSA version.

Most of the licensees managed to speed up Mosaic's operation. Files load faster (although the main speed limitation still comes from your modem—if you use a modem to access the Internet), in-line images display faster, and, in general, all aspects of the program involve less waiting time. Most of the licensees also reduced the amount of memory Mosaic uses while running and the amount of drive space occupied by the program.

Another key feature of many of these programs is that they are sold as part of a larger set of Internet tools. You can get the SLIP or PPP connection software, FTP, Gopher, e-mail, and other software in one package, all supported by the same company. If you are looking for an all-in-one Internet solution, this is the answer.

Most of these commercial versions are still very similar to the NCSA version in the way you use them. The fundamental Mosaic and World Wide Web features, covered in this book, work in essentially the same way. This chapter points out the differences, no matter what version of Mosaic you use, so you are able to make full use of this book.

This chapter describes several of the Mosaic programs that are commercially available. This is not a comprehensive list: there are several companies whose products are still in developmental stages. This chapter also discusses an older version of Mosaic from NCSA and explains why this version is still useful to some users. The following products are covered in this chapter:

- AIR Mosaic from Spry

- Enhanced Mosaic for Windows from Spyglass

- NCSA Mosaic version 1.0

- GWHIS Viewer from Quadralay

AIR Mosaic from Spry

AIR Mosaic is designed as the optimal tool for browsing the World Wide Web. Developed from NCSA's original Mosaic tool, AIR Mosaic incorporates more Windows functionality, and is easier to configure and customize. It's a 16-bit program (the most recent Mosaic is a 32-bit system).

AIR Mosaic features hotlists and advanced menu support: you can incorporate your own Internet finds and quickly access information. You can configure fonts, colors, and performance using only one configuration screen.

What Is AIR Mosaic and How Do You Get It?

The AIR series is distributed in two ways—in conjunction with publisher O'Reilly & Associates as part of Internet in a Box, and as part of Spry's AIR Series of TCP/IP programs. Contact O'Reilly & Associates at 800-998-4269 or **ibox@ora.com**, or Spry at 800-777-9638 or **info@spry.com.**

The following are the applications included in this suite:

- **AIR Mosaic.** This is the WWW browser. The features included in AIR Mosaic are described in the next section.

- **AIR Mail.** This is the e-mail handler for sending and receiving mail on the Internet. AIR Mail contains the printing, mail addressing, binary file attachments, and News folders.

- **AIR News.** This is the news reader for Usenet news. AIR News has several features, including personalized groups to read from, threading, and custom header support.

- **AIR Gopher.** This is the Gopher interface for searching and retrieving files in a menu driven environment.

- **Network File Manager.** This is the system's FTP utility, which lets you drag and drop files from an FTP site to File Manager. You can copy, create, delete, and move directories and files.

- **AIR Telnet.** This tool lets you connect to Telnet sites as if you were at the site itself, and you can have as many as 15 concurrent Telnet sessions. You can save custom sessions and automatic logins to your favorite sites.

The AIR series also has a GIF and JPEG viewer called ImageView and a uuencode/decode utility.

Features of AIR Mosaic

AIR Mosaic, then, is simply one of a number of applications that you get when you buy Internet in a Box or the AIR Series. AIR Mosaic is opened by double-clicking the GNN-AIR Mosaic icon in Program Manager.

> **Note**
>
> GNN stands for *Global Network Navigator*, a World Wide Web publication by O'Reilly & Associates—the same people who publish Internet in a Box. GNN is available to anyone traveling in Web-space, not just Internet in a Box users.

AIR Mosaic's features include the following:

- Hotlists let you add WWW documents to hotlists with folders and subfolders. You can add multiple hotlists to your AIR Mosaic menu for quick access and you can import NCSA menus from the MOSAIC.INI file—useful if you've been working with Mosaic and created menus.

- A straightforward Configuration dialog box lets you configure Mosaic preferences (colors, fonts, and default home page), viewers, and options. The External Viewers Configuration dialog box enables you to configure viewers or add new ones.

■ A *Kiosk* mode enables you to hide the toolbar and other information. Ideal for presentations, it also allows you to set up AIR Mosaic for unattended use. While Mosaic has Kiosk mode, it's "hidden"—you have to start the program using the -k parameter. But in AIR Mosaic you can simply click the Kiosk icon or select the Kiosk menu option.

■ A custom caching feature, so you can access documents you've already browsed in a session. While Mosaic also has caching, it's hidden away in the MOSAIC.INI file, while AIR Mosaic lets you set it from a dialog box.

■ Support for "proxy" servers for HTTP, WAIS, FTP, and Gopher. These let a user at a secure site bypass the security and get out onto the Web.

■ Print WWW document text and graphics as well as save or copy the document text.

Installing AIR Mosaic and Tools

The product's installation procedure is very straightforward. Run the Windows setup program from the first installation disk. The program asks you about each change it makes and tells you when to swap disks.

When you install AIR Mosiac, you are installing all the software you need to make a TCP/IP connection. Unlike many products that make installing such a connection difficult, Spry has done an excellent job of simplifying the procedure. In particular it has found a simple way to create a login script—and login scripts are the weak point in many Internet products.

> **Note**
>
> Installation is especially easy if you use SprintLink as a service provider. If you plan to use a different service provider's PPP or SLIP, check with Spry or your provider before purchasing AIR Mosaic to see if configuration files are available for that system. If not, see if you can get some help configuring the software to work with your provider. You will have to enter all the configuration data by hand, and create a login script using the system's Login Setup dialog box.

Note

You don't have to use Spry's dialing and connections software. If you already have a service provider and TCP/IP software (such as Trumpet shareware), you can install AIR Mosaic, skip the service provider section of the installation, and use AIR Mosaic with your current account. This may be the easiest way to use AIR Mosaic; however, you lose many of the advantages of Spry's all-in-one package.

Starting AIR Mosaic

To start AIR Mosaic, find the application—in the "Internet In A Box" program group if you are using that product (see fig. 10.1)—and double-click the GNN-AIR Mosaic icon. If you've already started your TCP/IP connection, AIR Mosaic starts right away, otherwise it starts the dialer and makes the connection.

Fig. 10.1
AIR Mosaic icons for Internet in a Box.

AIR Mosaic connects you to the Spry Inc. World Wide Web home page. This is a good place to look for other WWW resources and other Internet resources. From here, you can browse the Internet and connect to other home pages. When you become more experienced, you can build a library of home pages you like—using AIR Mosaic's hotlist feature.

The AIR Mosaic Console

The AIR Mosaic console consists of several components (see fig. 10.2). Note the following components:

Fig. 10.2
The AIR Mosaic
screen.

Document
title bar

Document
text

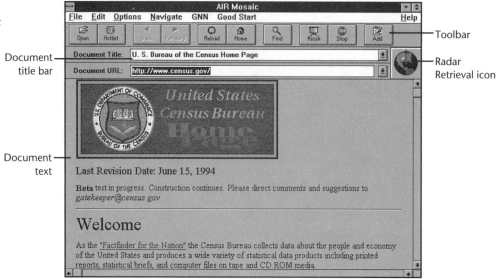

Toolbar

Radar
Retrieval icon

- **The Toolbar.** The toolbar contains shortcut buttons for AIR Mosaic menu items. You can change the style of the toolbar (Picture & Text, Picture only, and Text only). Open the **O**ptions menu and choose Toolbar Style.

- **The Document Title Bar.** The Document Title bar contains the Document Title and Document URL drop-down lists.

  You can go back to any of the previously accessed documents: select the title or URL from the lists. You can also change the number of documents displayed in these lists: open the **O**ptions menu and choose Configuration.

- The text of the document itself.

- **The Radar Retrieval Icon.** This serves the same function as the spinning globe in NCSA Mosaic.

Tip
The Radar Retrieval
icon, in the upper
right corner of the
AIR Mosaic con-
sole, spins while
the home page is
retrieved.

The Kiosk Mode

AIR Mosaic offers a special mode for displaying a data page. The Kiosk Mode hides all the console information except the actual document (in other words, the toolbar, status bar, document title bar, and the menu items and commands are hidden). This is useful if you give presentations—because it shows a lot of the screen—or if you set up Mosaic on an unattended work-station.

Kiosk mode is actually the same as the Kiosk mode in Mosaic, except that it's not hidden in AIR Mosaic. While Mosaic makes you start the program using the -k parameter, AIR Mosaic lets you start normally, then go to Kiosk mode at any time using the **O**ptions, **K**iosk Mode command, or by clicking the toolbar button.

> **Note**
>
> The shortcut movement keys of F (Forward) and B (Back) are very helpful when you move in this mode, because the Forward and Back commands are not available.

To exit the Kiosk mode, press Escape or Ctrl+K.

Browsing with AIR Mosaic

Hyperlinks in AIR Mosaic are indicated in the same way as the NCSA version: blue underlined text and boxes, or graphics surrounded by a blue border (you can change the color). As with the NCSA version, the mouse turns into a pointing hand over a hyperlink.

Opening Previous Documents

The Document Title and Document URL drop-down lists contain a listing of the last several documents you accessed in this session. (This is similar to the History feature but provides an easier way to access it.) The lists are identical, except one shows the title of the document (such as Spry Home Page) and the other shows that document's URL (**http://www.spry.com**). You can go back to any of the displayed documents by choosing the title or URL from the lists. (The latest version of Mosaic no longer has the Title drop-down list box.)

Using Hotlists

Hotlists in AIR Mosaic work quite differently from Mosaic. AIR Mosaic has a hierarchical system of hotlist folders that let you categorize the hotlist items.

You can access your hotlist in two ways:

- You can click the Hotlists toolbar button then double-click the item you want to go to in the Hotlists dialog box.

- You can make hotlists into drop-down menus, and choose them directly from the AIR Mosaic menu bar. Select the hotlist in the Hotlists dialog box, then click the Put this hotlist in the menu bar check box and choose OK.

Tip
You can convert any menu you create in NCSA Mosaic into a hotlist. See the end of this section for information.

The Hotlists Dialog Box

To get to the Hotlists dialog box, open the **F**ile menu and choose **H**otlists (see fig. 10.3). The Hotlists screen shows all the different Hotlists you have. AIR Mosaic comes with two default Hotlists pre-loaded—the GNN and Good Start hotlists—but you can add your own.

Fig. 10.3
The Hotlists dialog box contains two default hotlists.

A main Hotlist, such as the GNN Hotlist, has a flaming icon. Hotlists initially are shown closed: you can open the Hotlist by double-clicking the Hotlist icon (see figs. 10.4 and 10.5). Each Hotlist can contain individual WWW documents, or it can contain folders that house additional documents. You use folders and subfolders to organize your documents any way you want. The documents and folders are listed in a hierarchy, similar to the Windows File Manager.

Fig. 10.4
Double-click the GNN hotlist to show its individual items.

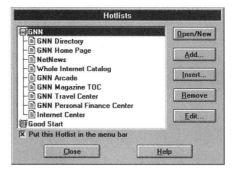

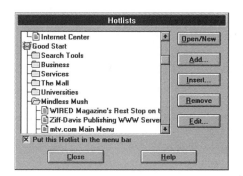

Fig. 10.5
The Good Start hotlist comes preconfigured with many interesting and useful sites arranged in folders.

In the Hotlists dialog box, you can create new hotlists, add new hotlist items, edit your existing items, or delete existing items.

To add a hotlist to the menu bar, you select Put This Hotlist in the menu bar. You can add as many hotlists to the menu that fit. When you choose this option, the selected Hotlist icon in the Hotlist dialog box changes to an icon containing the letter *M*. When you open one of these hotlist menus, you'll see a series of cascading menus, one for each folder in the hotlist.

Creating a New Hotlist

To create a new hotlist follow these steps:

1. Open the **F**ile menu and choose **H**otlists, or click the Hotlist button on the toolbar. The Hotlist dialog box appears (refer to fig. 10.5).

2. Click **O**pen/New. You see a Windows Open dialog box.

3. Enter a DOS name for the hotlist. Each hotlist is saved in a file with the HOT file extension.

> **Note**
>
> At this point, you can specify the name of an existing hotlist, to load the existing hotlist into the Hotlist dialog box.

4. Click OK.

   Another dialog box appears, asking you for the name you want to use for the hotlist (the name that will appear in the Hotlist dialog box). Use any name you want (keep in mind, though, that you may want to use this hotlist as an AIR Mosaic menu item, so you might want to keep the name short.) Type a name, and click OK. The hotlist is now created and appears in the Hotlist screen with a flaming icon.

Using Folders

You can create folders and subfolders to organize your information.

1. Highlight the hotlist or folder to which you want to add a new folder.

2. Click **A**dd and select Folder in the Add New dialog box that appears.

3. You are asked to name the Folder. Name it and click OK. You have created a new folder.

Adding Documents to a Hotlist

Now that you have a new hotlist and a new folder, you can begin adding documents. To add a document to a hotlist do the following:

> Open the **N**avigate menu and choose Add Document. This adds the document to the hotlist you are currently using—the last hotlist you selected. If you want to place the document into a folder within the hotlist, though, you'll have to use the following method.

> **Note**
>
> If a hotlist isn't selected, this command may not work properly. Using the Hotlist screen, as described below, allows you to specify where you want to add the document.

If you do not have a hotlist selected, use the following steps:

1. Open the **F**ile menu and choose **H**otlist.

2. Select the hotlist to which you want to add the current document.

3. Click **A**dd. You are asked if you want to add a document or a folder; select Document. The Add Document dialog box appears (see fig. 10.6). This contains the title and URL of the document you are currently viewing. You can change the name of the document. But do not change the URL!

Fig. 10.6
The Add Document dialog box.

IV

> **Note**
>
> You can also add a document you are not viewing to a hotlist. From the Hotlist dialog box, choose the **A**dd button, select the document, and then enter the URL address and title in the Add Document dialog box.

4. Click OK. The document you specified is added to the Hotlist you selected.

Special Feature: Importing NCSA Menus as Hotlists

If you previously used NCSA Mosaic, you may have built an extensive menu of favorite home pages and resources. You can use AIR Mosaic to convert these menus to AIR Mosaic Hotlists. To import an NCSA menu as a hotlist use the following steps:

1. Open the **O**ptions menu and click Import NCSA Menu as Hotlist. You see the Import NCSA Menu as Hotlist dialog box (see fig. 10.7).

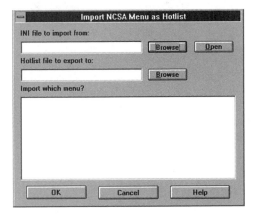

Fig. 10.7
The Import NCSA Menu as Hotlist dialog box lets you convert Mosaic menus to AIR Mosaic hotlists.

2. In the INI File To Import From text box, type the location and name of the MOSAIC.INI file where your NCSA menu information is stored. Click the **B**rowse button next to the text box to look through the directories on your PC and select the correct file. After you select the file, confirm that it is the correct file you want by clicking the **O**pen button.

3. Specify a hotlist file for this menu. Do not choose an existing hotlist unless you want to overwrite the information in that file. You can use **B**rowse to find a hotlist file and a directory for the file.

4. Select the menu from the NCSA MOSAIC.INI file you want to import (all of the menus in that file appear in a list) as shown in figure 10.8.

Fig. 10.8
The filled in dialog box with an NCSA menu selected.

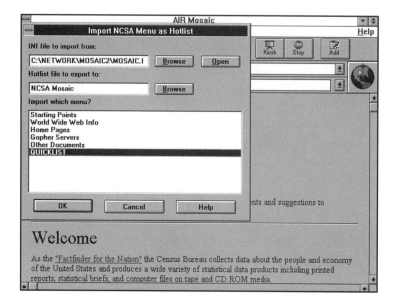

5. Click OK when you're ready to import the file.

Now you can return to the Hotlists dialog box to open the new hotlist you have just created.

After you've imported a menu to a hotlist, you can then place the hotlist on the menu bar if you wish, using the Put this Hotlist in the Menu Bar command.

Saving Documents

You can save WWW documents so you can open them later (using the Open Local File command) or so you can use the information in other documents (such as word processing documents). When you save documents, you are saving the HTML source document.

There are two ways to save documents: you can use Load to Disk Mode to save the document to disk as soon as you access it (as described below), or you can save the document source code to disk using the Document Source command.

1. Open the **O**ptions menu and choose Load to Disk Mode.

2. Click a link pointing to a document you want to save. The Save As dialog box appears.

3. Type a name and select a directory in which to place the file. (HTML files are saved as an HTM file in DOS.)

4. Click OK.

Here's the other method for saving a document you are already viewing:

1. Open the **F**ile menu and choose Document Source.

2. In the Document Source dialog box, select File, then Save As.

3. Type a name and select a directory in which to place the file.

4. Click OK.

If you see a message saying that the source is not available, it may be because you are using a cached document. Use the Reload command to reload from the original HTML file.

Configuring AIR Mosaic Options

You easily can configure AIR Mosaic using the Configuration dialog box. This dialog box allows you to specify options for displaying elements in the AIR Mosaic Console, such as the toolbar, status bar, images, text files, hyperlinks, and sounds. You can also set the proxy servers for AIR Mosaic, AIR Mosaic's fonts and colors, and which external viewers are used to view graphics, and play sounds and movies.

To access the Configuration dialog box, open the **O**ptions menu and choose **C**onfiguration (see fig. 10.9). The Configuration options are described in the sections that follow.

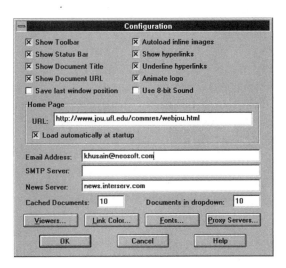

Fig. 10.9
The default Configuration dialog box (with the e-mail address and newserver filled in).

General Options

The General Configuration options, shown at the top of the Configuration dialog box, are almost the same as those in NCSA Mosaic. Some of the options in this dialog box are present in NCSA Mosaic, except they can be changed only by editing MOSAIC.INI. Some of the options are the same as in Mosaic, others are not:

- **Save last window position.** You can resize the AIR Mosaic Console window, in order to see more (or less) of a WWW document. If you want these size changes to be saved and used during your next AIR Mosaic session, check this option. (In Mosaic you open the File menu and choose Save Preferences to do this.)

- **Show hyperlinks.** This allows you to hide the hyperlink jumps in a Mosaic document.

- **Animate logo.** This refers to the radar indicator on the Document Title Bar. It takes additional time to animate this indicator logo. By default, the logo is turned on, because it tells you if a document or image is being retrieved. The time you save by turning off the logo animation, however, is not substantial. You probably only want to turn off the radar indicator if your connection is very slow.

- **Cached Documents.** This represents how many documents are cached, or kept active, in your PC's memory. If this number is 10, for instance, then 10 documents remain available to you. They don't have to be loaded to go back to them—they immediately appear. If you have a lot of available system memory, you can increase this number. Keep in mind, though, that a high number for cache can affect another application's performance, although AIR Mosaic's performance improves quite a bit. (To change the cache in Mosaic you must edit the MOSAIC.INI file.)

- **Documents in Dropdown.** This indicates how many of your last-accessed documents appear in the Document Title and Document URL drop-down lists (displayed beneath the toolbar). A value of 5 means that the last five documents you accessed display in these lists.

Viewer Options

The **V**iewers button in the Configuration dialog box lets you specify the external viewers you want to use. This option is available in NCSA Mosaic only by editing the INI file. AIR Mosaic offers a friendlier way to change the viewer settings. From the Configuration dialog box, press the **V**iewers button. The External Viewer Configuration dialog box appears, as shown in figure 10.10.

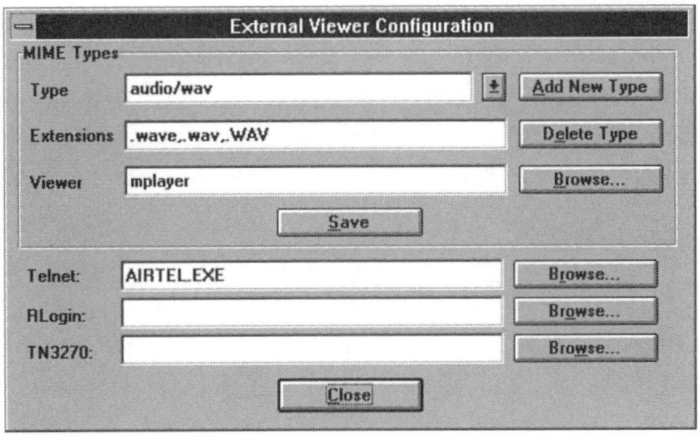

Fig. 10.10
The External Viewers Configuration dialog box presents an easy way to configure AIR Mosaic to use external viewers.

To see a list of resources (derived from the MIME multimedia specification) you are likely to find using AIR Mosaic, pull down the Type drop down list (see fig. 10.11). AIR Mosaic has default viewers set up for all resource types; however, it's unlikely that you actually have all of those viewers (or, if you have them, that they are in the right location). Therefore, you can reconfigure to make sure that all the resources you find work properly in AIR Mosaic.

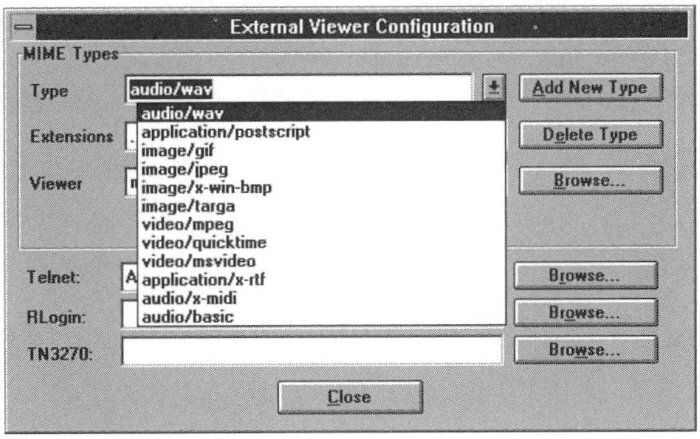

Fig. 10.11
The list of viewer types.

To redefine which viewer AIR Mosaic uses for a type of file:

1. Choose the data type from the Type drop-down list.

2. Type the full path and file name of the viewer you want to use in the Viewer field, or choose **B**rowse to find the viewer on your PC (when you locate the viewer and click OK, the Viewer field is filled in automatically).

3. Choose **S**ave. Note that you must choose Save for every type of viewer you want to configure.

4. Choose **C**lose when you are done configuring viewers. The changes take place immediately.

> **Note**
>
> You can also define the applications used by Mosaic for Telnet, rlogin, and tn3270. To do this, type the application you want to use in the appropriate field (choose **B**rowse to search your disk for the correct file and directory name). When you Close the dialog box, the changes you made are saved.

AIR Mosaic uses file extensions, found in the hyperlink that is created for the resource, to figure out what resource type the item is, and, consequently, what viewer to use. Therefore, you can create your own resource types and link viewers to them, so you can use items that have resource types not yet set up.

For instance, you can access a Gopher site with Mosaic and find some ZIP files. If you have an application that reads ZIP files (such as WinZip), you can define ZIP files in AIR Mosaic as a resource type associated with a viewer. To do this, follow these steps:

1. Click **A**dd New Type in the External Viewer Configuration dialog box (refer to fig. 10.10). Specify any name for the new type (such as zipped).

2. Type in the extensions to be considered as zipped files (zip and ZIP are used here).

3. Specify a Viewer name and path.

4. Choose **S**ave to store the new Viewer type.

Proxy Servers

AIR Mosaic allows you to specify any Proxy Servers to be used for getting WWW, FTP, WAIS, and Gopher information past Internet firewalls. Click the Proxy Servers button and specify the addresses of your Proxy Servers to have AIR Mosaic use those servers.

> **Note**
>
> A *firewall* is a system used to block outside access to a site for security reasons. The firewall can be bypassed by the system's users so they can access resources on the Internet, but to do so the system administrator must specifically allow connections to particular servers.

AIR Mosaic is a very nice system, one that has the added advantage of being bundled with TCP/IP software that is *very* easy to install.

Enhanced NCSA Mosaic for Windows from Spyglass

Enhanced NCSA Mosaic is a program published by Spyglass. As its name implies, it's a version of Mosaic created under license from the NCSA. Spyglass plans to sell the product to OEMs (Original Equipment Manufacturers) including IBM, DEC, and several others. If you purchase computer hardware from one of these manufacturers and it includes Mosaic, it is usually labeled with the hardware manufacturer's name, not Spyglass.

Spyglass is also sublicensing Mosaic to other software companies. These companies make refinements to the product and resell it. Again, you won't see the Spyglass name on these versions. They usually bear the name of the software company licensing it.

So, although you may not see Enhanced NCSA Mosaic for sale at your local computer store with that name, you may run across it bundled with another product you buy—or sold under another name.

Installing Enhanced NCSA Mosaic

Enhanced NCSA Mosaic is a 32-bit program. That means it's designed to run on a 32-bit operating system—Windows NT. But you can still run it in Windows 3.1 or Windows for Workgroups (16-bit operating systems), by installing the Microsoft Win32s software. That is covered in chapter 3, "Getting Mosaic for Windows Running," but Spyglass made it easy for you: they integrated the Win32s installation into the Mosaic installation.

The Mosaic installation program takes a look at your Windows setup and sees if you have Win32s installed. If not, it installs Win32s for you.

> **Caution**
>
> You may run into problems with Win32s if you have a LaserMaster printer (see chapter 3, "Getting Mosaic for Windows Running").

The installation program is a typical Windows setup program with no surprises. Run the setup program, start your Internet connection, and then double-click the icon created by the setup program.

What's New

When you start Enhanced NCSA Mosaic, you first notice the similarity to Mosaic (see fig. 10.12). However, there are some important changes—some you'll like and some you may not.

Fig. 10.12

At first glance Enhanced NCSA Mosaic looks much like NCSA Mosaic.

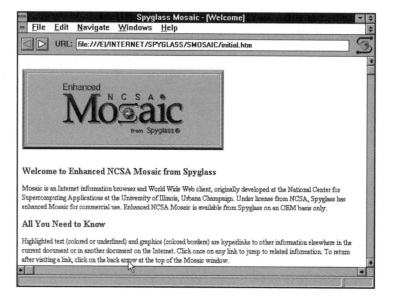

Start by looking at the obvious changes:

- There isn't a true toolbar, although back and forward buttons have been added to the URL line.

- The Mosaic icon is not a button—you can't click the icon to stop a transfer.

- There isn't a Starting Points menu.

- There is no Options menu. There are fewer options, and these are now reached through the Edit menu.

- The mouse pointer doesn't change when you point at a link. (But when the pointer goes over a link, the status bar displays the URL.)

- There are lots of menu-option changes.

As noted, there are some important changes from the freeware version. For instance, Enhanced NCSA Mosaic has a feature that changes the color of a link—if you click a link, read the document, then return to the previous document, the link changes color. That's handy if you're going through a document with many links you want to check—quickly you see which links you've already used.

The other important changes between these two versions of Mosaic are described in the following sections.

Copy and Save

The current version of basic Mosaic makes it difficult to save information from the current document. Enhanced NCSA Mosaic has that problem fixed.

First, you can copy all the text from the displayed document to the Clipboard. Then you paste it into any Windows application (word processing, for instance). This feature is implemented through the usual Windows method: open the **E**dit menu and choose **C**opy.

> **Note**
>
> The original NCSA Mosaic has the copy option on the Edit menu and there is button for it on the toolbar, but the feature does not work.

Also, you can save the document as a file. Follow these steps:

1. Open the **F**ile menu and choose **S**ave As. You see the typical Windows Save As dialog box.

2. Enter a file name and then select the type of file you want to create from the Save File as Type list box. You can save the file as Plain Text if you want; you get ASCII text, what you see in the document on your screen. You also can save as HTML; you get the text *and* the HTML codes—so you can use the page at a later date (by opening the **F**ile menu and choosing **O**pen Local).

3. Choose OK to save the file.

> **Note**
>
> When you save documents to a file using either method, inline graphics are not saved in the document. Also, the hyperlinks may not function correctly if you open the file locally. Hyperlinks that use relative addresses won't work when you save the file locally. See chapter 5, "Navigating with Mosaic," for a discussion of relative and absolute links.

Transferring Files

Spyglass tried to make Mosaic easier to use; however, in one way they made it harder—they hid the command used to download files. To download in NCSA Mosaic, you choose the Options, Load to Disk menu command, then click a link. Enhanced NCSA Mosaic doesn't have this option. Instead, you must press Control, then double-click the link. A Download To dialog box appears—this is the normal Save As dialog box, in which you can enter a file name and directory.

Multiple Windows

Enhanced NCSA Mosaic has something most other Web-browser publishers don't: the ability to have multiple document windows open at the same time. This means that you can run several Web sessions at the same time.

To open multiple windows and keep your current window open also, open the **F**ile menu and choose **N**ew Window. You can work in the new window, clicking on links and so on, while the previous window remains open. In fact, you can open more windows and have several sessions working at once (see fig. 10.13).

Fig. 10.13
Enhanced NCSA Mosaic lets you have multiple sessions working at once.

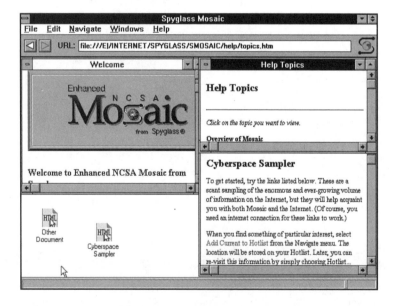

Use the **W**indows menu, and the maximize and minimize buttons, to manipulate these windows. You can tile or cascade them, or minimize them completely. You can use the **W**indows menu to jump to a particular window, or press Ctrl+Tab or Ctrl+F6 to move through each window in turn. You can also select Next from the document's window Control menu.

Each session can be in a different location on the Web. When you click a link in one of the document windows, it has no effect on the sessions in the other document windows.

Working with the Hotlist

Enhanced NCSA Mosaic does not let you add hotlist items to menus. It provides a Hotlist dialog box instead, which contains just one hotlist (see fig. 10.14). To use this feature, open **N**avigate and choose **H**otlist. You have to use it and then close it, though—you can't leave the Hotlist dialog box open while you work in the application itself.

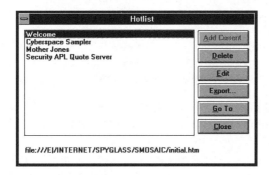

Fig. 10.14
The Hotlist dialog box is used to find your way back to your favorite FTP sites.

While you are traveling around on the Web, you can quickly add a document to your hotlist. Open the **N**avigate menu and choose **A**dd Current to Hotlist. You also can open the Hotlist dialog box and choose the **A**dd Current button. It is also that easy to delete a document from your hotlist: select the document and choose **D**elete. The document is removed from your list.

When you want to return to a document you have in your hotlist, you have to open the Hotlist dialog box and double-click the document, or select the document and choose **G**o To.

The Hotlist dialog box also lets you edit entries. Select the entry you want and choose **E**dit. A dialog box with the hotlist-entry title and its URL appears. You can modify the title in your hotlist, or copy the URL from the text box (to paste into a word processing or e-mail document, for example).

To create an HTML file from your hotlist, choose the E**x**port button. You see the Export Hotlist dialog box—a typical File Save dialog box. Give the document a name, select the directory to place it in, and then click OK. Enhanced

NCSA Mosaic not only creates the file, but also displays the file in the window. You immediately see what it looks like—each entry in the hotlist appears as a line in the document. Click the line to go to the referenced document.

Now you can use this document in the future. To load it to the window, open **F**ile and choose **O**pen Local. Now you can send the file to someone else—so they can use it in their WWW browser—or quickly reach the documents in your hotlist.

Using the History List

The History list shows all of the documents you viewed in a session. In Enhanced NCSA Mosaic, the History list works in much the same way as the hotlist. It uses the same dialog box, except that one button—Add Current—is disabled in the History list (refer to fig. 10.14).

To view the History list, open the **N**avigate menu and choose Hi**s**tory. After it is open, you can use it in the same way as the Hotlist. Double-click an entry to go to that document, or select the entry and choose the **G**o To button.

The **E**dit button lets you change the entry. You can use Edit to copy the URL for a particular document you view. The E**x**port button is also handy: you can create an HTML file showing your current session—a sort of interactive record of what you do. The next time you want to repeat a particular "journey" over the web, you open the HTML file (open the **F**ile menu and choose **O**pen URL), or you can send the session to someone else so they can follow your route.

Enhanced NCSA Mosaic Options

NCSA Mosaic has a menu full of options. Enhanced NCSA Mosaic, in the interest of simplicity, reduced the number of options available. Open the **E**dit menu and choose **P**references to see the Preferences dialog box, as shown in figure 10.15.

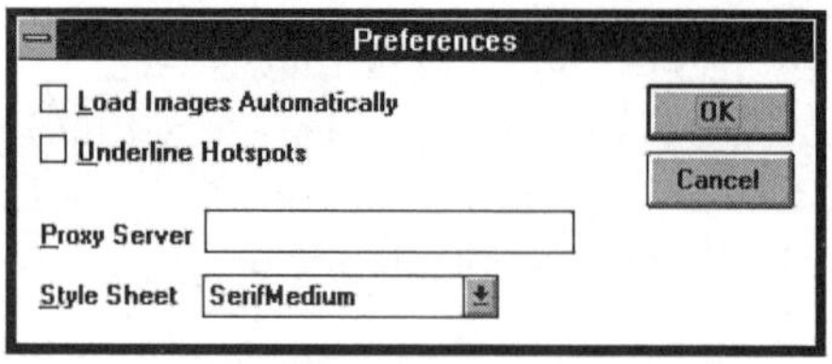

Fig. 10.15
The Preferences dialog box replaces Mosaic's Options menu.

The **L**oad Images Automatically check box turns inline images on and off. Turn them off to increase speed. (Inline images in HTML files on your hard disk are still displayed, but images in documents that have to be transferred across the WWW are not.)

The **U**nderline Hotspots check box turns on link underlining. You can see the links even if you leave this turned off, because they are a different color (you can't change the color of the links).

The **P**roxy Server list box lets you set up ways for secure systems to provide access to the outside world. If the program is being used on a secure World Wide Web server—one without any links to the outside world—you can enter the address of another server to access other WWW sites. You have to get the address of the server from your system administrator, because the administrator has to set up the connection.

Finally, the **S**tyle Sheet is Enhanced NCSA Mosaic's version of NCSA Mosaic's Fonts cascading menu (on the Options menu). Enhanced NCSA Mosaic lets you select a style sheet instead of setting up each font separately. Each style sheet is preconfigured with all the different fonts—headers, body text, and so on—set up correctly. So you don't create your own style sheet, you use one of Spyglass's preconfigured setups.

You may not like not having the flexibility to do exactly what you want; however, there are some advantages. A style sheet that suits you can save you the trouble of experimenting. If more than one person uses the program, it makes it easy to swap between different setups.

Where's the Home Page?

When Spyglass first started working on Enhanced NCSA Mosaic they decided to remove the Home Page feature. They thought many companies would want to control the home page and not allow their users to change it. On the contrary, Spyglass got so many requests for home page features, they had to put it back.

Some versions of Enhanced NCSA Mosaic have no way to change the home page, or a Home Page command that takes you back to the home page. Enhanced NCSA Mosaic's home page is designed as a local HTML file. The only way to go directly back to it is to open **F**ile and choose **N**ew Window (or press Ctrl+N).

Later versions of the program do let you change the home page: there is a text box in the Preferences dialog box, and a Go Home Page menu option.

Tip

If you turn off Load Images Automatically, you can open the **N**avigate menu and choose **L**oad Missing Images at any time to view the inline images in the current document.

Tip

The style sheets are kept in a file called SMOSAIC.INI. You can go into this file and modify the style sheets, save the file, and re-open Enhanced NCSA Mosaic.

IV

Other WWW Clients

Printing Documents

Enhanced NCSA Mosaic lets you print the current document, and you can add headers and footers to it. Open the **F**ile menu and choose Pa**g**e Setup to see the Page Setup dialog box (fig. 10.16).

Fig. 10.16

Add headers and footers to your printouts using the Page Setup dialog box.

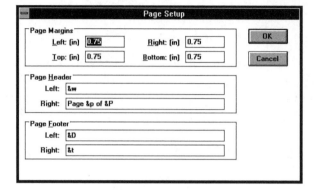

At the top of the dialog box, you enter the page margins. When you change the margins you change the word wrap (if you have very large margins, for instance, the program wraps the text to fit within those margins). In-line graphics cannot be wrapped, though, so if the margins are too small, some graphics don't print completely.

Below the margins, you enter the header and footer. In each case, you create text that is placed on the left and the right side of the page. The following are the codes used by the program to enter header and footer information:

Code	Entry
&d	Date MMM DD YYYY
&D	Date DD MMM YYYY
&t	Time, in 12-hour format
&T	Time, in 24-hour format
&p	Page number
&P	Total number of pages
&w or &W	Document title

You can combine these codes with any text you want, such as the following:

```
Fred's WWW Trip, &D, &t
```

Bits and Pieces

There are a few other changes—not necessarily significant but worth knowing nonetheless.

- The Find Again feature (**E**dit, Find Again) repeats the last search you carried out in the current document.

- To close the window you are working in, open the **F**ile menu and choose **C**lose, or open the **F**ile menu and choose Close All to close all of them.

- Help information is in HTML files on your hard disk, rather than on the net. Open the **H**elp menu and choose Mosaic **H**elp Page.

- Before calling Technical Support, open **H**elp and choose **A**bout Mosaic. Choose the **S**upport button to see information about your setup, including Mosaic version number and network information (such as the WINSOCK.DLL version). Choose the **S**ave button to save the information as a text file.

> **Note**
>
> Keep in mind, you cannot call Spyglass for technical support. You call technical support at the company who sublicensed your particular version of Spyglass Mosaic.

- Spyglass has created support for GIF, JPEG, and other media viewers built into Mosaic. Look for built-in viewers in some versions of sublicensed Spyglass Mosaic. (This eliminates the need to add external viewers, such as LView.)

Missing Features

So what can Mosaic do that Enhanced NCSA Mosaic does *not* do? There are a few things missing from Enhanced Mosaic:

- There isn't a Print Preview option.

- There isn't a Save Preferences option.

- No toolbar—toolbars are useful.

- There isn't a reliable way to stop a transfer. You can't click the globe icon to do so, as you can in freeware Mosaic. In some cases, pressing Escape locks the program.

- No way to add a menu of hotlist items—but that's because Spyglass wants the product to be simple to use. You still have the Hotlist dialog box.

- No list of useful sites on the Internet built into the menu—the home page does come with a "Cyberspace Sampler," though it's limited.

Enhanced NCSA Mosaic is a nice program, with some real advantages over freeware Mosaic—in particular, the ability to save the current document. Some of the omissions can be irritating. There should be a way to stop a transfer, for instance, and a way to change home pages.

NCSA Mosaic 16-bit Versions

You're probably wondering why a section on an older version of NCSA's Mosaic is included. After all, the newer version offers faster performance, more features, and fewer bugs. The reason is that the developers made one significant change in version 2 that may cause some to stay with version 1.

To speed up Mosaic, the developers made version 2 a 32-bit application. This means that you need a 32-bit version of Windows to run it. Currently, Windows 3.1, 3.11, and Windows for WorkGroups 3.11 are the most common versions of Windows—they are not 32-bit versions. They're 16-bit. Windows NT is a 32-bit system—if you have NT, there is no reason to use the old version of Mosaic.

> **Note**
>
> The first two test versions of Mosaic version 2, 2.0.1a and 2.0.2a, were 16-bit. If you are looking for new features and fixed bugs, but don't want to go to 32-bit, version 2.0.2a is the best option.

As you saw in chapter 3, "Getting Mosaic for Windows Running," Windows can upgrade to a 32-bit version by installing the free Win32s software. The downside is that Win32s is not 100% stable. There are complaints that it's buggy and doesn't work reliably with many existing applications. Because of this, many Windows users are reluctant to upgrade to Win32s. Most software vendors, whose programs have trouble under Win32, released updates and fixes so that their programs work in Win32. Microsoft released several updated versions of Win32s, which dramatically reduced the problems with Win32 incompatibilities.

> **Note**
>
> The authors and development staff on this book used the latest version of Mosaic, which is a 32-bit version. With only one exception, no problems with Win32s were experienced. The one exception is noted in chapter 3, "Getting Mosaic for Windows Running." The best advice is to back up your Windows directory and subdirectory before installing Win32s. If you do have problems, you can restore from your backup.

If you decide you are not ready to use the new version of Mosaic, the following few sections point out differences, mostly missing features, in 16-bit versions of NCSA Mosaic.

The Mosaic Screen

The Mosaic screen changed very little over the course of development. The screen in the 16-bit version is slightly different from the screen for version 2.0.6a, which is shown throughout the rest of the book (see fig. 10.17). Older versions have the document title with the URL below the toolbar instead of in the title bar. The other difference is that the Mosaic spinning globe icon is larger in the older version, because there is more room for the icon. These two changes make the document area of the screen smaller in older versions.

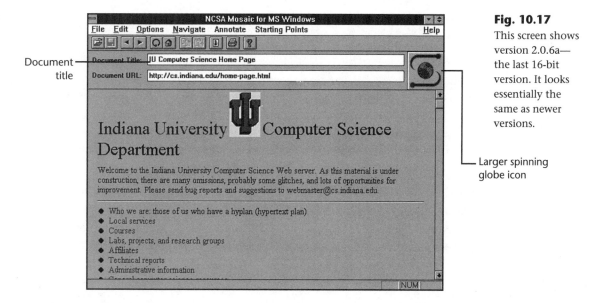

Fig. 10.17
This screen shows version 2.0.6a—the last 16-bit version. It looks essentially the same as newer versions.

Document title

Larger spinning globe icon

Missing Features in Older Versions

The following list details the major missing features and major bugs you may need to deal with when using the 16-bit versions. There are other minor bugs and esoteric changes not listed here.

- The print and print preview features do not work.

- Viewing or saving the document source does not work.

- Loading of local images and sound files deletes the file.

- Loading of local URLs produces errors and the file is not opened.

- Navigate back does not take you to the last document used in all cases.

- XBM images may load very slowly or result in an ERROR graphic.

- You cannot navigate by editing the Document URL line directly.

- Forms support is very buggy.

- UNIX file names may not be properly changed to legal DOS file names.

- The QUICKLIST hotlist size is limited.

- URL's without titles cannot be added to hotlists.

You may not want to mess with installing Win32s on your Windows system, in which case 16-bit Mosaic may be your only option—if you can put up with all the missing features.

Quadralay's GWHIS Viewer

GWHIS stands for *Global-Wide Help and Information Systems*, (and GWHIS is pronounced "gee-whiz," of course.) It's a system sold by Quadralay Corporation. GWHIS Viewer is the cornerstone of this system. GWHIS provides global on-line help. A corporation can link its applications to an on-line, networked help system that can be officewide, companywide, or even worldwide. GWHIS is ideal for providing access to ever-changing, up-to-date information. There are versions available for UNIX, PCs, and the Macintosh.

GWHIS is basically an extension of the World Wide Web, using GWHIS Viewer to read the on-line help and information documents created by the company. When a company employee or client uses GWHIS to refer to on-line documentation, he may be viewing documents somewhere else in the same building, in one of the company's buildings elsewhere in the world, or even at a World Wide Web site owned by another company or person.

GWHIS is the viewer that Quadralay provides to go with this system. They also provide a suite of related tools:

- **Search Engine.** A tool that lets you index and search large amounts of documentation.

- **API.** The GWHIS Application Programming Interface lets a company link its programs to GWHIS Viewer and Search Engine, so the program's users can access context-sensitive help. (If you want the jargon, the API "Internet enables" applications.)

- **HyperLink Editor/Librarian and Utilities.** These are tools for creating the HTML documents that are used for the World Wide Web.

While Quadralay sells the GWHIS Viewer as part of a larger "information system," it is of course a World Wide Web viewer, and can be used as a viewer in the same way you use Mosaic, Cello, or any other WWW viewer. In fact, GWHIS Viewer is licensed from the NCSA; it's a modified version of Mosaic.

You aren't likely to find GWHIS Viewer on a shelf in a retail computer store. Although Quadralay does plan to market this as a retail product, it appears that their primary customers are corporations that plan to make use of the entire Quadralay package as a corporate solution for all of the WWW needs. If this is the version of Mosaic your company is using, you'll find it similar to the other versions.

Installing GWHIS Viewer

GWHIS Viewer has a setup program that makes installing it quite straight-forward. The only catch is that the program is a 32-bit program. That means you must run it in Windows NT, or, if you are working with Windows 3.1 or Windows for Workgroups you must install the Win32s software. Quadralay distributes the Win32s software. You run the Win32s setup program and then install GWHIS. (If you have a LaserMaster printer, see chapter 3, "Getting Mosaic for Windows Running," for more information about installing the Win32s software.)

Installing GWHIS itself is very easy. It comes with a typical Windows setup program. Just run the setup program and follow the instructions to load GWHIS.

The version I used simply installed the program. Quadralay plans to improve the installation program soon, so it prompts you for information, such as which home page you want to use and which World Wide Web server.

What's New or Old?

Because GWHIS is a version of Mosaic, they look very similar (see fig. 10.18). The most significant change is that Quadralay uses an *earlier* version of Mosaic. Quadralay wants the program to match their UNIX version, so they aren't jumping forward with every change that appears in freeware Mosaic.

Fig. 10.18
GWHIS evolved from Mosaic and looks almost the same.

What does this mean to you? It means that some of the nice new features available with the very latest freeware Mosaic are not included in GWHIS Viewer. For instance, you can't type or copy a URL into the Document URL line near the top of the window—in the latest Mosaic, typing a URL and pressing Enter takes you to that document.

In addition, you can't add menus and menu items using a menu editor. GWHIS uses the old Mosaic method for creating menu items—you have to type them in the GWHIS.INI file. Make sure you get the right syntax, though. It's really not very hard, even though the GWHIS documentation doesn't give a lot of information about syntax. You can figure it out by looking at what's already in the GWHIS.INI file.

Also, the NCSA modified the recent version of Mosaic to make more room for the document—they moved the Document Title up to the title bar. This allowed them to reduce the size of the globe icon. GWHIS uses the old, two-line bar below the menu bar, along with the large globe icon.

Here are a few of the obvious changes you notice when you first open GWHIS Viewer:

- The toolbar is gone.

- A button bar is under the status bar.

- There isn't a Starting Points menu, but there are two new menus to take its place: Internet and HotList.

- There are lots of menu changes with menu options shuffled around. The Edit menu is gone, for instance, so the Find command is now on the File menu.

- For some reason, there's a File, Close Window command *and* a File, Exit Program command, both of which do the same thing.

The buttons at the bottom of the screen are the same—there's Back, Forward, Home, Reload, Open, and Close Window. It's a shame that they removed the toolbar, which had other useful commands, such as Load to Disk, Find, and Print. Quadralay could omit the Close Window button and put in a couple of other, more useful, items.

Hotlists and Menus

Quadralay has their own menus of neat places to go. GWHIS has two such menus: the Internet menu and the HotList menu. You can't change the Internet menu, at least not without messing around in the GWHIS.INI file. You can change the HotList menu, though. Find a document you want to add to the HotList menu and then open Navigate and choose Add Current to Hotlist. Changing the HotList menu, however, is not a great idea. First, if you want to remove an item from the HotList menu, you have to go to the GWHIS.INI file. Also, if you happen to select the Add Current to Hotlist command twice for the same document, it appears on the menu twice.

Perhaps a larger problem, though, is the size of the menu. You easily can add more hotlist items than the menu can display, especially if you're using a low-resolution video mode. When there are too many items on the hotlist, the whole menu shifts to one side—so you can't read *any* entry completely! So it's off to the GWHIS.INI file you go, to remove a few.

GWHIS Viewer Options

GWHIS Viewer also limits your ability to customize the program. You can't remove the button bar or status bar, though you can remove the Document Title and URL lines. You also can't modify the way the anchors (links) appear—at least not from within the application itself. You have to go to the GWHIS.INI file—again, this is how the older versions of freeware Mosaic used to handle it. There isn't a Change Cursor Over Anchors or Show Anchor URLs in the Options menu, nor is there an Extended FTP Directory Parsing option, or Show Group Annotations, or Use 8-bit sound. You can choose your fonts, and you can select Display Inline Images, of course, but that's about it.

From Here...

■ Chapter 3, "Getting Mosaic for Windows Running," is a good chapter to look at if you are interested in comparing the commercial versions in this chapter to NCSA's Mosaic.

■ Chapter 12, "Other Ways to Access the World Wide Web," describes alternative software packages for Web browsing that are not based on Mosaic.

Chapter 11

Other Versions of Mosaic for Macintosh

While the last chapter looked at the commercial versions of Mosaic that are available for Windows, this chapter looks at what versions are available for Macintosh.

So why would anyone be interested in purchasing a commercial version when the NCSA version is readily available for free use? As discussed in earlier chapters, many features that you might expect to finding working aren't. The commercial software companies are polishing many of the rough edges and adding some features that weren't finished in the NCSA version.

If you buy a commercial version of Mosaic, you may notice that files load faster (although the main speed limitation is still from the speed of the pipeline you have to the Internet itself; faster lines result in faster interaction), inline images display faster, and in general, all aspects of the program involve less waiting time. You also may find that a commercial version takes less memory and disk space than NCSA's version.

The first wave of commercial versions of Mosaic is very similar to the NCSA versions in the way that you use them. The essential Mosaic and World Wide Web features and concepts that are covered elsewhere in this book work in essentially the same way. This chapter points out the differences so that no matter what version of Mosaic you use, you will be able to make full use of this book.

The bad news for Macintosh users is that at this time, only one company, Spyglass, has developed a commercial version of Mosaic. To make matters worse, you can't even buy this version from them. However, other companies are developing Macintosh versions, that weren't available at the time of this writing.

> **Note**
>
> One Mac program for the World Wide Web that is available now is a shareware product called MacWeb. This is discussed in chapter 12, "Other Ways to Access the Web."

This chapter discusses the following:

- Where to get Enhanced NCSA Mosaic for Macintosh from Spyglass

- How to install Enhanced NCSA Mosaic for Macintosh from Spyglass

- The differences between the Spyglass program and the freeware NCSA version of Mosaic

Enhanced NCSA Mosaic for Macintosh from Spyglass

You can't buy Enhanced Mosaic in a retail software store. Spyglass is only interested in licenses with at least 10,000 users; you'll probably encounter S-Mosaic if you work for a large business or attend a large university.

> **Note**
>
> Spyglass has not been consistent with the name of this product. In some places it was called Enhanced NCSA Mosaic for Macintosh from Spyglass, Spyglass Mosaic for the Mac, S-Mosaic, and in others just Spyglass Mosaic. These names are used interchangeably in this chapter. In any event, you will probably see it with another name as companies that sublicense it are likely to put their own name on it.

Another possibility of getting a Spyglass version of Mosaic is by purchasing a sublicensed one. Spyglass plans to sell (or sublicense) the product to OEMs (Original Equipment Manufacturers). If you purchase computer hardware from one of these manufacturers and it includes Mosaic, it will usually be labeled with the hardware manufacturer's name, not Spyglass.

Spyglass is also sublicensing Mosaic to other software companies. These companies refine the product and resell it. Again, you don't see the Spyglass name on these versions, as they usually bear the name of the software company licensing it.

So while you may not see Enhanced NCSA Mosaic for sale at your local computer store, you may run across it under another name bundled with some other product you bought.

Performance Enhancements

S-Mosaic has a number of advantages over the original NCSA version. For starters, the standard 68K Mac version takes a mere 304K, compared to the lumbering 1.3M bulk of NCSA Mosaic version 2.00. Beyond that, it's fast and has plenty of new features. The key elements in Spyglass's plan, that have not been implemented yet, are a provision for credit-card based transactions and platform-independent document exchange.

Installing Enhanced NCSA Mosaic

Spyglass has three versions of Mosaic for the Mac: a 68K version, a PowerMac version, and a FAT version. Functionally, these are the same; each version is optimized to run on different Mac processors.

> **Note**
>
> In case you aren't up on the technical lingo, a "FAT" version of an application is one that has both 68K and PowerMac executables tucked inside itself: it's really big. When you install this application, the installer program figures out what kind of Mac you have and automatically gives you the right kind of executable without you having to worry about it.

Installation is simple. Just drag the icon for the version you want to use into a folder on your hard drive. There is also a MosaicMacHelp folder you should drag onto your hard drive (see fig. 11.1).

> **Note**
>
> The version of Mosaic from Spyglass discussed here is the version licensed to other companies to resell. The resellers may make changes in their retail versions, such as adding an installer or selling the three versions (68K, PowerMac, and FAT) separately, so don't be surprised if there are slight differences.

Fig. 11.1
The Spyglass Mosaic for the Mac folder contains three versions of the software (for different processors) and a help folder.

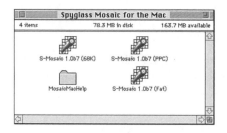

After you have Mosaic copied to your hard drive and if you have a SLIP or network TCP/IP connection, all you have to do is launch your Internet connection and double-click the S-Mosaic icon. After you start Spyglass, you can connect to any Web site with the same method used in the NCSA version.

What's New in Enhanced Mosaic?

When you start Enhanced NCSA Mosaic, the first thing you'll notice is that it looks pretty much like Mosaic itself (see fig. 11.2). There are, however, some important changes; some you may like, some you may not.

Fig. 11.2
At first glance Enhanced NCSA Mosaic looks much like NCSA Mosaic.

Back ─┐ ┌─ Forward

Progress indicator

Mosaic icon

URL: file:///Macintosh HD/Communications/Spyglass Mosaic for the Mac/MosaicMacHelp/initial.html

Welcome to Enhanced NCSA Mosaic from Spyglass

Mosaic is an Internet information browser and World Wide Web client, originally developed at the National Center for Supercomputing Applications at the University of Illinois, Urbana Champaign. Under license from NCSA, Spyglass has enhanced Mosaic for commercial use. Enhanced NCSA Mosaic is available from Spyglass on an OEM basis only.

All You Need to Know

Highlighted text (colored or underlined) and graphics (colored borders) are hyperlinks to other information elsewhere in the current document or in another document on the Internet. Click once on any link to jump to related information. To return after visiting a link, click on the back arrow at the top of the Mosaic window.

The easiest way to understand hyperlinks is to try one. To do so, click on this hyperlink. Note that the hyperlink changes color to indicate that it has already been visited. That's all you need to know to start exploring. For a listing of places to start exploring, click on the "Cyberspace Sampler" hyperlink below.

Cyberspace Sampler

Start by taking a look at the obvious changes:

■ There's no true toolbar, although back and forward buttons are below the title bar.

- The Mosaic icon is not a button—you can't click the icon to stop a transfer.

- There's no Options menu. There are fewer options, and they are reached through the Edit menu.

- As the pointer goes over a link the status bar displays the URL.

- A small progress indicator has been added to the left end of the status bar. This shows how much of a document or file has been transferred.

- The drop-down history list has been removed from the status bar.

- There are lots of menu-option changes.

Enhanced NCSA Mosaic may look the same, but there are some important changes from the freeware version. Let's look at the other important changes between these two versions of Mosaic.

Copy and Save

The current version of basic Mosaic makes it difficult to save information from the current document. This will change, but Enhanced NCSA Mosaic already has the problem fixed.

In Enhanced Mosaic from Spyglass, you can copy all the text from the displayed document to the Clipboard. You then can paste it into any Mac application (a word processor, for example). The copy and paste feature is implemented through the usual Mac method of opening the Edit menu and choosing Copy.

> **Note**
>
> NCSA Mosaic has the copy option on the Edit menu but the feature does not work.

There's still no way to select and copy just part of a document. It's all or nothing. There is also still no way to paste anything into Mosaic.

You also can save the document as a file. Open the File menu and choose Save As to see the Mac Save As dialog box (see fig. 11.3). Enter a file name, then select the radio button for the file type to save it as. You can save the file as Plain Text; which means all you get is ASCII text, which is what you see in the document on-screen. Or you can save the file as HTML; in which case you get the text *and* the HTML codes, so you can use the page at a later date (by opening the File menu and choosing Open Local).

Tip
Be sure to save the file with HTML at the end of the name. Spyglass Mosaic doesn't seem to know what to do with the file when you open it without this.

> **Caution**
>
> Although the Save As feature may appear to work in the NCSA's 2.0a6 version of Mosaic, it will crash your computer and the saved files will be unusable. This bug may be fixed in 2.0a8, however, we haven't had this version long enough to be certain.

Fig. 11.3

Saving a document in Spyglass Mosaic is a familiar process using the Mac Save dialog box.

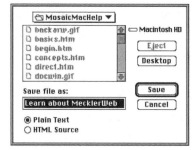

> **Note**
>
> When saving documents to a file using either the method described in this section or the method described in the next section, the saved file will not include the inline graphics in the document. Hyperlinks that use relative addresses won't work when you save the file locally. See chapter 5 for a discussion of relative and absolute links.

Transferring Files

While Spyglass has tried to make Mosaic easier to use, in one way they have made it harder—they've hidden the command used to download files. In freeware Mosaic you open the Options menu and choose Load to Disk, then click a link; there is no such option in Enhanced NCSA Mosaic. Instead, you must press Option and then click on the link. A Download To dialog box appears (the normal Save As dialog box) in which you can enter a file name and choose a folder. The dialog box also shows you the size of the file (see fig. 11.4).

The benefit of this method is that you can't forget that Load to Disk is selected and accidentally load to disk when you wanted to load the file on-screen. You have to press Option and click for each link to load to disk.

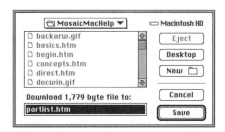

Fig. 11.4
Downloading a file is as simple as saving a file. Just use the Mac Save dialog box to choose a destination and name for the file.

Multiple Windows

To open another window, open the File menu and choose New Window. Then work in the new window the normal way, clicking links and so on. The other window remains open. In fact, you can open multiple windows and have several sessions working at once (see fig. 11.5.). This works in essentially the same way the NCSA Mosaic does.

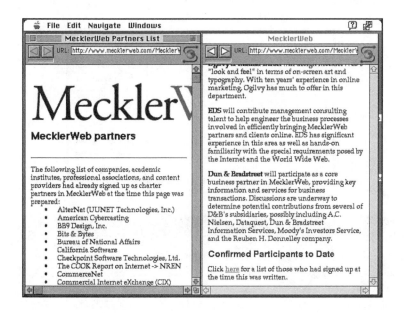

Fig. 11.5
Enhanced NCSA Mosaic lets you have multiple sessions working at once. This is a great feature for serious Web cruising.

Tip
You also can open a new window by pressing Control and clicking a hyperlink. The document for the link opens in the new window.

Spyglass has added a few features to help you work with these multiple windows. To arrange your open windows on-screen, open the Windows menu and choose Arrange Windows. To make any open window active, open the Windows menu and choose the name of the window (see fig. 11.6).

Fig. 11.6
All of the open
Mosaic windows
are listed in this
menu.

You can control the size of any window using the same methods used with any other Mac window.

Each session can be in a different location on the Web. When you click a link in one of the document windows, it has no effect on the sessions in the other document windows.

Working With the Hotlist

Enhanced NCSA Mosaic does not let you add hotlist items to menus. Instead, it provides a Hotlist dialog box (see fig. 11.7). To use this feature, open the Navigate menu and choose Hotlist.

Fig. 11.7
The Hotlist dialog
box is used to find
your way back to
your favorite FTP
sites. This default
Hotlist is empty.

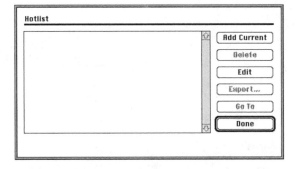

> **Note**
>
> While the default Hotlist in this version is empty, you can expect the licensees of Spyglass Mosaic to add some value for end-users by predefining some hotlist items for useful and interesting Web sites.

While you are traveling around on the Web, you can quickly add a document to your hotlist by opening the Navigate menu and choosing Add Current to Hotlist. Or you can open the dialog box and click the Add Current button.

When you want to return to a document that you have in your hotlist, open the dialog box and double-click the document. Or you can select the document and click the Go To button.

The Hotlist dialog box also lets you edit entries. Select the entry you want to edit and choose the Edit button. You'll see a dialog box with the hotlist-entry title and its URL. For example, you can modify the title that appears in your hotlist, or copy the URL from the text box to paste into a word processing or e-mail document.

There's also a Delete button for removing entries from your list, and a method for creating an HTML file from your hotlist. Choose the Export button and you'll see the Export Hotlist dialog box, a typical File Save dialog box. Give the document a name, and select the directory in which you want to place it, then choose the OK button. Enhanced NCSA Mosaic not only creates the file, but also displays the file in the window, so you can immediately see what it looks like—each entry in the hotlist appears as a line in the document. Clicking the line takes you to the referenced document.

You can use this document in the future, by loading it into the window, opening the File menu, and choosing Open Local. Or you can send the file to someone else, so they can use it in their WWW browser—it doesn't have to be Enhanced NCSA Mosaic, of course—to quickly reach the documents in your hotlist.

Tip
URLs for documents can change if a document gets moved to a different server or a different location on the server. If this happens to a document on your hotlist, use the Edit feature to update the URL.

Using the History List

The History list is a listing of all the documents you've viewed in the current session. In Enhanced NCSA Mosaic, the History list works in much the same way as the Hotlist. In fact, it uses the same dialog box, except that the Add Current button is disabled in the History list (see fig. 11.8).

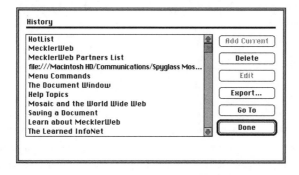

Fig. 11.8
The History dialog box shows all of the documents you have opened in this session.

To view the History list, open the Navigate menu and choose History. After the list is open, you can use it in the same way as the Hotlist. Double-click an entry to go to that document, or select the entry and choose the Go To button.

The Edit button lets you change the entry, though you probably won't want to. However, you may want to use it to copy the URL for a particular document you've just viewed. The Export button also is handy. You can create an HTML file showing your current session. This HTML is sort of an interactive record of what you've done. The next time you want to repeat a particular "journey" over the web, you can open the HTML file (by opening the File menu and choosing Open URL), or you can send the session to someone else so they can follow your route.

Enhanced Mosaic Options

NCSA Mosaic has a menu full of options. Enhanced NCSA Mosaic, in the interest of simplicity, has reduced the number of options available. Open the Edit menu and choose Preferences to see the Preferences dialog box shown in figure 11.9. This box is the replacement for Mosaic's Options menu.

Fig. 11.9
The Preferences dialog box replaces Mosaic's Options menu.

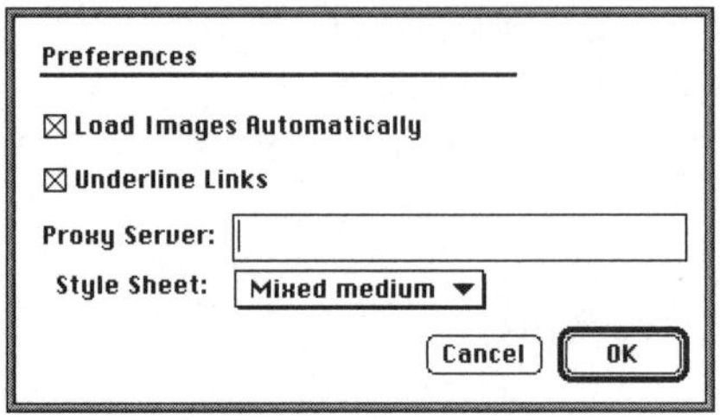

Tip
If you turned off Load Images Automatically, you can open the Navigate menu and choose Load Missing Images at any time to view the inline images in the current document.

The Load Images Automatically check box turns inline images on and off. Turn them off to increase speed. (Inline images in HTML files on your hard disk are still displayed, but images in documents that have to be transferred across the WWW aren't.)

The Underline Links check box turns on link underlining. If you leave this turned off, you are still able to see the links, because they are a different color (but you can't change that color).

Finally, the Style Sheet is Enhanced NCSA Mosaic's version of Mosaic's Styles dialog (from the Options menu). Each style sheet is preconfigured with all the different fonts—headers, body text, and so on—set up correctly. Instead of creating your own style sheet, by configuring each font individually, you use one of Spyglass's preconfigured setups (see fig. 11.10).

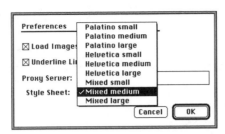

Fig. 11.10
This is the list
of style sheets
that come
preconfigured
with Enhanced
Mosaic.

You might not like using the style sheets—after all, you don't have as much flexibility—but there are some advantages. You will probably find a style sheet that suits you, saving you the trouble of experimenting. And if more than one person uses the program it makes it easy to swap between different setups.

Where's the Home Page?

When the people at Spyglass first started working on Enhanced NCSA Mosaic they decided to remove the Home Page feature. They thought many companies would want to control the home page, and not allow their users to change it. But Spyglass got so many requests for home-page features that they put it back in. However, the version I saw did not have this capability.

The current version of Spyglass Enhanced NCSA Mosaic has no way to change the home page, nor does it have a Home Page command that takes you back to the home page. Rather, the home page is set up as a local HTML file, and the only way to go directly back to the home page is to open the File menu and choose New Window, which opens a new window with the initial.html file as home.

Later versions of the program will let you change the home page. There will be a text box in the Preferences dialog box, and a Go Home Page menu option.

Bits and Pieces

The following are a few other changes Spyglass made to the NCSA version in their version, not necessarily significant, but worth noting:

■ To see the HTML source for the document you are viewing, open the Edit menu and choose View Source (see fig. 11.11). You can select a part of the document and press Command-C to copy it. You then must click OK to close the window before pasting this selection into another application.

■ To close all open windows, open the File menu and choose Close All.

Fig. 11.11
The Source
Window shows
the raw HTML
codes and text for
the document you
have open.

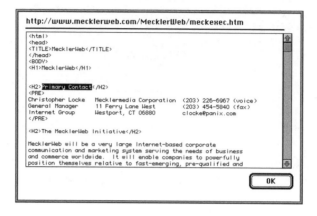

Missing Features

So what can Mosaic do that Enhanced NCSA Mosaic does *not* do? There are a few things missing from the Spyglass version:

■ There is no toolbar. Toolbars are useful, so it's a shame this is missing.

■ There's no reliable way to stop a transfer. You can't click the globe icon to do this, as you can in freeware Mosaic.

■ There's no way to add a menu of hotlist items—but that's because Spyglass wants the product to be simple to use. You still have the Hotlist dialog box, though.

■ None of the annotation features are included (although these features weren't working in the NCSA version until 2.0a8 either!).

■ Spyglass Mosaic has less control of the specifics of styles.

Enhanced NCSA Mosaic is a solid program, with some real advantages over freeware Mosaic—in particular, speed, size, and the ability to reliably save the current document. But some of the omissions are a little irritating. There should be a way to stop a transfer, for example, and to change home pages. However, for some, the smaller program size and faster operation may make up for these omissions.

Chapter 12

Other Ways to Access the World Wide Web

When it comes to Web cruising, Mosaic is probably the most recognized software for the job. But that doesn't mean it's the only option you have. Shareware programs are available for cruising the Web that are not based on Mosaic.

Another category of software takes the all-in-one approach a step further. In addition to giving you software that performs every task you need on the Internet, this type of software gives you a common interface to access all parts of the Internet. In most cases, this software comes from a service provider that has built a special interface to make using its service even easier. If you are looking for a no-hassle way to use the Web and don't mind sacrificing a few features for ease of use, this software may be for you.

You may be wondering why we have included this chapter in a book titled *Using Mosaic*. In a nutshell, most of these programs are so similar that the basic procedures you have seen throughout the rest of the book apply to these other products as well. The menu commands may be slightly different, (this chapter shows you the differences), but the procedures still operate the same way. So, if you are looking for an alternative product to use, or already have one, you can still use this book with whatever Web browser you choose.

In this chapter, you learn to use the following:

- Cello, a shareware program for Windows from the Legal Institute

- InterAp WebBrowser, a commercial Web browser based on Cello from California Software

- EINet's WinWeb and MacWeb shareware browsers for Windows and Mac

- NetCruiser, an all-in-one special Internet interface from NETCOM

- The Pipeline, an all-in-one system licensed to service providers all over the country

Cello

Cello is a Microsoft Windows-based multipurpose World Wide Web (WWW) browser that permits you to access information from many sources in many formats. You can use Cello to do anything that you would do in NCSA Mosaic.

Installation and Setup

Cello is freely available via FTP from **fatty.law.cornell.edu** in the directory /pub/LII/Cello. Download the cello.zip file. If you are already working with a WWW viewer, you can get Cello across the Web from **http:// ftp.law.cornell.edu/pub/LII/Cello.** (In this document you'll find a link currently called cello.zip. Set up your viewer to download, because clicking on the link causes the EINet site to send the WINWEB.ZIP file to your system.)

After you have retrieved the file, you should create a directory for Cello and unzip the program. (See chapter 3, "Getting Mosaic for Windows Running," for an example of how to use the PKUNZIP program.) You will also want to create an icon for Cello. See chapter 3 for an example of how to do this.

To use Cello, you need to either be on a network with a direct connection, or have a dial-in direct connection (SLIP, CSLIP, or PPP).

Using Cello

When you first start Cello, you see a large window with a standard Windows menu bar. A message box from the developers appears. Click on that box to remove it and you'll see the Cello home page (see fig. 12.1).

By default, Cello opens the local file shown in the document window in the figure. From here, you can click a hyperlink, enter a URL, or use a bookmark to move around the Web.

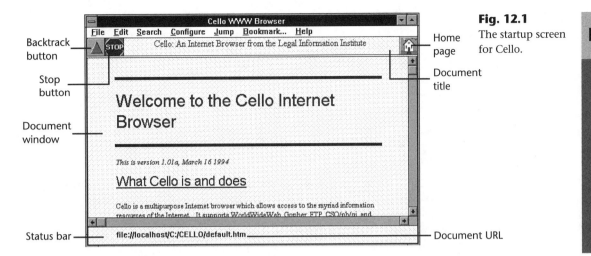

Backtrack button

Stop button

Document window

Status bar

Home page

Document title

Document URL

Fig. 12.1
The startup screen for Cello.

Hyperlinks in Cello

Hyperlinks in Cello are indicated by dashed boxes around the link as opposed to blue underlined text used in Mosaic. The cursor is in the shape of a crosshair. It changes to an arrow over a hyperlink.

Click the right mouse button on an item and Cello tells you what the URL for the link is (see fig. 12.2). You can then choose the Co**p**y button to copy the URL to the Clipboard if you want.

Fig. 12.2
The Current Anchor Informa-tion dialog box.

Using History

Cello keeps a list of the last 20 links in your session. It's too much of a hassle to go back with the backtrack key. To select a link you encountered earlier in a session, open the Main menu, choose Jump, and then select History. A dialog box appears (see fig. 12.3). Note how even failed connections are listed in the History box so that you can retry them.

Fig. 12.3

The History dialog box.

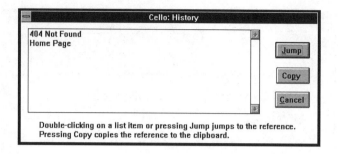

In this dialog box, you see a list of the last 20 links in your session with the latest session as the first element in the list. To jump to a link in this list:

■ Double-click the list item.

or

■ Single-click the list item and click the **J**ump button.

If you want to copy the link into the Clipboard for future use (in a home page, for example), you can use the **C**opy button. You can then paste from the Clipboard to your text editor.

Bookmarks

Mosaic's Hotlist feature is replaced by the Bookmarks feature in Cello. The major difference is that in Cello you have only one set of bookmarks, displayed in a dialog box. The bookmark list is limited to 50 items. In Mosaic you can have multiple hotlists, and place them into menus.

To add the current document to the bookmarks list:

1. Choose **B**ookmark from the menu bar. You see the dialog box shown in figure 12.4.

2. Choose **M**ark Current Document. The Name Your Bookmark dialog opens (see fig. 12.5).

3. Click OK to accept it or Cancel to abort naming this dialog box. If desired, you can change the name here. This won't affect anything except the name you see in the Bookmarks dialog.

4. Click Quit to dismiss the Bookmarks dialog box.

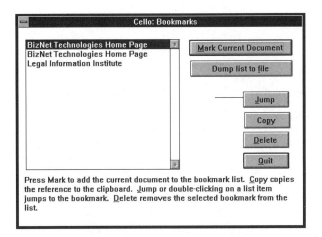

Fig. 12.4
The Bookmarks
dialog box.

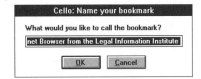

Fig. 12.5
The Name Your
Bookmark dialog
box.

Using Your Bookmarks

To use a bookmark, simply choose the **B**ookmark menu, then, when the
Bookmark dialog appears, click on the document you want to view and
choose **J**ump.

Saving Bookmarks in an HTML File

Cello enables you to copy your bookmarks into an HTML file, with each
bookmark becoming a link in the file. You can then use the HTML file as a
home page, or send it to a friend or associate so they can visit your favorite
sites. Unfortunately the HTML file is incorrectly formatted—it doesn't contain paragraph markers at the end of the lines, so all the links flow together
when viewed on-screen. Still, you can edit the file in a text editor. To create
the HTML file, follow this procedure:

1. Choose the **B**ookmark menu. The Bookmarks dialog appears.

2. Choose Dump list to **f**ile. A File Save As dialog box appears. Choose a
   file name and location and then click OK.

3. Click Quit to dismiss the Bookmarks dialog box.

Your bookmarks are written as a text file with the HTML codes for the URL addresses.

Copy a Bookmark

To copy a bookmark to the Clipboard, follow these steps:

1. Choose the **B**ookmark menu. The Bookmarks dialog box appears.

2. Choose Co**p**y and the bookmark is copied to the Clipboard.

3. A message box informs you that the bookmark was copied. Click OK.

4. Click Quit to close the Bookmarks dialog box.

You can then paste the bookmark into any other Windows application.

Delete a Bookmark

To remove a bookmark from the list, follow these steps:

1. Choose the **B**ookmark menu. The Bookmarks dialog box appears.

2. Select the list item with a single click.

3. Choose the **D**elete button. A confirmation dialog box appears. Choose OK to delete the bookmark.

4. Click Quit to close the Bookmarks dialog box.

Jumping to a Document by URL in Cello

Mosaic's Open URL feature is replaced by the Jump via URL command in Cello. To jump to a document by entering its URL, open the **J**ump menu and choose Launch via **U**RL. The Enter URL dialog box opens (see fig. 12.6). Enter the URL and choose OK.

Fig. 12.6
The URL dialog box.

To jump to a local file in Cello, you use the Launch via URL command. However, you need to precede the path and file name with

    file:::///localhost

and enter the path and file name in the form

```
c:/filename/filename
```

so the complete URL for a local file in cello is

```
file:://localhost/c:/filename/filename
```

Gopher and FTP sessions

Cello is actually more than a Web browser. It also has built-in Gopher and FTP utilities. Follow these steps:

1. Open the **J**ump menu and choose Launch **g**opher session or Launch FTP session. A dialog box appears (see fig. 12.7).

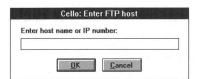

Fig. 12.7
The Enter FTP Host dialog box. The Gopher dialog box is similar.

2. Type the domain name or IP address of the Gopher or FTP server and then choose OK.

The main Gopher menu for this server appears. You get an error dialog box if a connection could not be made.

The methods for launching the other types of sessions (Telnet and TN3270) are very similar to the FTP or Gopher sessions.

Sending Mail

You can use Cello to send your current Web document to other users on the Internet. To mail files to someone, your e-mail address has to be configured. To do this, open the **C**onfigure menu and choose Your e-mail **a**ddress. Enter your address in the dialog box and choose OK.

To send a Web document to someone else, follow these steps:

1. Navigate to the document you want to e-mail.

2. Open the **F**ile menu and choose **M**ail file to. The dialog box shown in figure 12.8 appears. Your e-mail address is already filled in for you. The file itself doesn't appear in the dialog box but you see the message, `******Attached file follows******`.

3. Type the address of the recipient in the To: box

4. Type the header for the message in the Message: box.

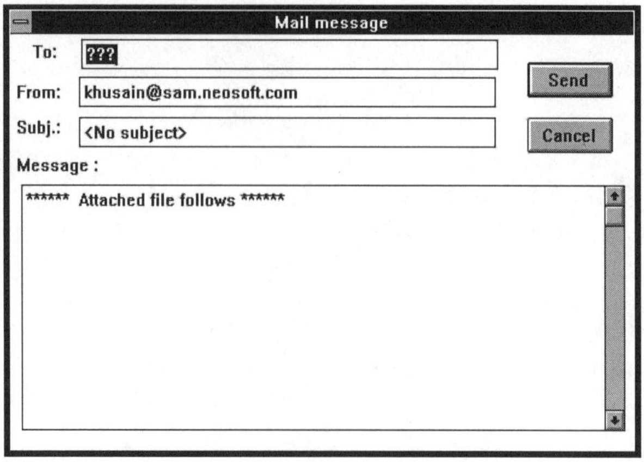

Fig. 12.8

The Mail Message
dialog box.

5. Click the Send button to send the file, or click Cancel to abort the transfer of this message.

The Signature File

Tip

Keep signature
files short and
terse. Long signa-
ture files annoy
many Internet
users.

If you create an ASCII file CELLO.SIG in the same directory as CELLO.EXE, Cello appends this signature file to all your outgoing mail messages. This ASCII file is simply a personal message you can append to all outgoing mail. Generally, this message lets the recipient know how to contact you; some people write very elaborate signatures. You are not required to attach a signature file to outgoing mail.

Customizing Cello

You can customize Cello for a number of features, some of which follow:

- **The home page.** Open the **C**onfigure menu, choose **F**iles and Directories, and then choose **H**ome Page. Enter the URL of the page you want to use as the home page.

- **The default editor to use.** By default this is Windows Notepad. If you want to change this to another editor, open the **C**onfigure menu, choose **U**se Your Own, and then choose **E**ditor. Type the full DOS path and file name of the editor.

- **File associations.** You can change these in the Extension section of CELLO.INI. Change the viewer used for a specific file extension by editing this file. To learn more about editing the MOSAIC.INI file, see chapter 3, "Getting Mosaic for Windows Running." You can edit the CELLO.INI file in the same way.

■ **Caching.** Cello caches files in the local memory on your machine or stores temporary files on the local-area network. Cello has a "low water-mark" as a number of bytes at which it starts deleting temporary files. Usually this is defaulted to 500K. That is, as soon as Cello sees that 500K or less space is left on the drive to which it's caching, it starts deleting the temporary files in the reverse order that they were visited. The oldest file used is deleted first. Open the **C**onfigure menu, choose **F**iles and Directories, and then choose **C**ache low watermark. Enter a value for the low watermark.

IV

Other WWW Clients

■ **Handling color images.** Getting 24-bit color images is a slow process under Windows. You can reduce the transfer time by turning on the Dither mode. This speeds up transfers of documents containing 24-bit color images, though it has no effect on other images. The picture will appear grainy, though. Open the **C**onfigure menu, choose **G**raphics, and then choose **D**ither to toggle the state between on and off.

■ **Using fonts.** You can change the fonts used to display various parts of Web documents. The options here are essentially the same as in Mosaic. (See chapter 3, "Getting Mosaic for Windows Running.") To change fonts in Cello, open the **C**onfigure menu, choose **F**onts, and then choose the page element—headings, list items, and so on—for which you want to change the font. The Font dialog box opens.

■ **Download directory.** To select another download directory, choose Configure, Files and directories, Download directory. Then type in the name of the directory in which you want to store your downloaded files.

■ **Automatic search dialogs.** When Cello displays an index docu-ment—one that lets you search a special Web index, it automatically displays the search dialog for you. If you don't want that to happen, choose Configure, Automatic search dialogs, to remove the check mark from this option.

■ **Changing Gateways.** You can specify which e-mail, WAIS, and newsgroup servers Cello should use. Open the Configure menu, and then select Mail relay, News server, or WAIS gateway and type the hostname.

Viewing and Saving Documents

Cello provides a quick and easy way to view the source document and save it to your hard disk. Choose the Edit, View source option, or the Edit, View as clean text menu options. Both options open Notepad. The former displays the HTML document, including the HTML codes. The latter strips out these codes, leaving the text. In both cases you can save the document using Notepad's File, Save option. (When you save an HTML file, you have to add the HTM extension manually.)

> **Note**
>
> Notepad cannot open very large documents. You can easily change Cello's setup to use Windows Write rather than Notepad. To do this, choose the **C**onfigure, **U**se your own, **E**ditor menu option, type **write** into the Choose editor dialog box, and then click OK.

InterAp from California Software

This section is about Web Navigator, an active, powerful tool for business and personal computer users to hunt and gather valuable information from the Web. The Web Navigator browser is an integrated part of a Windows-compatible suite of telecommunications services called InterAp, which stands for Internet Applications, from California Software (CSI).

The Web Navigator is a smoothly integrated part of the InterAp suite that includes e-mail, a Usenet newsreader interface, modem dialing, FTP, Telnet, and WAIS search services. Because this new Web browser is part of such a useful suite, it will interest customers seeking a single software solution to all their Internet access needs.

Web Navigator stands apart from Mosaic and some other browsers in that it holds a primary home page in the local client machine. On startup, the user immediately has a menu to view, rather than the message, Waiting for remote connection. You can replace your primary, local home page, which contains links that are subject to change, with a fresh, up-to-date home page that has new, unbroken links. Just download the new page from California Software. The section, "What Does It Looks Like," later in this chapter, covers this process.

IV

Note

California Software says they continue to have a friendly relationship with Thomas R. Bruce, who originally wrote and developed the web browser called Cello. Tom Bruce provides California Software with advanced technical advice.

Web Navigator and Cello (v. 1.01a) are very much alike, because the Web Navigator was built on and derived from Cello. This section shows you the important differences between Mosaic and Web Navigator, and shows you the major differences between Web Navigator and Cello, Web Navigator's parent.

Web Navigator is especially interesting because it uses the Windows tools of OLE 2.0 (Object Linking and Embedding 2.0) to integrate itself into a unified suite that deals with all your Internet needs. Also, because it approaches the idea of an initial home page in a new way, the Web Navigator is especially interesting.

Tip
Web Navigator (and the whole InterAp suite, for that matter) is compatible with TCP/IP LANs and SLIP and PPP connections that are WinSocket compliant.

Where Do You Get Web Navigator?

Web Navigator is the WWW part of the California Software InterAp suite. But remember, you should ask for InterAp by California Software rather than just the Web Navigator. InterAp will be sold both in retail software stores and directly from California Software.

Here is the contact information for California Software:

Surface Mail:
California Software Incorporated
4th Floor
4000 Civic Center Drive
San Rafael, California 94903
Voice: (415)491-4371
Fax: (415)491-0402
E-mail: Sales@calsoft.com
 Support@calsoft.com
FTP: **ftp.calsoft.com** or 199.4.105.10
WWW: **http://www.calsoft.com**

As usual in the software pricing business, the more copies you buy the more you save. Single users pay the highest prices, and large companies and organizations (who are a primary target audience for this sort of communications suite) can buy site licenses at lower costs per user.

The entire InterAp suite is priced at $295 (December 1994) for single users. Therefore, this browser can only be seen as a bargain if you want what California Software calls the *interoperability* of a single unified suite of Windows OLE 2.0 compliant telecommunications and Internet applications, rather than just the Web Navigator module.

InterAp can be quite a worthwhile investment if you already use other OLE 2.0 compliant programs, such as spreadsheets (for example, Excel 5.0), word processors (for example, Word 6.0), or graphics programs (CorelDRAW! 5.0, for example) and want the drag and drop and object linking and embedding features OLE 2.0 offers. This and other feature pros and cons are discussed in more detail in the section, "Advantages and Disadvantages," later in this chapter.

The InterAp suite is designed to be customizable, so that large companies and organizations can turn off individual modules if they are undesirable or unneeded. For example, if you already have a great e-mail reader that all your workers use and understand, you don't have to activate the e-mail program in the InterAp suite—you can just leave it turned off.

> **Note**
>
> Another Web Navigator feature you should know about is almost invisible. Web Navigator comes with its own WinSocket driver; it can supply WinSocket service if you need it.
>
> Web Navigator politely checks to see if you already have WinSocket installed, before it does any installing of its own. If it detects an installed WinSocket, Web Navigator announces that fact and moves on without installing another. To learn more about how to install and use WinSocket, see chapter 3, "Getting Mosaic for Windows Running."

What Does It Look Like?

This section gives you a first look at the Web Navigator interface (see fig. 12.9). It also describes the interface and the home page.

The InterAp interface is called the LaunchPad. If you double-click the InterAp Manager icon, the LaunchPad toolbar (shown in fig. 12.10) opens. Start the Web Navigator by clicking the globe icon.

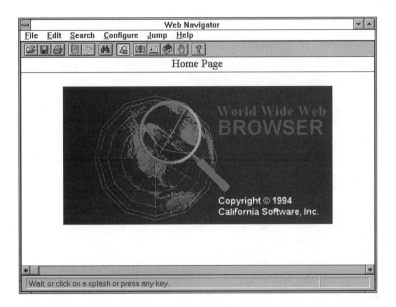

Fig. 12.9
Web Navigator
opens the World
Wide Web to any
Windows user.

Fig. 12.10
The LaunchPad
toolbar.

As mentioned above, Web Navigator loads a local home page from your hard
drive as soon as you turn on the Web Navigator. You have no initial lag-time
and you don't have to wait for a remote connection or for text and graphics to
be returned from a remote site. Figure 12.11 shows the top of the home page.

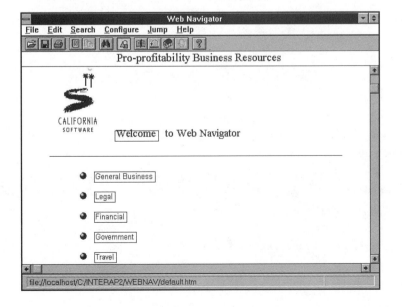

Fig. 12.11
Web Navigator
comes with its
own local home
page.

Tip
The Internet is much like a living thing—*always* changing. To accommodate change, California Software encourages users to download a new starting home page, with fresh new connections and up-to-date information.

This initial home page is only a sample. California Software gives you a fresh one any time you need it. Or you may want to have them custom design one just for your company or organization. Of course, you can always create your own.

This unique initial feature sets the whole tone for the Web Navigator—California Software wants to insulate you from the UNIX command line and all forms of TCP/IP gibberish by making each transaction simple, visually intuitive, and transparent.

Loading a Document by URL

Opening a URL in Web Navigator uses the same command as in Cello. Open the Jump menu and choose Launch via URL. Enter the URL in the dialog box and press Enter.

Bookmarks and History

Like Mosaic and Cello, it's easy to mark your place if you find something interesting that you may want to visit again. To place a bookmark in the open document, open the Jump menu and choose Bookmark. Then choose Mark Current document. The Bookmarks dialog box appears (see fig. 12.12).

Fig. 12.12
Cello's Bookmark dialog is given a facelift in Web Navigator.

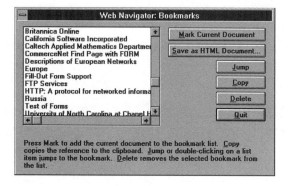

Just as in Cello, double-click a bookmark entry to immediately open that document. The remainder of the commands in this dialog box are used in the same way as they are in Cello.

Tip
If you forget where you are, so to speak, you can always click the right mouse button at the top, near the toolbar, and your current URL will appear in a pop-up box!

> **Note**
>
> The Save as HTML Document button in Web Navigator's Bookmark dialog box saves the bookmark list as an HTML file that you can open locally. This is the same as the Dump list to file button in Cello's bookmark dialog box.

Web Navigator's History feature is almost identical to Cello. But Web Navigator has a "spruced up" dialog box (as shown in fig. 12.13), and shows both
the URLs and document titles (Cello shows only the titles).

Moving a Bookmark

To move a bookmark from one group to another, copy it to the Windows Clipboard
using the Copy button in the Bookmarks dialog box. Open the new group (called a
bookmark category) into which you want to move the bookmark. Next, ask to
enter a new bookmark in the new group, and then use the Clipboard hot keys
(Shift+Insert) to paste the bookmark from the Clipboard to the new location. Return
to the bookmark's previous location and delete it. The final version of Web Navigator
may have a simpler way to move bookmarks, but this five-step method works.

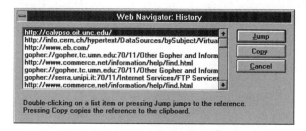

Fig. 12.13
The Web
Navigator's History
box is similar to
the dialog box in
Cello.

Convenient Function Keys

As you become more familiar with any Windows program, you find that
some menus and keystrokes are part of your normal routine. In many cases,
the most common mouse selections can be duplicated using function keys.
Because macros with mouse movements often fail to work properly, you need
hot keys if you are writing macros for your frequent tasks.

California Software has far exceeded both Cello and Mosaic on this issue by
supplying twelve function keys for the most common operations. Mosaic just
ignores function keys, and Cello uses only a couple.

California Software has provided a full complement of function keys—from
F1 to F12, so that you can use a single keystroke to accomplish a lot.

The Web Navigator hot keys are listed in table 12.1. This table lists the function or "f-keys", what the function key does, and on which drop-down menu
the function is found. The letters in boldface are the actual keys you press to
use the hot keys if the function keys are not available. (For more information
on using hot keys in Windows, please see your Windows manual.)

Table 12.1 Web Navigator Hot Keys		
Function Key	**Operation**	**Drop-down Menu**
F1	Help **C**ontents	(**Help**)
F2	**S**ave as	(**F**ile)
F3	**S**earch again	(**S**earch)
F4	View **S**ource	(**E**dit)
F5	Reload **D**ocument	(**F**ile)
F6	**P**rint	(**F**ile)
F7	Jump **U**p	(**J**ump)
F8	**B**ookmark	(**J**ump)
F9	**H**istory	(**J**ump)
F10	Invokes Hot Key menus, such as Alt	
F11	Return to Home **p**age	(**J**ump)
F12	**A**bort Transaction	(**J**ump)
Alt+F4	**C**lose	(Control Menu*)
Ctrl+Esc	S**w**itch	(Control Menu*)
Ctrl+C	C**o**py	(**E**dit)

As in all Windows applications, the hot key for accessing the Control Menu is Alt+Spacebar. Web Navigator offers another way, also. You can just press F10+Spacebar.

The next section, on California Software's NetScripts, is not strictly about Web Navigator, but is about how you can use an OLE 2.0 compliant Internet Web browser, such as Web Navigator, to create powerful interacting macros.

Viewing Source in Windows Write

A good decision on the part of California Software was to use Windows Write as Web Navigator's default word-processing program.

Cello uses Notepad for viewing text files (such as HTML source). It's possible that if you have Windows on your computer, you have (or had) Write on there also. Write came with Windows. Windows Write is a more capable program than Notepad and InterAp takes advantage of it. In particular Write can open very large documents, while Notepad cannot. (This is a limitation in Windows and Windows for Workgroups—Windows NT's Notepad can open large files.)

> **Note**
>
> You can easily change Cello's setup to use Windows Write rather than Notepad. See the section, "Viewing and Saving Documents," earlier in this chapter.

Other than that difference, the functionality of viewing source in Web Navigator is the same as in Cello. Write lets you either convert the incoming document to Write format, view the document as it is without conversion, or cancel the operation.

Starting Points

Web Navigator includes a convenient list of starting points that you may want to check out when Web cruising. The idea is the same as the starting points feature in Mosaic; you choose a starting point—a Web document that the InterAp developers think may be of use. To open a Web document, open the **J**ump menu and choose one of the documents listed at the bottom of the menu. You can get an updated list of starting points from California Software.

NetScripts Macros, Scheduler, and Web Fetch Objects

Because Web Navigator is OLE 2.0 compliant, and part of a full suite of Internet communications services, you can use Web Navigator as part of cross-application macro programs. The InterAp suite allows you to link programs on your computer to remote computers, using a process California Software calls *distributed object communications*.

InterAp does this with NetScripts, a Visual Basic scripting language that is fully compatible with Microsoft's Visual Basic. You can use NetScript macros to link Internet services such as WWW to your other OLE 2.0 compliant applications, such as Word 6.0, Excel 5.0, and CorelDRAW! 5.0.

Also included in the InterAp suite is a Scheduler; your NetScripts can use the Web at night (or whenever you want, such as daily or weekly at a certain time), for the fastest response times.

This ability to send and receive information from other OLE 2.0 compliant applications opens vast new automation opportunities, including Web Fetch objects, which are only briefly mentioned below.

> **Note**
>
> Although Web Navigator comes packaged with several pre-written NetScripts that may serve your initial, basic needs, California Software also offers to custom produce macros for your exact business needs.

Here are three examples of how you can get Web Navigator and OLE 2.0 to do complex work for you:

- You can prepare a Web macro to automatically retrieve a stock price at certain times each day from a remote Internet site. The retrieved price can then be placed in an OLE 2.0 compliant spreadsheet, and a spreadsheet macro can then be told to compare the price to preset values (or to percent change figures) you determine. If a target, preset level of price or change in price occurs, the spreadsheet macro is ordered to send an e-mail message to you, your stock broker, your clients, or anyone you want.

- If you find a Web site that you think would be especially interesting to a friend or customer, you can send them an e-mail message with a Web "Fetch" object attached to it. This gives another Web Navigator user more than a plain URL, because they won't have to type or cut and paste anything. All they do is click the Web Fetch object; they're connected to the remote site, automatically.

- To keep up to date on new developments, you can search the Web for new advances by topic area. Keyword searches are already available through WebCrawler and Veronica, but with Web Navigator, you can have the search done automatically daily, once a week, or once a month. Or in the middle of the night, with the result stored neatly in your word processor's format waiting for your return in the morning.

Help and Documentation

Context-sensitive help is available in Web Navigator, and the Windows hypertext help documentation looks very nice. Figure 12.14 shows the help contents page.

As the mouse cursor moves over the button-bar, yellow help "balloons" pop up to tell you what each button does. This is especially helpful when you are learning the new program.

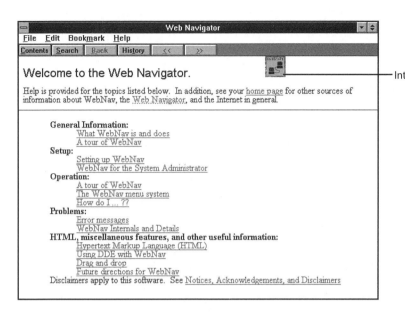

Fig. 12.14
The help contents page.

IV

Other WWW Clients

—— InterAp icon

Also, on the help contents page you'll find an integrated help service for the InterAp suite called INTERAP™ online help, including tutorials and visual demonstrations. To open this service, click the InterAp icon in the upper right part of the screen. Figure 12.15 shows you the opening page.

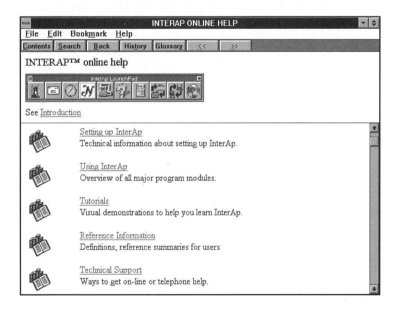

Fig. 12.15
An extra level of InterAp help is always available.

This INTERAP™ service is designed to stay on top of all other windows until you close it.

The bottom of the Web Navigator screen also contains a status line. If you open a drop-down menu up above, the status line always tells you in just a few words the most important tasks for which that menu is used.

Advantages and Disadvantages

While the unique function keys mentioned are not enough to sway a customer to purchase a $295 software program, they do once again demonstrate the customer convenience orientation of the Web Navigator. This section reviews the reasons you should consider buying this suite-with-a-web-browser, and a provides a few notes to check to be sure that it meets your needs.

Disk Cache of Entire Sessions

Web Navigator gives the appearance of more rapid responsiveness than old versions of Mosaic. In Web Navigator, as in Cello before it, the previous screens are stored on the hard disk and appear immediately. You can always tell if you are viewing a cached document by looking in the status bar—the [CACHED] indicator is shown as in figure 12.16.

Fig. 12.16
Cached pages are clearly marked in the lower-left corner when they are loaded.

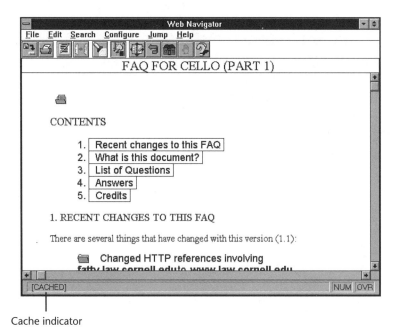

Cache indicator

Unfortunately, too many WWW sites still don't provide clear warnings about the sizes of the attached hypertext document. You can "accidentally" download a very large page or a series of graphics that takes several minutes to complete. With Web Navigator, you don't have to dread going back through that page later during your session because it was stored on your hard drive automatically. If you click a link to any previous page in the current session, it appears instantly.

California Software is adding another useful feature to Web Navigator (though it wasn't available at the time this chapter was written). You'll be able to save history lists for future use. Travel around the Web today, save the history, then come back and reuse the list next week or next month.

Drag and Drop (OLE 2.0)

One of the more important things that California Software means by "InterAp has interoperability" is that text can be moved to and from the Windows Clipboard, the InterAp e-mail program, and other OLE 2.0 compatible applications on the user's computer.

The addition of a Select All option on the Edit menu is one of the nicest new features in Web Navigator. This feature allows you to avoid clicking and dragging through an entire document to select it all. Once selected, the text can be moved to any OLE 2.0 compliant application, the InterAp e-mail program, or the Windows Clipboard. This is an especially welcome feature because NCSA Mosaic does not yet have a copy feature.

On-line Forms

Web Navigator has added support for on-line forms. These forms work in the latest versions of NCSA Mosaic, but not in Cello. (For a discussion of forms on the Web, see chapter 6, "Shortcuts to Favorite Places.") Figure 12.17 is a form from Encyclopedia Britannica Online's search service, and figure 12.18 is a similar form from CommerceNet's keyword search service.

To fill in a form, all you do is click the blank, and then start typing. Click each blank in turn to fill in a multiquestion form.

When you are ready, you indicate you are done by clicking Done, Go, Send, Search, or Submit. Some forms pages even let you reset the form if you want to start over again.

Fig. 12.17
You can fill in forms when you read Web pages to supply information or to search for information.

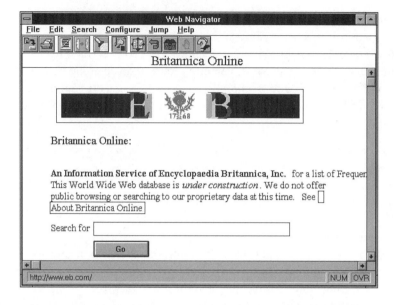

Fig. 12.18
CommerceNet allows you to clear the form if you want to start over.

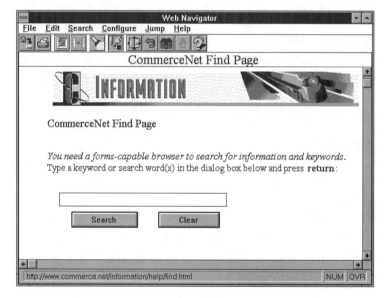

Abort Transaction

The excellent Abort Transaction feature started in Cello as a familiar red octagonal Stop sign. (Clicking this Stop sign performs the same function as clicking the spinning globe in Mosaic.) Abort transaction can be used when you discover a remote site is sending you too much material, when you want a short text, or when another priority presents itself during your busy workday.

Windows 32-bit Mode Is Not Required

Web Navigator makes full use of one of the most advanced Windows features, OLE 2.0. On the other hand, it doesn't require that Windows 3.1 users upgrade to 32-bit mode, as does Mosaic. Web Navigator runs quickly, and has advanced features such as session caching, without the trouble, hard disk space requirements and fear of major change that upgrading your Windows version from 16-bit to 32-bit processing may cause.

The Bottom Line

The bottom line is that with full OLE 2.0 compatibility and well-developed second generation web browser services (session caching, bookmark management, and so on), Web Navigator is an exciting new entry in the Internet software arena that first-time users and long-time users can both enjoy.

WinWeb from ElNet

WinWeb is a neat little World Wide Web viewer from ElNet (Enterprise Integration Network), a service provider owned by Microelectronics and Computer Technology Corporation (MCC). ElNet has created a Web site they call ElNet Galaxy, and the main Galaxy document appears as WinWeb's home page—though you can select whatever page you want as the home page, of course. And, like Mosaic, WinWeb is free for noncommercial use. There's also a Macintosh version, MacWeb.

Installing WinWeb

At the time of writing ElNet had released Version 1.0 A2 of WinWeb; that's an alpha version, a prerelease version. Version 1.0 A2 is out there, and you can use it, but don't be surprised if you run into bugs. When I used WinWeb, though, I found it to be pretty stable.

You can find WinWeb at the **ftp.einet.net** FTP site, in the /einet/pc/winweb directory. Or, if you are already working with a WWW viewer, you can get WinWeb off the World Wide Web at **http://galaxy.einet.net/ElNet/ WinWeb/WinWebHome.html**. (In this document you'll find a link currently called /einet/pc/winweb/winweb.zip. Set up your browser to download, because clicking on the link causes the ElNet site to send the WINWEB.ZIP file to your system.)

When you download the ZIP archive file, extract the WinWeb files into a directory you've created for WinWeb. Create a Program Manager icon for the program. Start your Internet connection, double-click the icon, and WinWeb starts. You can see the Galaxy home page in figure 12.19; you see this page when you first start WinWeb.

Fig. 12.19
The WinWeb window, showing the default home page.

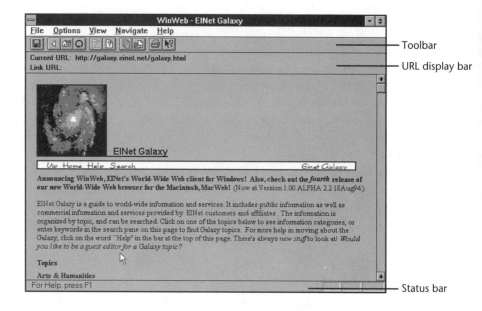

Toolbar

URL display bar

Status bar

You don't have to use this page as your home page. If you prefer to use another—the one provided by your service provider, for instance, or even one on your computer's hard disk—open the **O**ptions menu and choose Set **H**ome Page. The Set Home Page dialog box appears (see fig. 12.20).

Fig. 12.20
The Set Home Page dialog box lets you choose the home page you see each time you start WinWeb.

The **E**lNet Galaxy Home Page option is the default option, but you have two other choices. If you have already navigated the viewer to the page you want to use as the home page, simply select the **C**urrent Page option and then choose OK. Or type the URL of the page you want to use into the **U**RL text box and then choose the OK button.

The WinWeb Toolbar

Let's take a quick look at the WinWeb toolbar, which you can turn off using the **V**iew, **T**oolbar menu option if you prefer. The toolbar buttons are shown in figure 12.21.

- **Save to File.** Turns on loading documents to file (the same as Options, Load to File).

- **Back.** Returns to the previous document (the same as Navigate, Back).

- **Home.** Displays the home page (the same as Navigate, Home).

- **Reload.** Reloads the current document (the same as Navigate, Reload).

- **Search.** Lets you search the current document (the same as Navigate, Search).

- **Search ElNet Galaxy.** Lets you search the ElNet Galaxy WWW system (the same as Navigate, Search ElNet Galaxy).

- **History.** Displays the History List (the same as Navigate, History List).

- **Hot List.** Shows or removes the Hot List (the same as Navigate, Hotlist).

- **Print.** Prints the current document (the same as File, Print).

- **Help.** Turns the mouse pointer into a help pointer—clicking a screen component then displays a help file for that component.

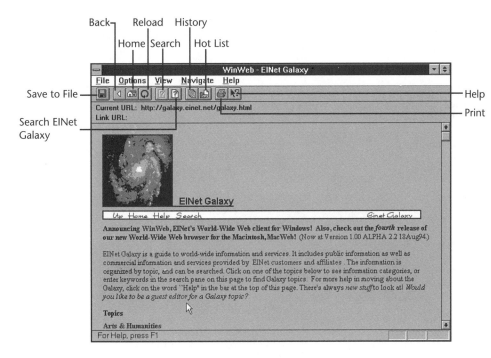

Fig. 12.21
The WinWeb toolbar has some very useful tools.

Note

Version 1.0 A2 does not have an on-line help system for the program; all the help tools, including buttons and menu options, do not work at present.

Using WinWeb

WinWeb is not as sophisticated as Mosaic or some of its derivatives, but for many users its simplicity more than makes up for that. It doesn't have as many options as Mosaic, but what it does have is pretty well designed. It's also smaller than Mosaic—the executable file takes up about a third as much disk space as Mosaic—and uses less memory. But perhaps most important is that it's a 16-bit application, so Windows 3.1 and Windows for Workgroups users don't need to add the Win32s 32-bit upgrade. The Win32 versions of Mosaic will outperform it, but WinWeb is faster and more stable than the early 16-bit NCSA Mosaic 1.0.

The basics are the same as with any WWW viewer; you click links to go places. When WinWeb is transferring a document it displays a small dialog box with a Cancel button inside it. You can just click the button to stop the transfer.

Let's look at the other navigational tools (see the menu commands in table 12.2).

Table 12.2   The Navigation Menu Commands

Command	Action
Navigate, **B**ack	Displays the previous document.
Navigate, **H**ome	Displays your home page (which is set using the Options, Set Home Page command).
Navigate, Load **U**RL	Displays a dialog box in which you can type a URL. When you choose the OK button, the document is displayed.
Navigate, Reload	Reloads the current document.
Navigate, **C**ancel	Cancels the current document-loading operation. Use this if you clicked a link and the document is taking too long to load.
Navigate, **S**earch	Searches the current document. You can enter a search keyword.

Command	Action
Navigate, Search ElNet **G**alaxy	Even if you are not currently at the ElNet Galaxy home page, you can still search the Galaxy system for information.
Navigate, His**t**ory List	Displays the History List, so that you can go back to a previous document.
Navigate, Hotlist	Displays or closes the Hotlist. Use the Hotlist to take a shortcut to documents you saved in the Hotlist earlier.

Using the Hotlist

Mosaic uses a Hotlist, a sort of bookmark system, to help you find your way back to documents you know you will return to. WinWeb has a similar system, though the current version doesn't let you add the Hotlist to the menu bar. Instead, there's a Hot List dialog box that you can keep open, or open when you need it.

If you are viewing a World Wide Web document that you think you'll want to return to, choose **N**avigate, Hot**l**ist. The dialog box shown in figure 12.22 appears.

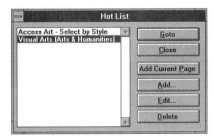

Fig. 12.22
Use the Hot List dialog box to keep a record of your favorite WWW documents.

Choose the Add Current **P**age button to see another small dialog box, into which you can type an item name, or accept the document title. Choose the OK button in that dialog box and the entry is added to the Hot List box.

You can also add items to the Hot List box without going to the document first. Choose **A**dd to see another small dialog box, this time with space for an item name and its URL. Type both in and choose the OK button to add the entry to the list.

When you've finished adding items to the Hot List dialog box, close the box by clicking the **C**lose button. You don't have to close the box, though. This dialog box is always on top—it remains above all your other Windows applications, WinWeb included. You can push the dialog box off screen just a little, but have it ready when you want it.

When you need to go to one of the documents you've added to your Hotlist, and if you didn't leave the box open, use the **N**avigate, Hot**l**ist option again to open it. Then simply double-click the document to which you want to go. Or select the document and click the Goto button.

Using the History List

The History List can also stay open all the time. Choose the **N**avigate, His**t**ory List menu option. The History dialog box appears (see fig. 12.23). It is quite small when you first open it, but you can enlarge it using the Control menu's Size command or the window's borders.

Fig. 12.23
Use the History dialog box to return to documents you viewed earlier.

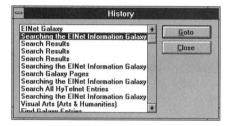

The dialog box shows you all documents you've viewed in the current session. Double-click one to go to it, or select it and choose the Goto button.

Saving Files

WinWeb uses a similar system to Mosaic for downloading files from the World Wide Web. When you find a link that is a connection to a file (a link that when clicked begins a file transfer), choose the **O**ptions, **L**oad to File command.

Tip
You can use this method to load an HTML file to your hard disk. If you click a normal link, you see the Save As dialog box. When you save the document, it is saved as an ASCII HTML file that you can then modify and use as, for example, your home page.

Now WinWeb is in Load to File mode. Each time you click a link, the Save As dialog box appears. (You see this box even if the link is a normal document-to-document link.) Select the directory in which you want to place the file, and the file name you want to use, then choose the OK button. The file transfers to your hard disk.

Printing a Document

You can print from WinWeb using the same procedure you use in Mosaic. WinWeb also has a print preview function that works essentially the same way as Mosaic's.

Customizing WinWeb

You have a few ways to customize WinWeb; use the **V**iew menu to get to the tools that let you do so (perhaps the View menu needs to be renamed).

WinWeb has a tool for selecting the fonts you want to use for various types of document text. Open the **V**iew menu and choose **F**onts to see the dialog box shown in figure 12.24.

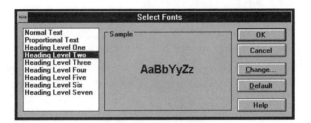

Fig. 12.24
Use the Select Fonts dialog box to determine how documents are displayed.

Click the type of text you want to change, and the dialog box shows you how that text is currently set up. Choose the Change button to see a typical Windows Fonts dialog box, in which you can modify the font—remember that you can change font color, not just typeface.

Notice also that WinWeb's Select Fonts dialog box has a Default button. Choose this button if you want to return the selected font to its default setting—useful if you've been goofing around with the fonts and don't like what you've done to them.

You can also change the **H**ighlight Color and **B**ackground Color by selecting these options from the **V**iew menu. The Highlight Color is the *link* color, what would be called the *anchor* color in Mosaic; this is the color of the text (or of the border around the graphic) that you click to display another document or download a file. The Background Color is the color of the WinWeb background. In both cases use the Windows Color dialog box—the one that is used by the Windows Control Panel—to select the color you want.

The other three options on the **V**iew menu are **T**oolbar, **S**tatus Bar, and **U**RL Display. These options turn those three items on and off. The URL Display is a line that appears below the toolbar and menu bar that shows the current document's URL, and the URL of the link to which the mouse pointer is pointing.

Tip
The more of these items you remove, the more space you have to view your WWW documents.

Another very important option is the **O**ptions, Load **I**mages command. Use this to turn the display of inline graphics on and off. If you are using WinWeb on a telephone line—through a SLIP or PPP connection—this capability is very important, because displaying all those inline graphics can take a long time.

MacWeb from EINet

 MacWeb is a World Wide Web viewer from EINet (Enterprise Integration Network), a service provider owned by Microelectronics and Computer Technology Corporation (MCC). They have created a Web site they call EINet Galaxy, and the main Galaxy document appears as MacWeb's home page—though you can select whatever page you want as the home page, of course. And, like Mosaic, MacWeb is free for noncommercial use. There's also a Windows version, WinWeb.

Installing MacWeb

At the time of writing EINet had released Version 1.00 A2.2, a prerelease version. This version is available, and you can use it, but don't be surprised if you run into bugs. When I used MacWeb, though, I found it to be pretty stable.

You can find MacWeb at the **ftp.einet.net** FTP site, in the /einet/mac/ macweb directory. Download the file macweb.latest.sea.hqx to get the latest available version. Or, if you are already working with a WWW viewer, you can get MacWeb off the World Wide Web at **http://galaxy.einet.net/ EINet/MacWeb/MacWebHome.html.** (In this document, you'll find a link currently called macweb.latest.sea.hqx. Set up your browser to download, because clicking the link causes the EINet site to send the file to your system.)

When you download the sea archive file, extract the MacWeb files to a folder you've created for MacWeb. That's it. You've installed MacWeb. Start your Internet connection, double-click the icon, and MacWeb starts. You can see the MacWeb home page in figure 12.25. You see this page when you first start MacWeb.

> **Note**
>
> In the 1.00 A2.2 version, loading graphics is off by default. This figure shows the home page with the graphics on.

> **Note**
>
> For details on installing and starting an Internet connection on your Mac, see chapter 4, "Getting Mosaic for Mac Running."

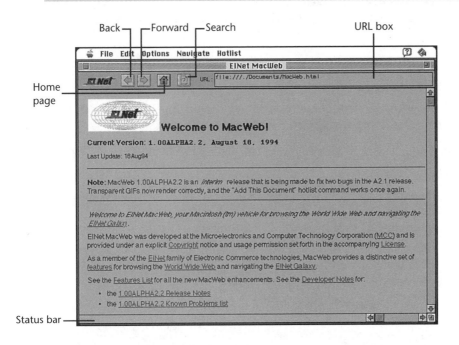

Fig. 12.25
The MacWeb window, showing the default home page.

The home page file is a local file called MacWeb.html saved in a folder named Documents in the folder where you extract MacWeb. You don't have to use this page as your home page. If you would prefer to use another—the one provided by your service provider, for instance, open the File menu and choose Preferences. The Preferences dialog box appears (see fig. 12.26).

The MacWeb Home Page is the default page, but you can enter any other URL address here.

Tip
If you have already saved some document URLs in a hotlist, you can copy the URL for a page and paste it into the box for the home page.

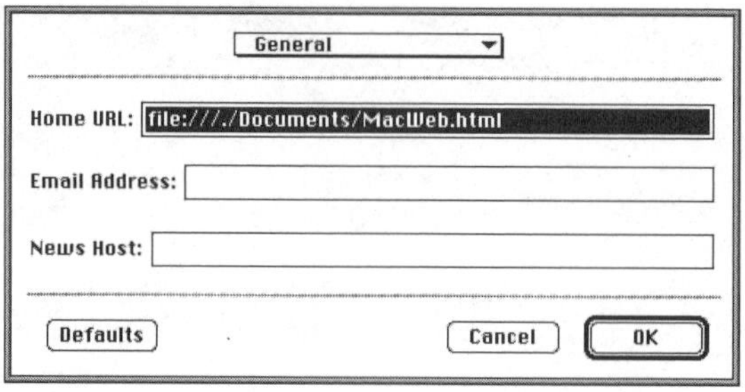

Fig. 12.26
Among other options, the Preferences dialog box is where you choose the home page you see each time you start MacWeb.

The MacWeb Toolbar

Let's take a quick look at the MacWeb toolbar. The toolbar buttons are in figure 12.27.

- **Backward.** Returns to the previous document (the same as Navigate, Back).

- **Forward.** Goes to the next document in the history list if you are not at the last document (the same as Navigate, Forward).

- **Home.** Displays the home page (the same as Navigate, Home).

- **Search.** Lets you search the current document (the same as Navigate, Search; however, this was not working in the A2.2 version I saw).

Fig. 12.27
The MacWeb toolbar has some useful tools.

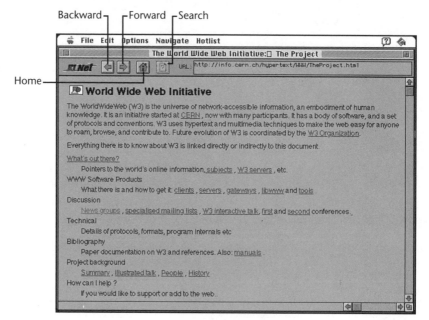

Using MacWeb

MacWeb is not as sophisticated as Mosaic or some of its derivatives, but for many users its simplicity more than makes up for that. It doesn't have as many options as Mosaic, but what it does have is pretty well designed. In fact, the design is so good that you should notice much faster performance. You will also find that MacWeb takes less memory to run (about 2M is suggested with a 700K minimum compared to a 3M suggested and 2M minimum for NCSA's latest release). And it requires a mere 400K of hard disk space compared to 1.3M for NCSA.

The basics are the same as with any WWW viewer; you click links to go places. When MacWeb transfers a document, it displays a small dialog box with a Cancel button inside it. You can just click the button to stop the transfer.

Let's look at the other navigational tools—you can see the menu commands in table 12.3. Notice that all the navigation commands are not under the Navigate menu.

Table 12.3 The Navigation Commands	
Command	**Action**
Navigate, Forward	Displays the next document.
Navigate, Backward	Displays the previous document.
Navigate, Home	Displays your home page.
Navigate, History	Opens a submenu History List so that you can go back to a previous document.
Navigate, Search	Searches the current document. You can enter a search keyword. (Does not work in the alpha2.2 version.)
Navigate, ElNet Galaxy	Opens the ElNet Galaxy Home Page.
Navigate, ElNet	Opens the ElNet Home Page.
Navigate, MacWeb Home Page	Opens the MacWeb Home Page.
File, Open URL	Displays a dialog box that you can type a URL into. When you choose OK, the document is displayed.
File, Reload	Reloads the current document.

Using the Hotlist

Mosaic uses a Hotlist, a sort of bookmark system, to help you find your way back to documents you want to return to. MacWeb has a similar system. The current version has the Hotlist as part of the menu bar.

If you are viewing a World Wide Web document that you think you'll want to return to, open the Hotlist menu and choose Add This Document. The document is immediately added to your Hotlist.

When you need to go to one of the documents you've added to your hotlist, open the Hotlist menu and choose the document to go to. Figure 12.28 shows this menu with items added.

Fig. 12.28
The Hotlist with two documents added.

Two documents added to hotlist

Using Multiple Hotlists

MacWeb scheme for multiple hotlists isn't as slick as the NCSA version (there's no way to add more than one hotlist to a menu and you can't create hierarchical submenus), but its simplicity is nice compared to NCSA. Like the NCSA version, you can create unlimited numbers of hotlists (the only limit is the drive space to store them). MacWeb stores each hotlist as a separate file. So, if you want to send a particular Hotlist to a friend or colleague so that they can easily get to the documents on your list, just give them a copy of your hotlist file.

To start a new hotlist file, open the Hotlist menu, choose Hotlist Operations, and then choose New.

> **Note**
>
> If you have made any changes to your currently open Hotlist, you will be prompted to save them before you open a new one.

After choosing New, your hotlist will have no entries in it. You can now add any new items to it as described earlier in this chapter in the section "Using the Hotlist."

To open another Hotlist, open the Hotlist menu, choose Hotlist Operations, and then choose Open. In the dialog box, choose the name of the hotlist you want to open.

To save hotlists, open the Hotlist menu, choose Hotlist Operations, and then choose Save. If the hotlist has already been named and saved, it is saved immediately. If this is the first time you are saving it (or if you open the Hotlist menu, choose Hotlist Operations, and then choose Save As), you need to enter a name and choose a folder for the hotlist.

When you use the Save As command, you have the option to save the hotlist as a different file type. You can save this as a MacWeb Hotlist, a MacMosaic Hotlist (to use with NCSA's Mosaic hotlist feature) or you can save it as an HTML document to create a Web document that you can open (see fig. 12.29).

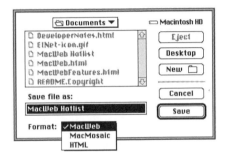

Fig. 12.29
The three format options for saving a hotlist.

One final worthwhile feature is the ability to edit hotlists. This feature is similar to the edit feature in NCSA Mosaic. To edit an item on the open hotlist:

1. Open the Hotlist menu, choose Hotlist Operations, and then choose Edit. The dialog box shown in figure 12.30 opens.

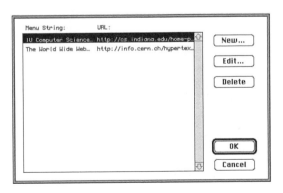

Fig. 12.30
Select the item to edit here.

2. Click the item to edit.

3. Click the Edit Button. The dialog box shown in figure 12.31 appears.

Fig. 12.31
Change the name
or URL of the item
here.

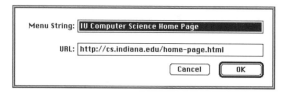

4. Make any desired changes to the Menu String or the URL, and then
click OK twice to close the two dialog boxes.

Sorting Your Hotlists

Here's a feature that must have been designed just for the terminally unorga-
nized like myself. After adding a dozen items to a hotlist, you may notice it is
difficult to find a particular entry. To organize your hotlists, follow these
steps:

1. Open the Hotlist menu, choose Hotlist Operations, and then choose
Sort.

2. This opens another sublevel in the menu with these two options:

   By Menu String. Sorts alphabetically according to the name of the
   entries in the hotlist.

   By URL. Sorts alphabetically according to the document URL. The
   entries are still displayed by name, though.

   Choose one of these options and the currently open hotlist is sorted.

Using the History List

To access the History List, open the Navigate menu and choose History. A
submenu with all the documents from this session opens (see fig. 12.32).
Choose the document you want to open.

Fig. 12.32
Use the History list
to return to
documents you
viewed earlier.

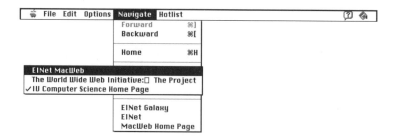

Customizing MacWeb

You have a few ways to customize MacWeb; open the File menu and choose Preferences to get to the tools that let you do so. You get three sets of options here.

The first is the same dialog box where you change your home page (this dialog box was described earlier in the section "Installing MacWeb"). See figure 12.33.

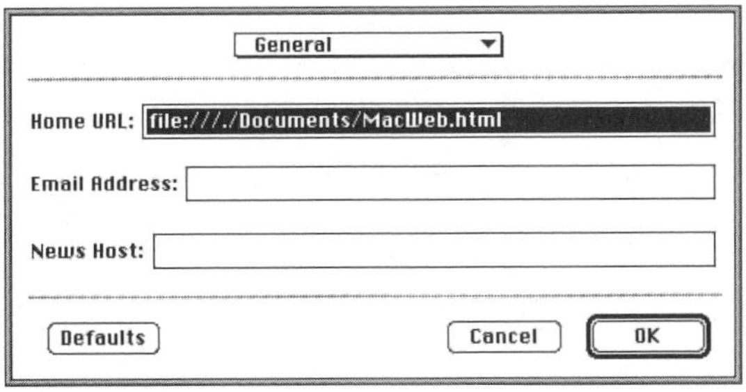

Fig. 12.33
Customizing the home page, e-mail address, and news host.

If you plan to use MacWeb for e-mail or newsreading, you should fill in the appropriate information in this dialog box. See coverage of these features in NCSA Mosaic in chapter 4, "Getting Mosaic for Mac Running."

Selecting the Files/Folders item from the drop-down list at the top of the dialog box changes the dialog box to the one shown in figure 12.34.

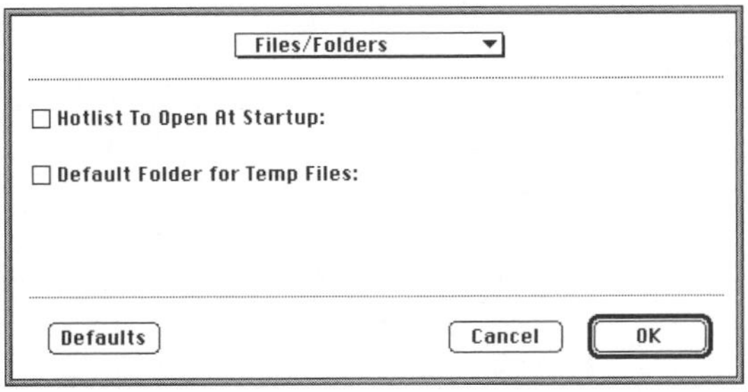

Fig. 12.34
Customizing the hotlist and temp folder.

To customize the hotlist to open when MacWeb starts or the default folder for temp files (MacWeb temporarily stores files on your drive when downloading large files to view), select the appropriate checkbox. A standard Open dialog box appears; select the hotlist or folder you want.

Finally, if you select the Format option from the drop-down list at the top of the dialog box, the dialog box in figure 12.35 appears.

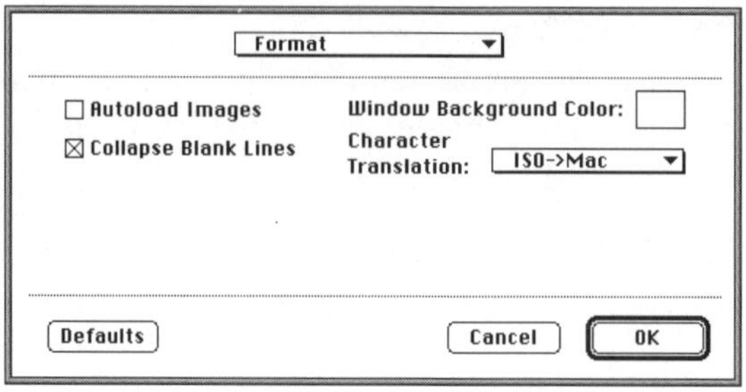

Fig. 12.35
MacWeb lets you
modify several
Web options.

The most commonly used option on this dialog is Autoload Images. When selected, inline images are automatically loaded. If not selected, you can open the Options menu and choose Load Images to load inline images.

The other options in this dialog box are:

■ Collapse Blank Lines. Shrinks documents that you view so that you never have more than one empty line in a row (some people try to format documents by having five, ten, or more blank lines in a row as spacers).

■ Window Background Color. Lets you select a background color for Web documents.

■ Character Translation. Opens a drop-down list of character sets you can use for various foreign languages.

Font Options

MacWeb has a nice little tool for selecting the fonts to use in various types of document text. Open the Edit menu and choose Styles to see the dialog box shown in figure 12.36.

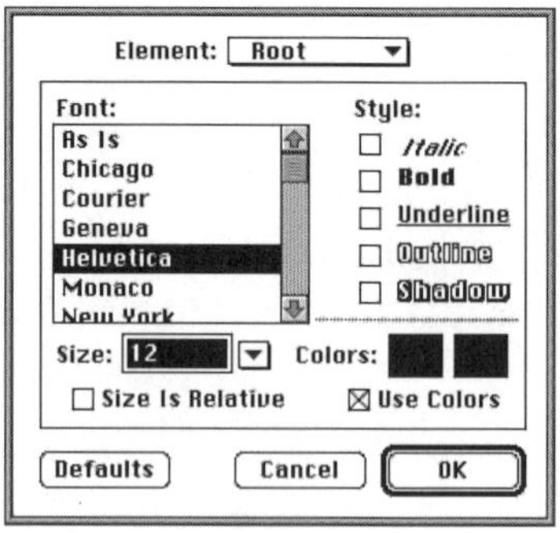

Fig. 12.36
Use the Styles
dialog box to
determine how
documents are
displayed.

Click the element drop-down list to display the types of text you can change and select the item you want to change (see fig. 12.37). The dialog box shows you how that text is currently set up. Choose the new font styles you want to use, and then click OK.

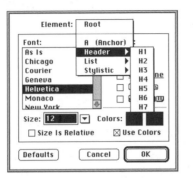

Fig. 12.37
Use the drop-down list of elements to choose the type of text to change.

Multiple Windows

Like NCSA Mosaic, MacWeb allows multiple independent open windows. To open a new window, open the File menu, choose New or press the Option key on the keyboard and then click a hyperlink.

Helper Applications and Suffixes

Changing the Helper applications (applications used to view images in JPEG, MGEG, or QuickTime, StuffIt Expander, and so on) is done in essentially the same way as in NCSA. To get to these options:

1. Open the Options menu and choose Helpers. The dialog box shown in 12.38 appears.

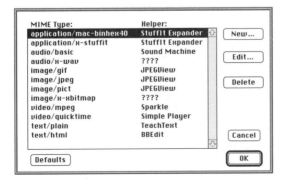

Fig. 12.38
This shows a list of all the file types and their helper applications.

2. Select a type from the list to edit.

3. Click the Edit button. The dialog box shown in figure 12.39 appears.

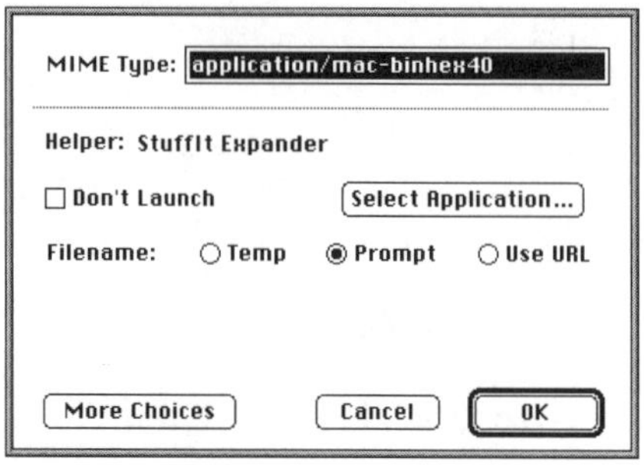

Fig. 12.39
Options for the
selected helper.

```
┌──────────────────────────────────────────┐
│  MIME Type: │application/mac-binhex40│    │
│  ........................................  │
│  Helper: StuffIt Expander                 │
│  □ Don't Launch        [ Select Application... ] │
│  Filename:  ○ Temp  ● Prompt  ○ Use URL  │
│                                            │
│  [ More Choices ]   [ Cancel ]  [  OK  ]  │
└──────────────────────────────────────────┘
```

4. Here you can choose a different file (MIME) type for the application, a different application for the file type, whether to start the application when a file of its type is downloaded, and whether to use a temporary file name, be prompted for a file name, or use the URL as a file name when downloading files.

5. To see even more choices click More Choices (see fig. 12.40). The defaults in this dialog box depend on the file type chosen. Make any needed changes, and then click OK.

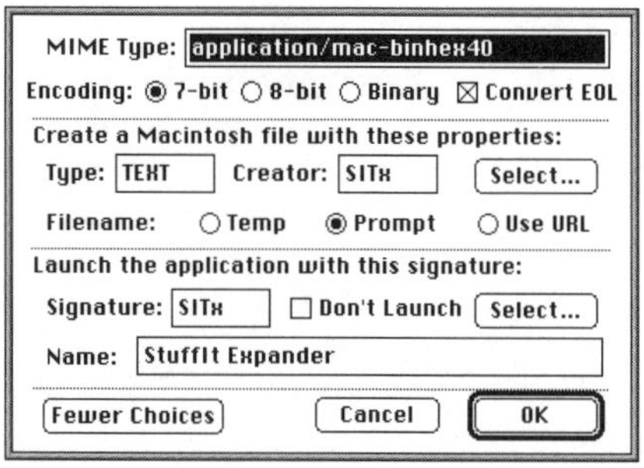

Fig. 12.40
More options for
the chosen helper
application.

```
┌──────────────────────────────────────────┐
│  MIME Type: │application/mac-binhex40│    │
│  Encoding: ● 7-bit ○ 8-bit ○ Binary ☒ Convert EOL │
│  Create a Macintosh file with these properties: │
│  Type: [TEXT]   Creator: [SITx]   [ Select... ] │
│  Filename:   ○ Temp  ● Prompt  ○ Use URL │
│  Launch the application with this signature: │
│  Signature: [SITx]   □ Don't Launch [ Select... ] │
│  Name: [StuffIt Expander]                  │
│  [ Fewer Choices ]   [ Cancel ]  [  OK  ] │
└──────────────────────────────────────────┘
```

6. Click OK to close the dialog box and to accept the changes.

The part of the file name after the period is called the file suffix. To change the file suffixes, open the Edit menu and choose Suffixes (see fig. 12.41). Macs can usually identify file types, but they can't always identify files transmitted on the Internet. These default settings should be okay for most uses, but if you find that a particular file suffix opens an application for the wrong file type (for instance, StuffIt opens to view a picture rather than your image viewer opening to view the picture) you may need to change the settings.

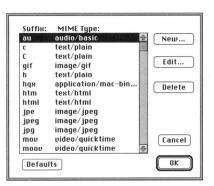

Fig. 12.41

The suffixes are on the left and the file type is on the right. These types correspond to the types from the helpers dialog boxes.

Select an entry, and then click Edit. You'll see the box shown in figure 12.42.

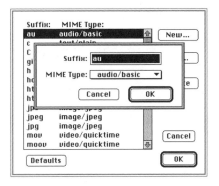

Fig. 12.42

Use this dialog to change the suffix or type.

Enter the suffix in the box provided or select a file type from the MIME Type drop-down list.

For more details on Helper applications, see chapter 4, "Getting Mosaic for Mac Running."

Viewing the Source for a Document

MacWeb gives you three options for viewing the underlying HTML document source. To view any of these, open the Options menu, choose View Source, and then choose Generated, Retrieved, or Retrieved+Headers. The best way to see this difference is to look at examples, as shown in figures 12.43, 12.44, and 12.45. Your text helper application opens all these. Depending on what information beyond the basic text you need, choose the appropriate option. You can copy and paste using the commands for your text editor.

Fig. 12.43

Viewing Source Generated option.

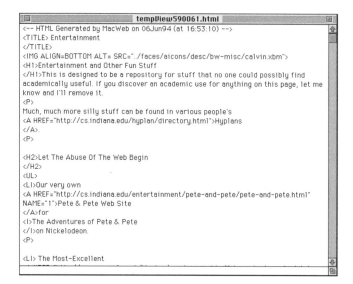

Fig. 12.44

Viewing Source Retrieved option.

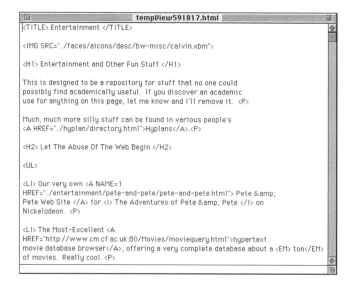

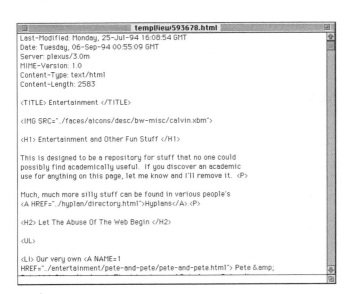

Fig. 12.45
Viewing Source
Retrieved+Headers
option.

NetCruiser

NetCruiser is a Windows program that works with the NETCOM system.
NETCOM is a large Internet service provider—they created NetCruiser to give
their customers an easy-to-install way to get a suite of easy-to-use Internet
tools. NetCruiser only works with NETCOM—you can't buy the software and
install it on other systems.

A remarkable thing about NetCruiser is that it uses a PPP connection, yet is as
easy to install as the average Windows program. There's no need for you to
worry about entering IP addresses or anything complicated like that—
NetCruiser handles it all for you. All you need to enter is your name and
address, the COM port you are using, the type of modem, and so on. Because
the software only works with one system, the NETCOM system, it knows how
to communicate with that system—there's no need for you to set up communications parameters. NetCruiser even has a command that automatically
downloads and installs the latest software upgrade. On the Internet, well-
designed, easy-to-use software is the exception, not the rule—and NetCruiser
is a delight to work with.

What's There

After you've installed and started NetCruiser, you'll find a well-designed
Windows interface with a variety of Internet tools: e-mail, newsgroups,
Telnet, FTP, a Gopher client, finger, and, most importantly for us, a World
Wide Web browser. To get to the browser, click the WWW button in the

toolbar—it's the one with a picture of a web, of course. Or choose the **I**nternet, **W**orld Wide Web - Browser menu option. You see the screen in figure 12.46.

Fig. 12.46
NetCruiser's World Wide Web Browser is a well-designed program that's fast and easy.

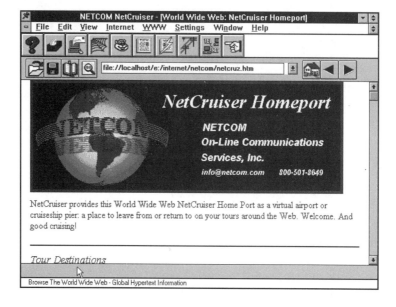

You use NetCruiser in much the same way you do Mosaic—click the links to go somewhere. But before we get into detail about working with this program, let's have a quick look at how to customize it.

Configuration Options

When you open the WWW Browser, a couple of things happen to the menu bar. A new menu appears, WWW, and another option appears on the Settings menu. Open the Settings menu and choose the WWW **O**ptions and you'll see the dialog box in figure 12.47.

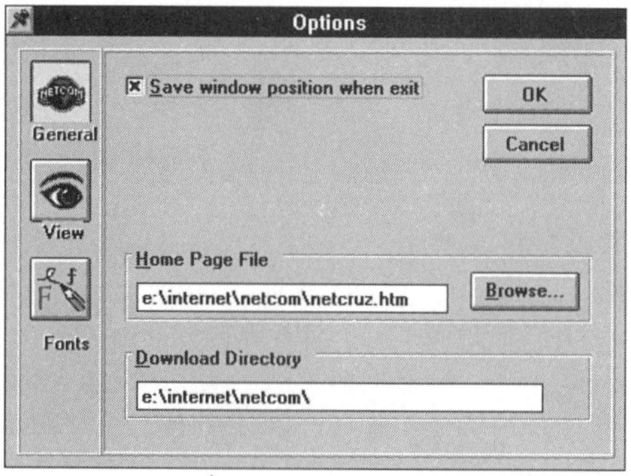

Fig. 12.47
The Options dialog box lets you set up your WWW Browser.

When you first open this box you see the General options. To make sure the window is the same size the next time you open the browser, choose **S**ave window position when exit. This option is useful because otherwise the window is small when it opens and you have to maximize it. You can also select the home page you want to use; by default, the home page is a file that was installed on your hard disk. Finally, you can specify the **D**ownload Directory, which is the directory in which you want to place any files downloaded during a WWW session.

Choose the View button, and the dialog box changes (see fig. 12.48). Here you can define a few characteristics of the documents you are going to view. Choose the Background Color button to select the background color and the Anchor Color button to select the link colors. (Remember, in WWW-speak the hypertext links that you click to display a document are often known as *anchors*.)

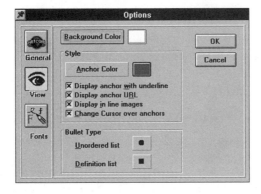

Fig. 12.48
The View options let you define what many of the document elements look like.

You can also modify how the links will look in a few other ways. You can choose Display Anchor **w**ith Underline to place an underline below each text link, Display Anchor U**R**L, to put the URL in the status bar when you point at a link, and **C**hange Cursor over Anchors to turn the pointer into an arrow when it passes over the links. Clearing the Display **i**n Line Images check box makes sure that inline images are not transferred, which speeds up your session somewhat.

You can also change the types of bullets used in your documents by choosing the bullet buttons at the bottom of the dialog box. In each case a dialog box appears with several choices.

Choose the Fonts button to see the different fonts defined for the documents (see fig. 12.49). Each button has the name of the type of font, and even displays the name in the format that you have selected, so that you can see all elements as they will appear in the documents. To change one, choose the button and select the type of font you want from the Fonts dialog box that appears.

Fig. 12.49
The Fonts options let you select each document font type.

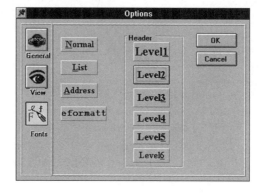

The NetCruiser Toolbar

Tip

To make a little more room for your WWW sessions, open the View menu and choose Toolbar to remove the large NetCruiser toolbar.

When you open the WWW Browser, you actually have two toolbars, the large one under the menu bar, which lets you select the different NetCruiser modules (FTP, Telnet, WWW, and so on), and a slightly smaller one that is for the WWW Browser itself.

Figure 12.50 shows the buttons you can find on the toolbar.

- **Open Local File.** Opens an HTML file.

- **Save to Disk.** Displays a Save As dialog box so that you can save the current document on your hard disk (as an HTML document).

- **Bookmark.** Opens the Bookmark dialog box.

- **Find.** Displays the Find dialog box, so that you can search the current document.

- **Home.** Displays the home page.

- **Back.** Goes to the previous document.

- **Forward.** Goes to the next document.

- **Stop.** This button only appears while the browser is transmitting information. Click it to cancel the transmission.

Open local file
Bookmark
Back
Save to disk
Find
Home Forward

Fig. 12.50
The NetCruiser
toolbar.

IV

Other WWW Clients

The Menu Options

Let's take a quick look at the menu options that you can use for your WWW session (see table 12.4).

Table 12.4 NetCruiser's World Wide Web Menu Options	
Command	**Purpose**
File, **V**iew Text File	Lets you view a text file that you have downloaded.
File, **V**iew Graphics File	Lets you view a graphics file that you have down-loaded.
File, **O**pen WWW File	Opens an HTML file on your hard disk.
File, **S**ave	Saves the current document as an HTML file on your hard disk.
Edit, **F**ind	Searches the current document for a particular word or phrase.
Edit, Find **N**ext	Repeats the search.
View, **S**ource File	Displays the HTML file so you can copy portions of it to the Clipboard.
WWW, **L**oad to Disk	Changes the browser to "download mode" so that when you click a link, a file is downloaded to your hard disk.
WWW, **B**ack	Displays the previous document.
WWW, **F**orward	Displays the next document.
WWW, **H**ome	Displays the home page.
WWW, His**t**ory	Displays the History list.
WWW, **R**eload	Reloads the current document.
WWW, Book **M**ark	Displays the Book Mark dialog box.
Settings, **W**WW Options	Lets you customize your WWW browser.

Working with Bookmarks

NetCruiser has a simple bookmark system that is adequate, but by no means great. When you want to place a bookmark, choose the **W**WW, Book **M**ark option or click on the Bookmark toolbar button. You see the Book Mark dialog box (see fig. 12.51).

Fig. 12.51

The Book Mark dialog box provides an adequate but simple bookmark system.

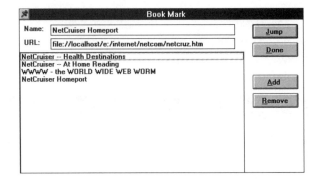

Choose the Add button to place the bookmark into the dialog box. To go to one of the bookmarks, choose the Jump button. You can also remove bookmarks with the Remove button and close the dialog box with the Done button. You can't edit entries; there's no way to save any changes you make in the Name and URL text boxes. You can, however, copy the URL from this box and paste it into another Windows application (highlight the text in the URL box and press Ctrl+C to copy it to the Clipboard).

The History List

If you want to see where you've been in the current session, choose WWW, History. You see a very simple dialog box (see fig. 12.52) in which you can double-click an entry to return to that document, or select it and choose the Jump to button. Unfortunately there's a serious problem with the History list—it displays URLs, not document titles. Which is easier to remember, "WWWW - the World Wide Web Worm" or "**http:// www.cs.colorado.edu/home/mcbryan/WWWW.html?**"

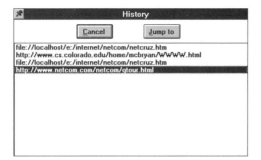

IV

Other WWW Clients

Fig. 12.52
The History dialog box provides a simple way to return to an earlier document.

Viewing Graphics

NetCruiser's WWW browser has a couple of built-in, automatic viewers, one for text and one for graphics. Click a link that transfers a JPG file, for instance, and that file is transferred to your disk and then displayed in the Graphics viewer (see fig. 12.53). You can also open the graphics and text viewers from the File menu, and load a variety of different file formats from your hard disk. You can view BMP, GIF, JPG, and XBM files. These types cover most, but not all, graphics file types you will run across (GIF and JPG are probably the most common formats used for pictures on the Web).

Fig. 12.53
Graphics are displayed in NetCruiser's graphics viewer (You can find Dr. Fun's cartoons at **http://sunsite.unc.edu/Dave/drfun.html.**)

What Can't It Do?

A number of useful features are missing from this browser. It can't copy text from the current document, or save the document as a text file (without the HTML codes that is—it can save it as an HTML file). Freeware Mosaic can't do this right now, either, but it should be able to soon, and some other commercial browsers can.

The bookmark system is very simple, also. There is no way to create menus or hotlists, and no way to export the bookmark list so that others can use it or so that you can load it from your hard disk as an HTML document. (You can't do this with the History list, either, which is a nice feature of some browsers.)

Viewer support is fairly limited, too. There are built-in text and graphics viewers, but no sound support, and no way to add your own viewers. For instance, if you click "Shut up boy!" at the **http://cc.lut.fi/~mega/ simpsons.html** WWW site, NetCruiser will transfer the AU file and put it on your hard disk—but you won't hear Homer Simpson shout at his son.

Also, although you can turn off inline images, you can't view selected images—it's all or nothing. In other words, if you are not getting in-line images and want to view just one image or the images in a particular topic, you have to turn inline images back on. Other browsers, including freeware Mosaic, have commands that let you work with inline images turned off (for speed), but still view selected images.

Finding NetCruiser

If you'd like to try NetCruiser, you have to contact NETCOM. There's a $25 registration fee for the NetCruiser system (which gets you the software). Then you have to pay $19.95 a month, which gets you 40 peak hours and unlimited use on weekends and from midnight to 9 a.m. during the week. Use more than 40 peak hours and you have to pay $2 per hour. NETCOM has local telephone numbers all over the country, so you probably will not have to pay long distance rates on top of these charges. For more information about NetCruiser, contact NETCOM:

> NETCOM
> 3031 Tisch Way, 2nd Floor
> San Jose, CA 95128
> (800)353-6600
> (408)345-2600
> Fax:(408)241-9145
> E-mail:info@netcom.com

NetCruiser is a very nice system, and its WWW Browser is pretty good, too. It's very easy to use, and very quick (because it's a PPP connection as opposed to a SLIP connection). The browser doesn't have the flexibility and features of Mosaic, however. That's probably okay for most users, but the advanced user will prefer a little more power.

Few people are going to get NetCruiser just for the WWW browser. They are going to get the product because it's a well-designed, all-in-one Internet tool, with a consistent user interface that is easy to install and to use. We need to see more of this type of tool on the Internet.

The Pipeline

The Pipeline is a unique Internet system. It's designed to be used over phone lines, but it's not a SLIP, CSLIP, or PPP connection. It isn't a simple dial-in terminal connection. It's what The Pipeline has called *Pink SLIP,* their own packet-switching protocol.

SLIP, CSLIP, and PPP are all TCP/IP (Transmission Control Protocol/Internet Protocol) protocols. A *protocol* is a set of rules that define how two systems can communicate; the protocol used by the Internet is TCP/IP, a packet-switching protocol. The data transmitted is broken into packets, sent, and then put back together by the system receiving the data.

The Pipeline decided to create their own system because they wanted a packet-switching terminal system. Rather than giving all their clients dial-in direct accounts—in which the user's computer becomes a host on the Internet—they wanted to use a simpler system, in which each user's computer is a terminal on The Pipeline's system. That way they wouldn't have to worry about setting up IP addresses for each user, for instance. But they still wanted to provide all the benefits of a dial-in direct account, and for that they needed packet switching.

For example, users working with packet-switching systems—whether SLIP, CSLIP, PPP, or The Pipeline—can run multiple sessions. They can download a file from an FTP site (or even several files) at the same time they work on the World Wide Web. By creating their own packet-switching system, The Pipeline has more control over how the system works, and can actually make multiple sessions work more smoothly than with dial-in direct connections. For instance, they are adding error-correction to Pink SLIP, to make transmissions more reliable. The design of The Pipeline's user interface makes multiple sessions quite simple to start. With most TCP/IP FTP software, for instance, you'd have to open several FTP programs to run several sessions. With The Pipeline, you just double-click each file you want to download— you don't really start an FTP program (The Pipeline does it all for you in the background).

Installation and Setup of The Pipeline

The Pipeline software was designed to be used with The Pipeline service. The Pipeline is a service provider based in New York. It has three ways to connect: dial the New York number, dial a SprintNet number from almost anywhere in the United States (you'll pay extra for the connection, though), or, if you have a local service provider, dial your service provider and connect to The Pipeline using an rlogin connection. (If you use rlogin, you have to pay both your service provider and The Pipeline for connect time, but it may be less than long-distance charges.)

There's another way to use The Pipeline software, though. The Pipeline is being licensed to service providers throughout the country. You may find a local service provider that uses the software.

To get a demonstration of The Pipeline software, or to find out if there's a service provider in your area using the software, contact The Pipeline by one of these methods:

> The Pipeline
> 150 Broadway
> Suite 1710
> New York, NY 10028
> Phone: (212)267-3636
> Fax: (212)267-4380
> E-mail: info@pipeline.com
> Modem: (212)267-6432 (login as guest)
> Telnet, Gopher, FTP: **pipeline.com**

Note that you may be able to download The Pipeline software from the **pipeline.com** FTP site, though the site is often unavailable.

Once you have the software, simply run the SETUP program to install it onto your hard disk. When you first run the program you will have to enter the configuration information—the number you want to dial, the COM port you want to use, and so on. It's all fairly straightforward, though. (At the time of writing, you could not use the rlogin method for a demonstration session, only for access once to The Pipeline.)

Using the Web Browser

The Pipeline is an integrated system that has all the usual Internet tools—FTP, Telnet, Internet Relay Chat, e-mail, newsgroups, and so on. But of course we are here to talk about the World Wide Web. Let's take a look at what's available, and how it works.

> **Note**
>
> At the time of writing, The Pipeline had just released a beta version of its Web software, and it lacked a number of features that will be in the final released version. The program I used when writing this chapter, and the figures you see here, aren't exactly the same as the version available now.

You can run the Web browser in a couple of ways. The Pipeline has, until now, been based on a Gopher menu system. The main window has a list of options that you can double-click—these options are actually Gopher menu items. But you can replace this system with the Web browser, so that every time you open The Pipeline you are shown the browser, not the Gopher menu.

To do this, open the Options menu and choose Web browser. (You can go back to the Gopher menu screen at any time by choosing this option again.) You'll see something like the screen in figure 12.54.

Tip
You can run multiple web sessions. Each time you choose the Internet, World Wide Web option, or press Ctrl+W, a new Web window opens. If you are in a Web window, you can click the Open URL toolbar button (see the next section "Using the Toolbar.").

Fig. 12.54
The Pipeline main screen, once you've selected the Web browser.

If you prefer to keep the Gopher main menu, and just start the Web browser occasionally, you can choose the Internet, World Wide Web option, or press Ctrl+W. The dialog box in figure 12.55 appears. Enter the URL of a web site you want to use (or select from the drop-down list box, in which you'll find URLs you used in previous sessions). When you choose the OK button, a new window opens, in which your Web session begins (see fig. 12.56).

Fig. 12.55
This dialog box saves the URLs you've used in the past, so you can quickly select them.

Fig. 12.56
The Pipeline's browser displays each page in a separate window.

Using the Toolbar

Notice the two toolbars. The one on the left side of the main window is a way to get to the other Pipeline services—e-mail, talk, newsgroups, and so on (see fig. 12.56). But the one at the top of the Web browsers contains buttons related to the web (see fig. 12.57).

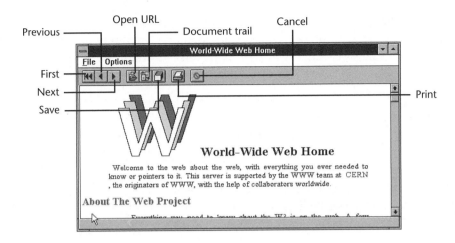

IV

Other WWW Clients

Fig. 12.57
The Pipeline's browser displays each page in a separate window.

Here are descriptions of each of these buttons:

- **First.** Go to the first document you looked at in this session.

- **Previous.** Go to the previous document.

- **Next.** Go to the next document.

- **Open URL.** Open a URL.

- **Document Trail.** Displays document trail—a history list.

- **Save.** Saves the current document on your hard disk.

- **Print.** Prints the current document.

- **Cancel.** Cancels the current transfer.

Using the Document Trail

The Pipeline browser calls its history list a *document trail*. At the time of writing the feature wasn't fully implemented. However, the drop-down list box in the main window to the left of the toolbar buttons contains the document trail (refer to fig. 12.55). Simply click the down arrow to see the list, and then click the document you want to return to.

Using Inline Images

As with most browsers, The Pipeline's browser lets you turn off inline images to speed up transfers. In the beta version this could only be done from a Web browser window, not the main window (though the released version will probably have the option in the main window, also). Choose Options, Expand Inline Images to turn the images on and off. The inline images will be replaced with asterisks in braces ([*]), and, in some cases, with Pipeline icons.

What if you want to view one of the missing inline images? Simply click the image and The Pipeline opens it for you.

Using a Home Page

In the first released version the Web browser may not have a way for you to change the home page directly—you can do so by modifying the PIPELINE.INI file, but there may not be a menu option that lets you.

Future versions will have better home page support, and may even have HTML editing tools. These will let The Pipeline's users create HTML files and place them on The Pipeline's computer, providing quick and easy Web publishing.

What Else?

When this chapter was written, some of the Web browser's features weren't working—such as the document trail. Pipeline promises that certain other features will be added before the software is released. Here's what the browser should have by the time you read this:

- **Forms support.** The WWW browser lets you enter data into HTML documents that contain interactive forms.

- **Viewers.** You can view most graphics files you find on the web and listen to most sounds by simply clicking the link. The Pipeline's built-in viewers will do the rest.

- **Video support.** This won't be available in the first release of the Web browser, but will be added later.

- **Home Page.** A Pipeline home page is created (the beta version was using the CERN home page).

How Does It Compare?

It's difficult to tell just how The Pipeline's browser will compare to Mosaic. It's a much simpler system, but it's also much easier to use—it has fewer features, but what there is you will find easier to work with.

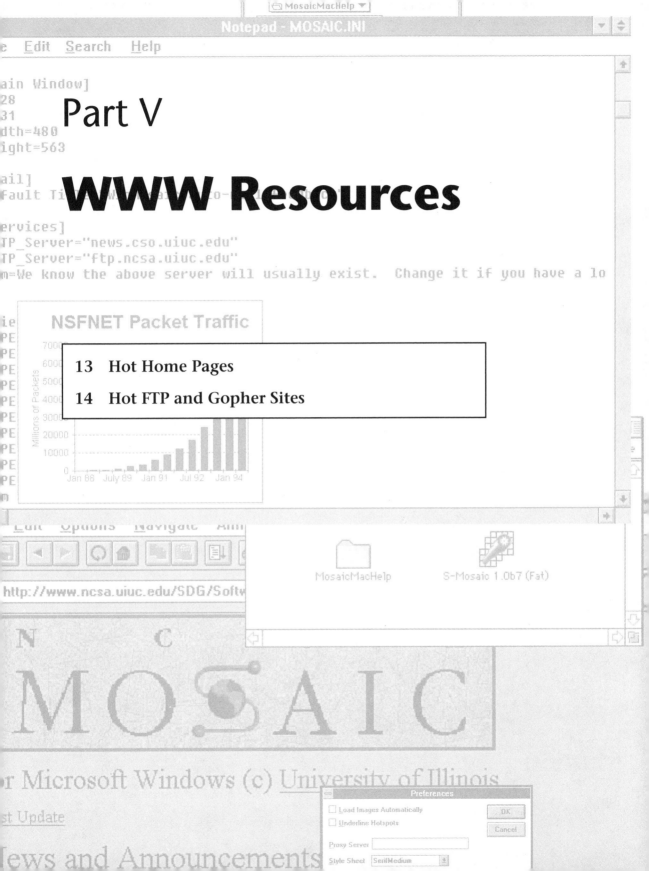

Part V

WWW Resources

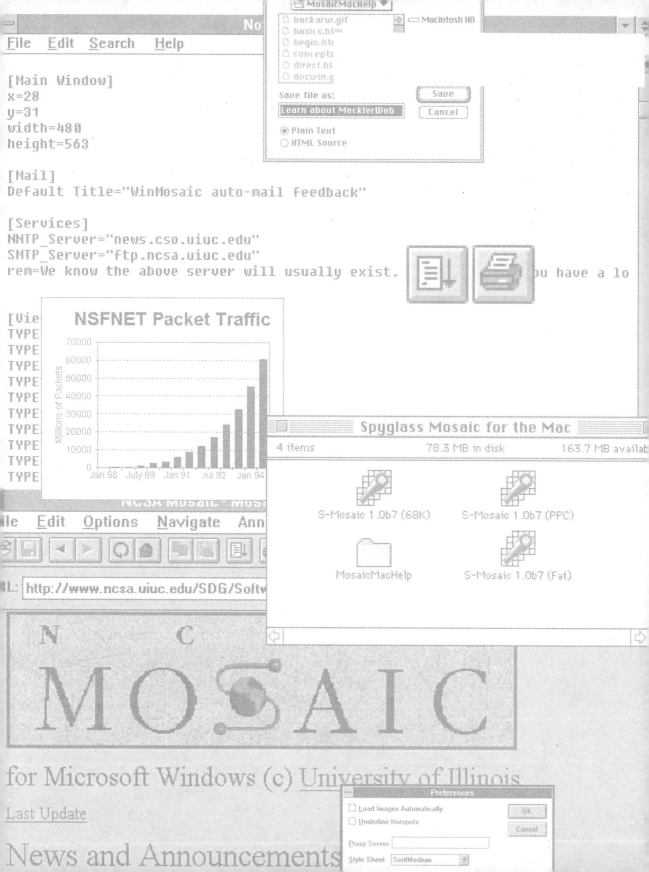

File   Edit   Search   Help

No...

```
[Main Window]
x=28
y=31
width=480
height=563

[Mail]
Default Title="WinMosaic auto-mail feedback"

[Services]
NNTP_Server="news.cso.uiuc.edu"
SMTP_Server="ftp.ncsa.uiuc.edu"
rem=We know the above server will usually exist.         ou have a lo

[Vie
TYPE
TYPE
TYPE
TYPE
TYPE
TYPE
TYPE
TYPE
TYPE
TYPE
```

MosaicMacHelp ▼

□ backarw.gif
□ basics.htm
□ begin.htm
□ concepts
□ direct.ht
□ docwin.g

⊂ Macintosh HD

Save file as:
Learn about MecklerWeb

Save
Cancel

◉ Plain Text
○ HTML Source

NSFNET Packet Traffic

70000
60000
50000
40000
30000
20000
10000
0

Millions of Packets

Jan 88   July 89   Jan 91   Jul 92   Jan 94

Spyglass Mosaic for the Mac

4 items   78.3 MB in disk   163.7 MB availab

S-Mosaic 1.0b7 (68K)   S-Mosaic 1.0b7 (PPC)

MosaicMacHelp   S-Mosaic 1.0b7 (Fat)

NCSA Mosaic - Mos...

ile   Edit   Options   Navigate   Ann

RL: http://www.ncsa.uiuc.edu/SDG/Softw

N   C
MOSAIC

for Microsoft Windows (c) University of Illinois

Last Update

News and Announcements

Preferences

☐ Load Images Automatically   OK
☐ Underline Hotspots

Cancel

Proxy Server

Style Sheet SerifMedium

Chapter 13

Hot Home Pages

Now that you know how to use Mosaic, you are probably wondering what's out there on the Web. You may have a particular interest that you want to satisfy by using the Web. The good news is that with the explosive growth that the Web has undergone, you can find Web pages on almost every topic imaginable.

The bad news is that it isn't easy to find the pages you want when you need them. You can use a Web search page (as described in chapter 6, "Shortcuts to Favorite Places") but this may or may not help you find what you need.

Another way to find something on the Web is to let someone else find it for you. That's what we've done in this chapter. We have scoured the Web and found the best, most interesting, most useful sites on the Web and categorized them for you.

While this will be more than enough sites to keep you busy, it is only a start. If you have a special interest that isn't in this listing, take a look at Que's *Using the World Wide Web*. That book lists and describes approximately 2,000 Web sites by category. The sites in this chapter are a sample of that book's listings.

Entertainment and the Arts

Cardiff's Movie Database

URL address: **http://www.msstate.edu/Movies**

Have you ever watched a movie and couldn't remember the name of the actress or actor who had a certain part? Or placed a bet with a friend that you could name the entire cast of *The Maltese Falcon*? Or wondered how many movies Henry Fonda and Paul Newman were in together? If you've ever had questions about a movie regarding plot, characters, actors, actresses, directors, writers, or anything else, this is the home page for you!

Fig. 13.1

You can search Cardiff's WWW Movie Database to find out about films and the people who played a role (acting, writing, and directing) in each movie.

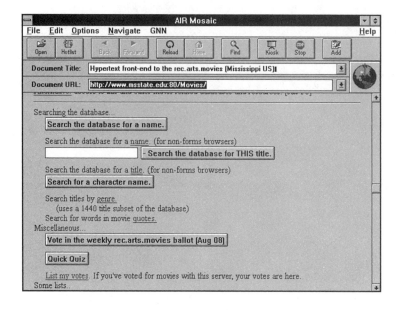

A hypertext front-end to the **rec.arts.movies** newsgroup database, this is a wonderful example of interactive information. The home page provides you with a variety of search boxes where you can enter names of characters, actors, or movie titles to begin your search. The information is vast. The database contains more than 85,000 listings of actors and actresses, some 34,835 titles (including TV series), and 1,500 plot summaries.

As an example of how this works, enter the last name HOLDEN for a name search. This query delivers a list of approximately 35 Holdens (Amy Holden Jones, the writer; David Holden, the writer; Gloria Holden, the actress, and William Holden, the actor). Now click on William Holden to get a list of some 72 films he acted in. You didn't know he was a character in the 1967 film *Casino Royale*? Click on this film name and you get a description of the film that tells you it was a James Bond spoof originally written by Ian Fleming, and that many other actors and actresses, including Woody Allen, were in the film.

EXPO Ticket Office

URL address: **http://sunsite.unc.edu/expo/ticket_office.html**

This is a WWW must-visit! The home page refers to the EXPO Ticket Office as "the world's most exciting electronic exposition." This isn't far off. From the home page, you can jump onto one of six guided tour buses that take you to one of the six EXPO pavilions (buses leave every few microseconds). Selections include:

The Vatican Exhibit—with precious maps, books, and manuscripts.
Soviet Archive—the first public display of secret Russian records.
1492: An On-Going Voyage—examines the events that settled the "new world."
Dead Sea Scrolls—describes the history and discovery of these artifacts.
Paleontology Exhibit—fossil life from the University of California, Berkeley.
Spalato Exhibit—the history and architecture of this Roman village.

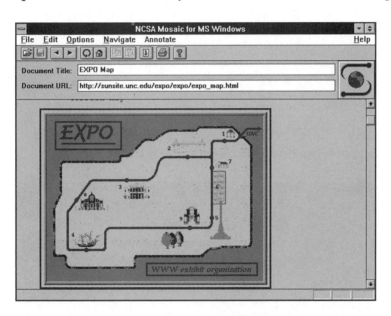

Fig. 13.2
Jump on board an interactive bus tour and visit six interesting pavilions at the EXPO Ticket Office.

Most of the information and multimedia exhibits have been donated by the Library of Congress. What makes this Web resource unique is the interactive manner in which you move through information. As you move through one of the pavilions, a little icon of footsteps appears to help guide your journey. From the home page, you can jump to an almost three-dimensional map that shows the location of the pavilions and includes an audio clip. There is even an EXPO restaurant, Le Cordon Bleu, for the weary traveler. Every day of the week there is a different menu; Wednesday's special is split pea soup with bacon, sorrel, and lettuce. Inline GIF images display your electronic lunch. Have fun!

Traditional Folk Song Database

URL address: **http://web2.xerox.com/digitrad**

This server provides a searchable index of the Digital Traditional Folk Song database. The database contains the lyrics and music for thousands of folk songs, many very esoteric. Some even include audio sample files that you can play back. Dick Greenhaus and his friends are credited with developing this collection.

To find a song, perform a keyword search. Search results bring up a list of songs that either contain or relate to your search word. You click a song name to retrieve the lyrics. A search using the word "Russian" delivers "It's Sister Jenny's Turn To Throw the Bomb," while a search for the keyword "Spring" produces four songs: "Birds In the Spring," "So Early In the Spring," "Flower Carol," and "Spring Glee." This is a fun and extensive resource—try it out!

The Online Museum of Singapore Art & History

URL address: **http://king.ncb.gov.sg/nhb/museum.html**

Fig. 13.3
Travel around the world, and back in time when you download images from this on-line collection of historical artwork from the Museum of Singapore.

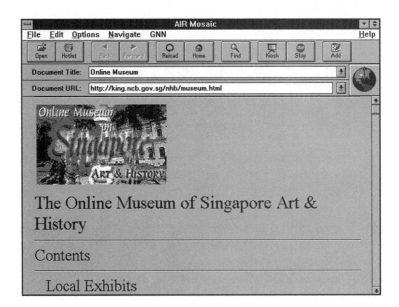

Art history offers a unique opportunity to appreciate artistic endeavors from another era and a chance to learn about society and life at a particular point in time. The Online Museum of Singapore Art History lets you explore paintings and documents by early Singaporean artists. One of the exhibitions is a collection of 19th-century prints of Singapore. When you click on the title for a print, a picture of the artwork appears along with a description of the piece and an overview of the artist. This particular exhibition is quite interesting because many of the prints show you images of Singapore in the early 1800s—so not only do you get to travel halfway around the world to view the artwork, you also travel back in time.

For example, when you select "Plate 5: View from the Mouth of the Singapore River, 1830," you get a wonderful image that shows a view of Singapore from the mouth of the river. You can "look" upstream and see where European merchants used warehouses for their products. View and save the pictures as JPEG files—even start your own personal museum of images on your PC. You can also learn about the artists, engravers, and specific details about each print, such as their size (this one was 31.5 x 23 cm) and where they are currently stored or displayed. Other choices from the main menu include:

> **Pioneer Artists**—Early Singapore artists
> **Raffles Revisited**—A history of the founder of Singapore
> **Ponts des Art**—Explores the influence on area artists who studied in France
> **From Ritual to Romance**—An exhibition of paintings inspired by Bali

Star Trek: The Next Generation

URL address: **http://www.ee.surrey.ac.uk/Personal/STTNG/index.html**

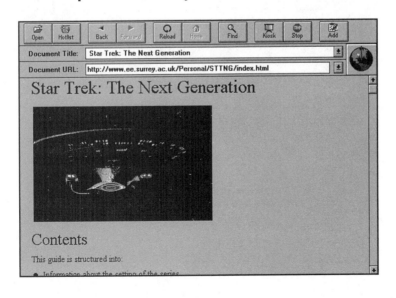

Fig. 13.4
Connect with this Star Trek Web site to find out whether Klingons really like humans.

V

WWW Resources

It is the year 2364 and the phrase, "Beam Me Up" transmits across the galaxy. This WWW server is located in the UK, where, despite its non prime-time slot, ST:TNG (the abbreviation for *Star Trek: The Next Generation*) often came in as one of the top 10 rated shows for BBC2, sometimes the highest rated show on the channel. The home page has so many links you won't have time to visit the Holosuite. There is information about the cast, guest roles, descriptions of all major alien species (even the nasty Borgs), episode summaries, and movie rumors. A trivia section will keep you busy with facts like Professor Steven Hawking (the famous physicist) is the only person to ever appear "as himself" in the show. Here is one example of an episode summary:

"Peak Performance"

"A simulated war game turns deadly when the crew is ambushed by a Ferengi battleship. With the Enterprise crippled in the attack, Picard must try to get Riker, Geordi, and the others back on board."

Business

CommerceNet

URL address: **http://www.commerce.net**

Fig. 13.5
The CommerceNet Home page. Additional information can be accessed by clicking inside one of the boxes.

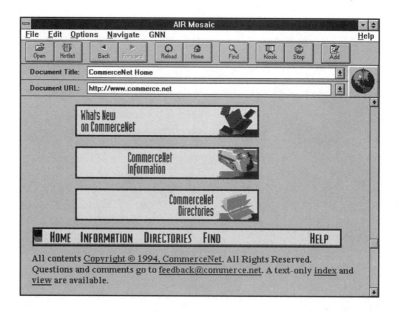

From marketing and selling products to transmitting electronic orders and payments, Silicon Valley-based CommerceNet focuses on the business applications of the WWW. Many of the world's largest companies, including Intel, Apple, Lockheed, Bank of America, and Dun & Bradstreet, have joined the initial phase of CommerceNet to create a virtual storefront. Any size business, from an individual's home business to a multinational corporation, can join CommerceNet to promote their products and services. From the CommerceNet home page you can jump to a directory of all the companies involved with CommerceNet. If these companies operate Web servers, you can jump directly to them. When CommerceNet is complete, you will be able to get detailed product information, do on-line price comparisons, and conduct financial transactions electronically.

Half the initial funding for CommerceNet comes from a Federal grant made under the government's "Technology Reinvestment Program" (TRP), which is sponsored by the Defense Department's Advanced Research Projects Agency (ARPA), the National Institute of Standards and Technology (NIST), the National Science Foundation (NSF), and other government agencies. Matching funds come from the State of California and participating companies.

CommerceNet's goal is to make public computer networks such as the Internet "industrial strength" for business use. CommerceNet will address issues including low-cost, high-speed Internet access using newly deployed technology such as Integrated Services Digital Network (ISDN) services and multimedia software. CommerceNet will support a range of commercial network applications such as on-line catalogs, product data exchange, and engineering collaboration. It will also offer outreach services such as technical assistance to small- and medium-size businesses that want to access public networks. CommerceNet is currently testing a system that uses public key cryptography and a version of Mosaic known as Secure Mosaic (**http:// south.ncsa.uiuc.edu/security.html**) to ensure the security of financial transactions over the vast Internet. Initially, CommerceNet will serve the needs of businesses and customers in California, but service is expected to extend around the world in less than two years.

The CommerceNet consortium is sponsored by Smart Valley, Inc., a non-profit organization chartered to create a regional electronic community, and the State of California's Trade and Commerce Agency. Enterprise Integration Technologies, a company that specializes in electronic commerce, is leading the effort. If you want to become an on-line vendor on CommerceNet, you can either place informational pages on-line at the CommerceNet server, or set up a private WWW server and connect it to the CommerceNet. Subscribers who pay an annual fee receive training and are listed in CommerceNet's

V

WWW Resources

vendor directory—a logo or listing connects to your server. Sponsors who pay a larger annual fee receive advanced training classes and the opportunity to participate in the governance of the network.

(For more information on CommerceNet, send e-mail to **info@commerce.net**.)

Hong Kong WWW Server

URL address: **http://www.hk.super.net/~rlowe/bizhk/bhhome.html**

Fig. 13.6
On this home page, use the scroll bar to view additional information about doing business in Hong Kong.

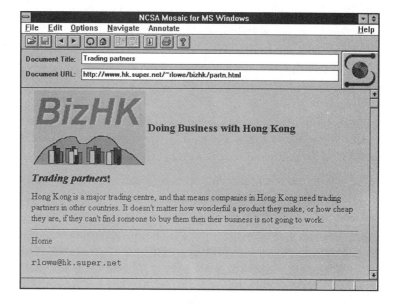

This server offers a wealth of information about doing business with Hong Kong, which, as many business people know, is a leading manufacturing and financial center, and a gateway to doing business with China. A link to BizHK provides a trade contacts service. This home page matches Hong Kong businesses with potential trading partners worldwide. More information is available by sending e-mail to **rlowe@hk.super.net**.

Via this server, you can access a database of more than 1,000 companies in Hong Kong. You can click alphabetically through the database and find company contacts, financial data, product information, addresses, and phone numbers. Special sections focus on two major areas for business opportunities: the Hotel, Tourism, and Travel industry, and Textiles, Fabrics, and Clothing. The home page also has links to economic statistics that relate to Hong Kong, and press releases about business trade, such as an overview of the imports and exports between Hong Kong and the United Kingdom.

The World Bank

URL address: **http://www.worldbank.org**

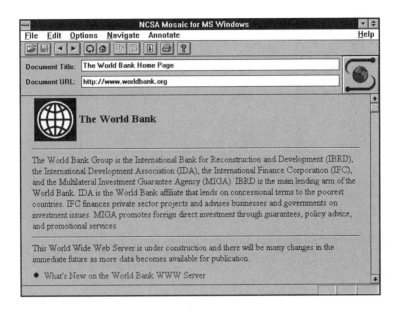

Fig. 13.7
The World Bank
home page.

If you need to find out what is going on in international finance, or trends in the economies of specific countries, this is the Web server for you! The World Bank Group consists of

- *The International Bank for Reconstruction and Development (IBRD).* The primary lending arm of the World Bank.

- *The International Development Association (IDA).* The World Bank affiliate that lends funds on concessional terms to poor countries.

- *The International Finance Corporation (IFC).* Finances private sector projects and advises businesses and governments on investment issues.

- *The Multilateral Investment Guarantee Agency (MIGA).* Promotes foreign direct investment through guarantees, policy advice, and promotional services.

You can jump from the home page to two areas that contain a wealth of information on the financial status, economic development projects, and social and environmental conditions in countries around the world. Some of the available information is found in books, articles, and documents in the World Bank Publications section (many of which are for sale). A second area, the World Bank Public Information Center (PIC), maintains a variety of economic reports and environmental data sheets. You can view these reports online or download and print one copy. The World Bank maintains copyright on all information. Here are a few examples of these reports:

- Privatization and adjustment—Bangladesh

- Public finance reforms in the transition—Bulgaria

- Policies for private sector development—Caribbean countries

- Environment and development: challenges for the future—Indonesia

- Nutrition and national development: issues and options—Morocco

- Social protection during transition and beyond—Russia

EINet Galaxy

URL address: **http://galaxy.einet.net/galaxy.html**

This is a guide to world-wide information and services. It includes public as well as commercial information and services provided by EINet customers and affiliates.

Fig. 13.8

A peek at some of the many sites you can access via EINet Galaxy's home page.

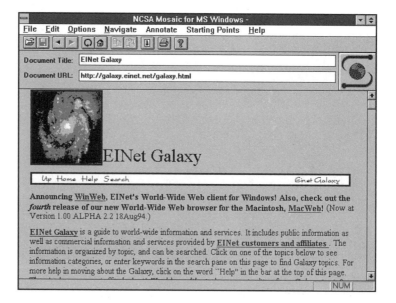

The site provides an overview of the latest release of WinWeb, a World Wide Web browser for Microsoft Windows, along with downloading instructions.

Similar information is provided for MacWeb, a Web browser for Macintosh computers.

EINet Galaxy's most exciting feature from an information-access point of view, is its generous collection of links to home pages on a variety of topics.

The Business General Resources link takes you to a range of business-related sites, including the Koblas Currency Converter, a comparative chart of currency values that is updated every week.

Canadian Airlines International Ltd.

URL address: **http://www.CdnAir.CA**

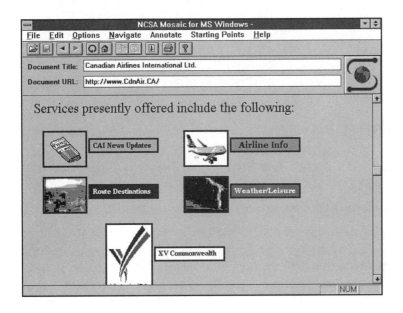

Fig. 13.9
This home page provides information about Canadian Airlines.

This home page provides service and information about "Canada's premier customer-driven airline." Buttons point to the services presently offered via the home page. These include the ability to query flight arrival and departure databases and to obtain pricing information. News updates as well as weather and leisure information for the traveler are also provided. As shown in the figure, the site also includes clickable route maps of the airline's service areas. Although this site is as yet incomplete, it has the potential to be a very useful and user-friendly information repository.

Fig. 13.10
Click on the
Weather/Leisure
icon to get this
information.

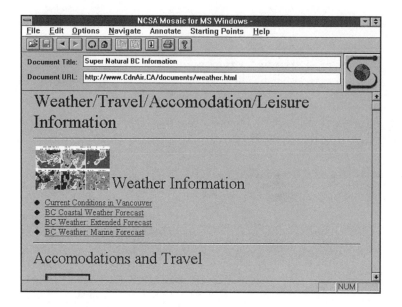

Computing

National Center for Supercomputing Applications (NCSA)

URL address: **http://www.ncsa.uiuc.edu/demoweb/demo.html**

If you want to learn more about the Mosaic WWW browser, update your
version of the software, or simply explore interesting Web links, then travel
to the server at the National Center for Supercomputing Applications
(NCSA)—the same organization that gave birth to Mosaic. This home page
provides a fantastic demonstration of the multimedia capabilities of Mosaic
and the Web. The page begins with an overview of the history of Mosaic,
complete with audio messages. There is a brief explanation of hypermedia,
complete with a picture of Vice President Al Gore. The home page also has
more than 100 links (with short descriptions) to Web sites around the world.

You can also jump to the NCSA Mosaic home page (URL address **http://
www.ncsa.uiuc.edu/SDG/Software/Mosaic/
NCSAMosaicHome.html**), which has links that focus on information resources specific to Mosaic. You can find out about the latest developments
and features of this browser, such as a version that will ensure security of
financial transactions via the Internet.

Another useful link from the home page is to the NCSA "What's New" page. This page offers a chronological listing of new WWW resources. The listings start with the week that you connect, and date back about three weeks. Each listing includes a brief description, and the name of the resource is a hyperlink to that Web server. Here are two examples:

> "The office of USA Vice President, Al Gore, announces *FinanceNet*, providing access to financial management documents and information pertaining to all levels of government: foreign, Federal, state and local."

> "The World's Greatest Rock 'n Roll Band is proud to announce their very own Web Server. They are the *Rolling Stones* and they are now giving you the best place in netland for the real Stones fan to hang out."

In both instances the highlighted text (shown here in italics) represents a link. If these descriptions have peaked your interest, the FinanceNet address is **http://www.financenet.gov**, and you can find the Rolling Stones at **http://www.stones.com/**.

Apple Computers, Inc.

URL address: **http://www.apple.com**

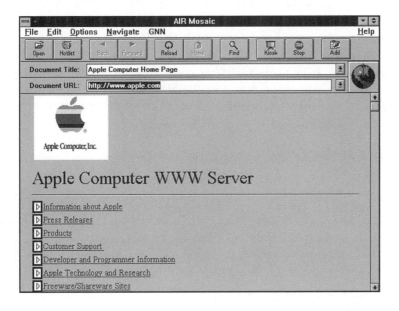

Fig. 13.11
Visit this home page if you use an Apple Computer product or service.

V

WWW Resources

Apple Computers continue to develop unique, computer-based products and services. The Apple Newton is a hand-held personal digital assistant (PDA) that manages information and can be used to send electronic mail messages to and from remote locations. The Power PC is a high-speed computer that uses both Macintosh and IBM-compatible files and programs, and E-World is a commercial on-line service similar to CompuServe or America Online.

Perhaps you need to learn how to expand your 4MB PowerBook 150 to 8MB RAM, or you'd like to participate in a local Apple User Group. You can learn about these products and services when you connect to the Apple WWW home page. The main menu offers the following selections:

> Information about Apple
> Press releases
> Products
> Customer support
> Developer and programmer information
> Apple technology and research
> Freeware/shareware sites
> User groups
> Internet resources sponsored by Apple

About 50 percent of these links open hypertext documents that contain other links and informational documents. The other half connect to Gopher menus where you navigate through easy-to-understand subdirectories to get the information you need. The Freeware/shareware sites link offers a list of non-Apple places where you can get free advice and software applications for many different Apple products. Examples include the University of Michigan (**ftp://mac.archive.umich.edu/mac/**); Washington University (**http://www.uwtc.washington.edu/JonWiederspan/MacSupportOnInternet.html**); and the University of Iowa (**ftp://newton.uiowa.edu/pub/ Newton Software**).

Do It Yourself—PC Lube and Tune

URL address: **http://pclt.cis.yale.edu/pclt/default.htm**

The PC Lube and Tune (PCLT) home page represents the ultimate in electronic "self-service"—first you learn about a subject, and then you apply that knowledge to suit your needs. PCLT supplies introductions, tutorials, directions, and education on technical subjects for ordinary computer users through hypertext articles. Examples of a few of the articles include:

> Introduction to PC Hardware
> Introduction to SNA
> Introduction to TCP/IP
> PC Serial Communications

"Windows on the World" (a project to add Internet software to Windows and OS/2)

InterNIC Provides WWW On-Line Guide

URL address: **http://www.internic.net**

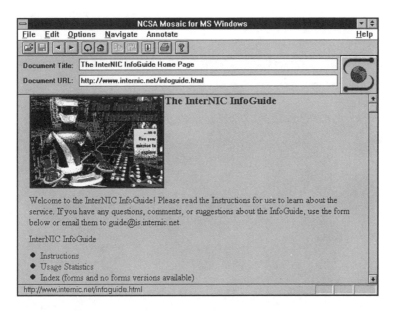

If you could only visit one WWW server for information about the Internet, this would be the place to go. The Internet Network Information Center, known simply as InterNIC, was established in January of 1993 by the National Science Foundation and went into operation on April 1, 1993. The InterNIC is a collaborative effort of three organizations that work together to offer a variety of services, which include providing information about how to access and use the Internet, assistance in locating resources, and registering network components for Internet connectivity. The goal of InterNIC is to make network-based information accessible to researchers, educators, and the general public. The term "InterNIC" comes from the cooperative effort between Network Information Centers, or NICs.

From the InterNIC home page, you can access Information Services, provided by General Atomics; Directory and Database Services, provided by AT&T; and Registration Services, provided by Network Solutions, Inc. The Information Services InfoGuide (**http://internic.net/infoguide.html**) is an on-line source of information about the Internet, offering pointers to on-line resources, Internet organizations, access providers, usage statistics, basic and advanced user guides, and a hypertext version of the National Science Foundation Network News. There is a simple electronic index, similar to a library card catalog system, where you select an index based on subject, title, and author, then follow hyptertext links to specific documents, images, sounds, or video. Another source of on-line information are Scout Reports, weekly reports that keep users aware of current network activities and offer reviews of new WWW and Internet resources. The reports contain hyperlinks to the resources mentioned.

ISDN—High Speed On-Ramp to the Digital Highway

URL address: **http://www.pacbell.com/isdn/isdn_home.html**

Fig. 13.13
The Pacific Bell home page provides an overview of Integrated Services Digital Network for both beginners and advanced computer users.

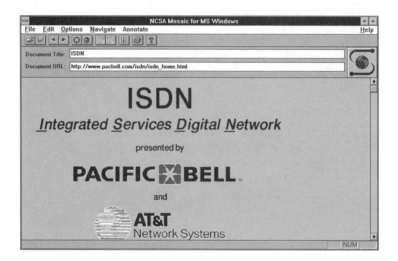

Pacific Bell and AT&T Network Systems present information on ISDN, Integrated Services Digital Network. ISDN is a high-speed, digital telephone service delivered to businesses and homes over standard copper telephone wires. ISDN offers usage-based pricing, is easy-to-use, and provides high speed data service with voice capability. You can access inline graphics that illustrate how you can use ISDN for Internet access, telecommuting, and video conferencing. Links included in this home page include:

ISDN overview
How to order ISDN to learn more
Receive FREE ISDN e-mail updates
ISDN for Internet access
ISDN for video conferencing
ISDN for telecommuting

Pacific Bell ISDN service options and rates

ISDN-related products and services

Try Cutting-Edge Computer Applications at MIT

URL address: **http://tns-www.lcs.mit.edu/tns-www-home.html**

Fig. 13.14
MIT's Telemedia, Networks, and Systems Group WWW server lets you try some of the cutting-edge applications of computer-network multimedia.

The MIT Laboratory for Computer Science is an inter-department laboratory that focuses on research in computer science and engineering. The Telemedia, Networks, and Systems Group (TNS) is a research group at the MIT Laboratory for Computer Science. The group studies topics in distributed multimedia systems—the hardware, software, and networks that enable multimedia information to travel to computers.

The TNS home page offers hyperlinks that help you navigate the world of computers and computing. For example, you can jump to the WWW Index to Multimedia Information Sources. Another interesting link is to *The National Information Infrastructure: Agenda for Action,* where you can hear a speech by Secretary Brown on the topic of The National Information Infrastructure, and view clips of the video "Toward a National Information Infrastructure."

Novell Inc. World Wide Web Homepage

URL address: **http://www.novell.com**

Novell's home page makes good use of the WWW's graphic capability. It is just a system designed to help answer questions you have about Novell or its products. The categories, which include technical support databases, searchable FTP and Gopher archives, an on-line product buyer's guide, and linkage to the Novell European Support Center, are represented by a row of books resting on a bookshelf.

Fig. 13.15
Novell's novel home page, which uses a bookshelf metaphor to point to different categories of information.

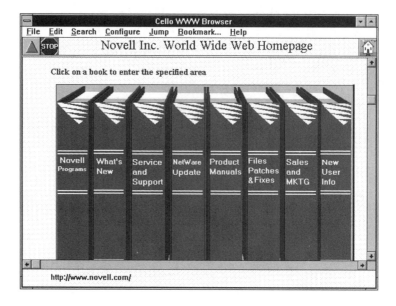

The book metaphor doesn't carry through smoothly to all the links at the site. In fact, most of the links are to plain text files or Gopher servers. But the page demonstrates how navigation of Internet hypertext files can be facilitated when familiar metaphors and motifs are used.

Education

The Teacher Education Internet Server

URL address: **http://curry.edschool.virginia.edu/teis**

This Web site proves that you're never too old to learn. It represents a combined effort between the Society for Technology and Teacher Education, the University of Virginia, and the University of Houston. The entire focus of its resources is the exploration of ways in which the Internet/WWW can benefit global teacher education programs. The home page includes a graphic picture of a schoolroom. The icons in the picture link to the resources. For example, a microscope links to science information, a bookshelf links to reading resources, and the telephone on the wall links to telecom and networking information. If you don't have graphics capability or have difficulty with the image links, there are four hypertext links just beneath the image. These, in turn, open a world of educational resources. The Whole TEIS Gopher opens doors to electronic publications like the Journal of Technology and Teacher Education; and Interface, an IBM teacher preparation grant school newsletter; as well as documents for subjects that range from social studies to international education. Other home page links include Special Ed, Math Education, and Reading, and Language Arts.

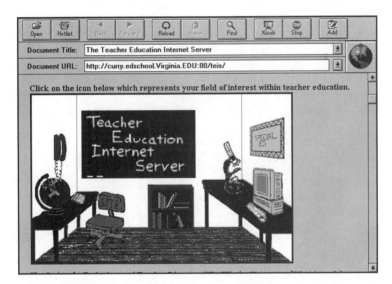

Fig. 13.16
Explore the Web's educational resources as you click your way through a hypermedia image of a classroom.

V

WWW Resources

DeweyWeb

URL address: **http://ics.soe.umich.edu**

This Web server is a Sun Sparcstation 2 located at the University of Michigan School of Education. It is an experiment that uses the WWW to facilitate communication between students and classrooms around the world. Links from the home page include the following highlighted items.

■ *The ICS World Forum.* The ICS (Interactive Communications Simulations) World Forum is a computer-mediated conference in which 30 schools follow the adventures of the International Arctic Project, where explorers train for an expedition across the Arctic. The project helps students analyze challenges from different perspectives as they role-play characters from many walks of life. Ghandi, William Bennett, Rachel Carson, and Pope John Paul II are some of the individuals who have "attended" the World Forum.

■ *DeweyWeb and the Journey North.* The DeweyWeb was inspired by the work of the University of Michigan ICS and the Indiana University World School for Adventure Learning. These projects attempt to expand the classroom experience with reports from scientists and explorers, as well as linking distant schools together through telecommunications. The information in the DeweyWeb experiment is closely aligned to the World School's activities, and is therefore called "The Journey North." When you go to the Journey North, you receive the news, issues, and opinions that surround the Arctic Adventure.

Fig. 13.17
Designed primarily for K–12 education, the DeweyWeb home page provides access to interactive exploration about global political and scientific exploration.

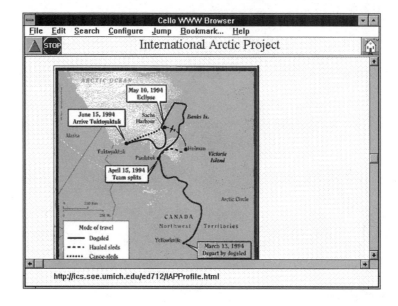

Between ICS and the World School, various telecommunications and networking technologies help serve and gather information from classrooms. DeweyWeb builds on this experience and delivers information that comes from scientists and explorers, and gives students an opportunity to contribute their own observations and discussions.

Indiana University

URL address: **http://www.indiana.edu**

Indiana University is a public university comprised of a residential campus in Bloomington, Indiana, a major urban campus in Indianapolis, and six other campuses located in Gary, South Bend, Fort Wayne, Kokomo, Richmond, and New Albany, Indiana. The University currently serves 94,000 students, employs nearly 17,000 faculty and staff, and has a budget in excess of $1 billion. It is one of the largest institutions of higher education in the United States.

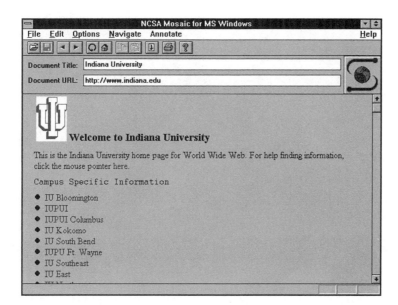

Fig. 13.18
Astronomy, law, music, and philosophy are a few of the departments you can connect to from the Indiana University home page.

Indiana University's WWW home page presents a variety of information about the degree programs and has links to each of the eight campuses. A good start, which gives you some idea of how large this institution really is, is the link to a list of Internet servers on all IU campuses. You'll find links here to the astronomy, computer science, law, music, philosophy, and numerous other departments and schools—even the Indiana University Press. But be warned, even though it's user friendly, you can get lost just like on a real university campus. Other resources include news, weather, address books, library and research services, and access to Telnet resources.

Geography—What Do Maps Show?

URL address:
http://info.er.usgs.gov/education/teacher/what-do-maps-show/index.html

If you've ever gotten lost, you know how important a good map can be. How do you read a map? What do map symbols represent? These are just a few of the topics and lesson plans that you can find on this Web site. The focus is information and resources for educators who teach upper elementary and junior high school classes; the goal is to teach students how to use and understand maps. In addition to links for step-by-step lesson plans, there are online posters and reproducible activity sheets.

Fig. 13.19
Good map reading skills last a lifetime. This WWW home page provides lessons and material that teach those skills.

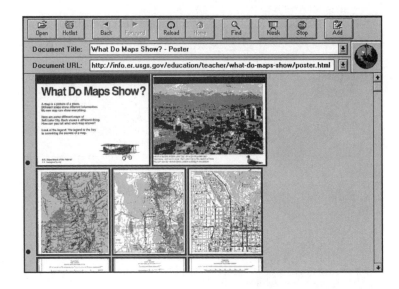

The on-line color poster is a wonderful resource. The poster shows several different views of Salt Lake City. There is an aerial photograph, a relief map, a road map, a topographical map, and a three-dimensional terrain map. You begin with small "thumbnail" images of these maps and click your way through to get ever larger images—final images can print as 8 1/2" x 11". Students will be able to learn the difference between these maps and understand how to read the legends and keys. From the home page you can jump to a list of USGS materials that is available for educational purposes. It's a great WWW application.

Patch American High School

URL address: **http://192.253.114.31/Home.html**

This WWW site really illustrates what a teacher with motivation, students with talent, and a diverse educational program can accomplish. The school is located at Patch Barracks, headquarters for the United States European Command (US EUCOM) in Vaihingen, a small section of Stuttgart, Germany, and serves dependent youth of American military and civilians stationed throughout 19 countries.

Students and faculty at Patch share some of their European experiences on the Web. Home page links include a picture of the school's mascot and a multimedia exhibition about the D-Day Normandy Invasion. Definitely check out the "What's New" section. One link brings up a multimedia presentation about the Maulbronn Abbey.

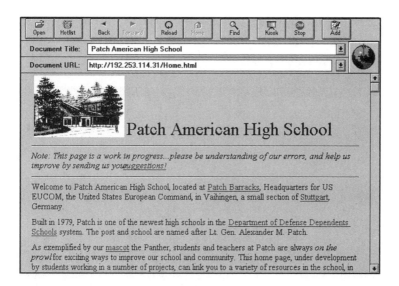

Fig. 13.20
This is the home page for a school that serves the dependent youth of American military and civilians in 19 countries. It offers a variety of educational resources that relate to European history and events.

Other home page links include:

- *Student Art Galleries*. Examine artwork by students.

- *The Arab-Israeli Conflict*. An interactive communications course.

- *Biology Department Zoo*. Jump to a breakdown of the living world that includes insects, reptiles, and birds. Be sure to check out the picture of Louise, a ten-year-old boa constrictor at the zoo.

- *Music*. The world band and recent concerts.

If you are a K–12 educator, this might be a good site to begin an interactive classroom project. The school's e-mail address is **WWW@patch-ahs.dsi.net**.

Government

FedWorld

URL address: **http://www.fedworld.gov**

Have you ever read a newspaper article or listened to a radio report that cites a government study or report? This WWW site is the place to go if you want to see that report for yourself. The National Technical Information Service maintains this home page to help people deal with the challenge of accessing the vast amount of U.S. Government information. How vast? NITS provides users access to over two million documents, studies, and databases, and adds about 1,300 titles each week. This WWW server is extremely popular and has been accessed more than a half million times.

Fig. 13.21
FedWorld represents a collection of hyperlinks to millions of government publications.

From the home page you have three main choices. First, you can go to the FedWorld FTP Site, which includes information on business, health, the environment, the White House, and the National Performance Review. Second, you can link to the FedWorld Telnet site, which has information on about 50 different agencies—you can order publications and learn about federal job opportunities. Third, you can click an alphabetical index that will help you locate and access specific federal WWW sites. Rather than displaying a long list of servers, the alphabetical section has subject categories, such as Environmental Resources, which then opens a menu of servers that focus on that topic. This is a good starting point to jump into the U.S. government.

Library of Congress

URL address: **http://lcweb.loc.gov/homepage/lchp.html**

If your local library doesn't have the book or resource you need, then take an electronic trip to the digital card catalogs and shelves at the Library of Congress WWW home page. Each week approximately 5,000 people log into this server. If you are looking for a specific book (by author, subject, or title) click on the icon that begins a Telnet session to LOCIS (**telnet://locis.loc.gov**), the Library of Congress Information System. The menu selections at LOCIS include:

1. Library of Congress Catalog

2. Federal Legislation

3. Copyright Information

4. Braille and Audio

5. Organizations

6. Foreign Law

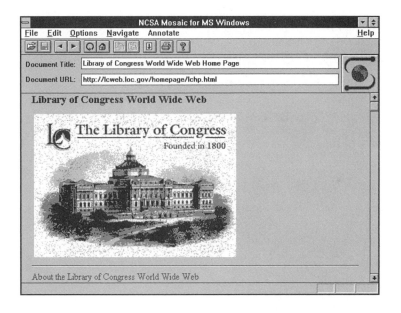

Fig. 13.22
The Library of Congress WWW home page is your gateway to the world's largest collection of information about published works.

To Search Use First Word	Examples
Subject	browse solar energy
Author	b faulkner, william
Title or series	browse megatrends
Partial LC call #	b call QA76.9
LC record #	loci 80-14332

The home page also sports links to some great exhibits and collections. The American Memory Project focuses on American culture and history, and catalogs numerous items and digital reproductions including prints and photographs. You weave your way through a few links into the collections page where you find photographs from the Civil War (1861-1865) by Matthew Brady; portraits of literary figures and artists by Carl Van Vechten (1932-1964); and color photographs from the Farm Security Administration (1938-1944).

Another home page link is the Country Studies. This represents a series of documents that examine the political, social, and economic conditions in countries around the world such as Ethiopia, Egypt, Philippines, and South Korea. If you are researching a project or paper, check out the Global Electronic Library that offers links to several WWW indexes and search tools.

State of North Carolina

URL address: **http://www.sips.state.nc.us/nchome.html**

Fig. 13.23
The North Carolina WWW home page lets you access a wonderful multimedia encyclopedia that offers information about the 400-year history of the state.

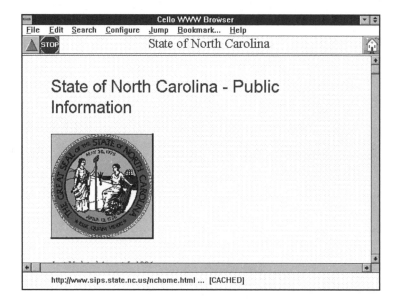

What do Sir Walter Raleigh and the Wright Brothers have in common? They both played an important role in the history of North Carolina. This state takes the bull by the horns when it comes to the Information Age. From the home page, go to the FAQ document, which does a good job of explaining how the state and state agencies are taking advantage of electronic communications. There is also a link to North Carolina and the Information Superhighway.

Several public agencies have contributed to the resources you can access from this home page. If you want to find out what elected representatives are doing, jump to the status of bills from the North Carolina General Assembly. Other home page links include:

>Center for Geographic Information and Analysis
>Division of Environmental Management
>Office of State Personnel Job Vacancies
>State Library
>Cooperative Extension Service
>Institute for Transportation Research and Education (ITRE)
>Research Triangle Institute (RTI)
>Weather In North Carolina

The State Library maintains an electronic multimedia guide to the Old North State—the North Carolina Encyclopedia. This fun and easy-to-use resource for adults and children combines text and visuals to give the reader a good understanding of the state's economy, educational and cultural assets, and the state's system of government. There are also overviews of the geography, the 100 counties, and the 400-year history of the state. It's a great tool for education, tourist promotion, and business information.

National Capital FreeNet (NCF)

URL address: **http://www.ncf.carleton.ca/**

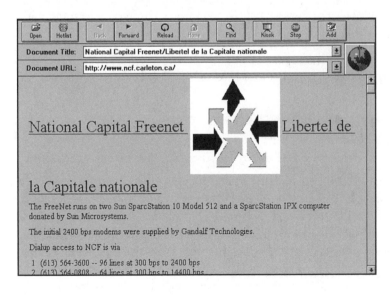

Fig. 13.24
Located on a Web server in Canada, the home page for the National Capital FreeNet has links to thousands of documents and resources for both the region and the country.

This URL address provides WWW access to the Ottawa, Canada FreeNet. The home page has a menu that offers five selections. The first and second choices are "Survival Guides" for new users (#1 is in English and #2 is in French). These selections bring up menus that provide advice on topics such as "Navigating Menus" and "Using the File System." Selection #3, NCF Information, jumps to the NCF FreeNet main menu, where you will find approximately 18 different service areas. There aren't a lot of fancy graphics here, but you could spend days going through all the links from this menu. A few examples include:

- **The Government Center.** Where you can weave your way to reports on Canadian national politics or to an organizational chart of the Ottawa police.

- **Professional Associations.** Find out about the Canadian Association of Journalists or other associations.

- **Schools, Colleges, and Universities.** Links range from Global Education to the Ottawa Board of Education.

- **Science, Engineering, and Technology Center.** Topics range from museums to women in engineering.

From the home page, menu item 4 brings you to the NCF message of the day, which is a list of new services and information resources. Finally, menu item 5 brings up a hypertext "GO" list. This is an alphabetical listing of all the special interest groups (SIGS) that offer information or news group messages via the NCF.

Health

Abdominal Training FAQ

URL address:
http://clix.aarnet.edu.au/misc.fitness/abdominal-training.html

If you want to keep your abdominal area in tip-top shape, or simply want to eliminate a "spare tire," this is the WWW address for you! Located at the University of Queensland, Australia, this series of Frequently Asked Questions is an introduction to the basic principles of training the abdominal area. The creation of this set of WWW documents was motivated by frequent questions on the topic in the newsgroup **misc.fitness**. You can also get this information via anonymous FTP from **rtfm.mit.edu** in (**ftp://rtfm.mit.edu/pub/usenet/misc.fitness/Abdominal_Training_FAQ**). The table of contents has links to individual documents that provide advice on common questions about mid-section exercise. These include:

Question 4: How do I exercise the abs?
Question 5: What's wrong with situps?
Question 6: What are good ab exercises?
Question 7: Is there a specific order I should do exercises in?

HealthNet

URL address: **http://debra.dgbt.doc.ca/~mike/healthnet**

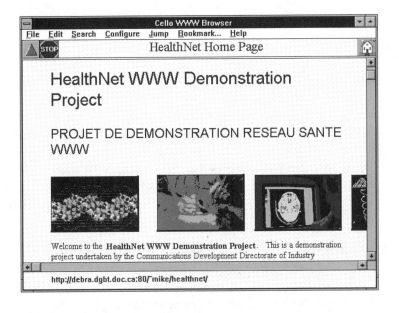

Fig. 13.25
The hyperlinks on the HealthNet home page bring you to government agencies and educational institutions around the world.

HealthNet should be one of the fist destinations in your exploration of health and medicine on the Web. Developed by the Communications Development Directorate of Industry Canada, the main goal of the project is to raise awareness about health-care applications for the Information Superhighway. HealthNet uses the WWW to educate health-care providers, governments, private groups, and any individuals who have an interest in health care and about what types of electronic health services are currently available and the future developments that may be feasible.

The HealthNet WWW Demonstration Project accomplishes this education in two ways. First, it provides a comprehensive set of hypertext links to medical and health-care resources currently available on the Internet/World Wide Web. Second, it provides an interactive hands-on resource for demonstrating future medical and health-care applications for the Information

Superhighway. HealthNet hyperlinks take you to the following categories of health-related information:

- Biotechnology initiatives and health-care human resource planning

- Clinical and administrative applications

- Government health-care sites

- Health-care applications for the electronic highway

- Hypertext list of Internet health-care resources and contact information

- Medical and health research applications

- Medical education and community health applications

The HealthNet WWW Demonstration Project is an international and collaborative effort. Available publicly via the Internet, it welcomes participation from anyone who wants to contribute ideas, materials, or comments. For updates on the HealthNet WWW Demo, or to keep up on other topics related to health-care networking in Canada, subscribe to the HealthNet listserv. Send a message to: **listserv@calvin.dgbt.doc.ca** with the message "subscribe healthnet and place your name" in the body of the text. You may want to review the procedures for sending electronic mail covered in chapter 1, "What is the Internet."

U. S. Department of Health and Human Services

URL address: **http://www.os.dhhs.gov**

Fig. 13.26
This Web server provides access to a vast amount of information that U.S. government agencies maintain on documents and programs related to health.

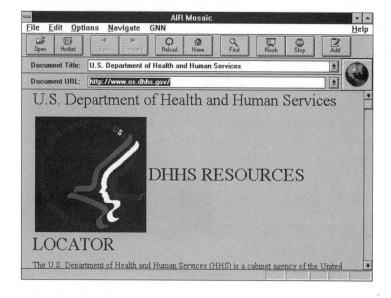

A cabinet agency of the United States Federal Government, the U.S. Department of Health and Human Services (HHS) focuses on programs that both maintain and improve the health and well-being of the nation's population. The agency emphasizes programs that help children, the elderly, persons with disabilities, and the poor. The department administers social security benefits, prevents and controls disease, deals with alcohol and drug abuse, conducts and supports medical and biomedical research, promotes child development, and assures the safety and efficacy of drugs. HHS administers nearly 300 grant programs that directly serve or assist one out of every five Americans.

The purpose of this WWW server is to provide information on the mission, programs, organization, initiatives, and activities of the U.S. Department of Health and Human Services. From the top of the home page you can jump to an alphabetized listing of specific programs that begin with "AIDS Related Information" and finish with "Social Security Statistics." There is also a link to the Catalog of Federal Domestic Assistance Programs (**http://www.sura.net/gsa.html**), which the General Services Administration maintains. From this server you can perform searches to locate information about financial and non-financial assistance programs. The HHS home page also provides links to information and resources made available by the various organizations that comprise HHS and other health-related agencies. Here are a few places you can jump to:

Health Organization	Internet/WWW address
Centers for Disease Control (CDC) FTP	**file://ftp.cdc.gov**
Food and Drug Administration (FDA) Telnet— "bbs"	**telnet://fdabbs.fda.gov**
National Center for Food Safety and Applied Nutrition (CFSAN)	**http://vm.cfsan.fda.gov/index.html**
National Center for Toxicological Research (NCTR) Gopher	**gopher://gopher.nctr.fda.gov**
National Institutes of Health (NIH)	**http://www.nih.gov**
National Institute of Allergy and Infectious Diseases (NIAID) Gopher	**gopher://gopher.niaid.nih.gov**
National Institute of Mental Health (NIMH) Gopher	**gopher://gopher.nimh.nih.gov**
National Institute of Environmental Health Sciences (NIEHS) Gopher	**gopher://gopher.niehs.nih.gov**
National Library of Medicine (NLM)	**http://www.nlm.nih.gov**

Palo Alto Medical Foundation

URL address: **http://www.service.com/PAMF/home.html**

A nonprofit organization, the Palo Alto Medical Foundation encompasses a research institute, and health-care and education divisions. At the facility approximately 160 physicians provide medical care for more than 110,000 people. Scientists conduct research in the areas of human health concerns, including immunology and infectious diseases, cholesterol metabolism, heart and cardiovascular dynamics, and cancer cell biology. Instructors in the health-care division teach classes in a wide variety of areas related to health promotion, including early diagnosis and prevention.

From the home page you can access the monthly publication HealthNews (**http://www.service.com/PAMF/healthnews/home.html**), which is published by the Palo Alto Medical Clinic/Health Care Division of the Palo Alto Medical Foundation for Health Care, Research and Education. There are also links to a community health calendar, and health education and support groups.

Rapid changes are occurring in the U.S. health-care system. The quality of care, rising costs, and benefits are some of the important issues that face individuals, companies, and medical providers. The hypertext link "The Symposium—Can Managed Care Heal America?" (**http://www.service.com/ PAMF/symposium.html**) brings you to documentation on this conference, a follow-up of five separate conferences that address the costs and administration of health care.

Stanford University Medical Center

URL address:
http://med-www.Stanford.EDU/MedCenter/welcome.html

The Stanford University Medical Center (SUMC) is internationally recognized for its outstanding achievements in teaching, research, and patient care. From the home page you can jump to a page of phone numbers for the departments in the Medical Center, and there are numerous links to other biomedical resources. You can also follow links to detailed information about the facilities and services of the following entities, which are part of SUMC.

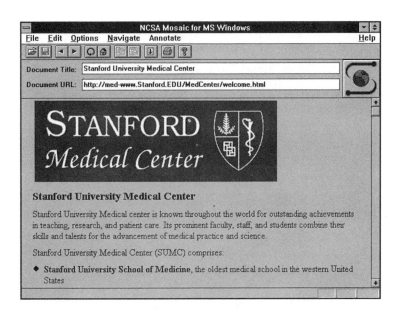

Fig. 13.27
When you jump to this home page you access the information resources of the oldest medical center in the Western United States.

V

WWW Resources

■ *Stanford University School of Medicine (SUSM)*

Through its educational programs, SUSM conducts extensive research in many areas of medicine.

■ *Stanford University Clinic*

The Stanford University Clinic is made up of more than 100 outpatient clinics where members of the medical school faculty focus their activities in medical practice and medical education.

■ *Stanford University Hospital*

The Stanford University Hospital is a university owned, nonprofit organization that provides acute and tertiary care to local, national, and international patients.

■ *Lucile Salter Packard Children's Hospital at Stanford*

Lucile Salter Packard Children's Hospital is an independent, nonprofit pediatric teaching hospital that provides acute and tertiary care exclusively for children.

History and Geography

Scrolls from the Dead Sea

URL address:

http://sunsite.unc.edu/expo/deadsea.scrolls.exhibit/intro.html

Fig. 13.28
Scientists and archeologists unravel the mysteries of the Dead Sea Scrolls—find out how when you visit this interactive exhibit.

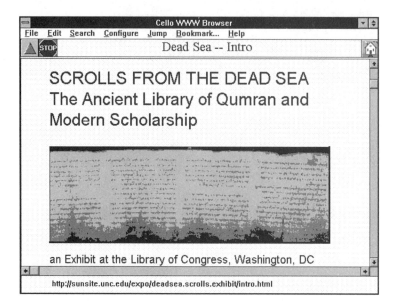

The Ancient Library of Qumran and Modern Scholarship sponsors this exhibit. The physical exhibit is located at the Library of Congress in Washington, D.C.—the WWW server is at the University of North Carolina. There are many questions about these mysterious scrolls. Are they indeed authentic? Who were the people who wrote and then carefully hid them? What was the world like when they were written?

This interactive, multimedia exhibit describes the historical context of the scrolls and the Qumran community where they may have been produced. You can read about and relive the story of their discovery—2,000 years after they were hidden. The exhibit encourages viewers to learn about the challenges and activities of archeology and scroll research.

United States Geological Survey (USGS)

URL address: **http://info.er.usgs.gov**

This site uses the multimedia aspects of the Web as a powerful tool for education and exploration. Everywhere you turn there is another clickable image, icon, map, or link. The home page opens with a short introduction that tells you the USGS was established by an act of Congress in 1879 as an agency of the Department of the Interior.

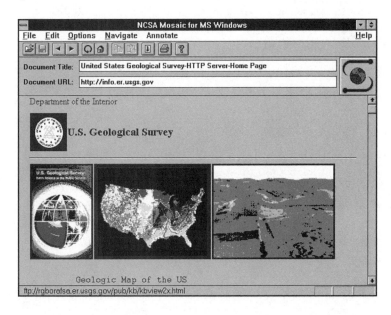

Fig. 13.29
This WWW home site will give you a new perspective on land and natural resources in the United States.

Three large inline images are on the screen—a color picture of a USGS brochure, a color map of the United States that indicates geological contours, and a picture of a mountainscape. Each of these images is a clickable link to other resources. The brochure links to:

National Earth Science Issues
Overview of USGS Services and Activities
Fact Sheets

The color map brings you to Online Files for USA Geology, where you can either view a large image of USA Geology or connect to and download ARC information files. The final image, the mountainscape, loads a digital MPEG movie. Some of the other areas you can visit include:

■ The USGS library system, the largest earth-science library in the world. Find out what individual collections offer (including maps).

■ A list of publications and fact sheets, such as Geology and Human Activity in the Florida Keys or the International Strategic Minerals Inventory report series. Many of these publications are free or have a small fee—you'll learn how to get them.

- The Digital Data Series provides information about USGS electronic data such as a geologic map of the sea floor of the Western Massachusetts Bay constructed from digital sonar images, photographs, and sediment samples. These data sources are available as CD-ROMs.

- Employment opportunities with the USGS

World Map—Xerox PARC Map Viewer

URL address: **http://pubweb.parc.xerox.com/map**

Sponsored by Xerox PARC, this hypermedia world map viewer is custom-made for the WWW. The home page presents a global map. Position your mouse on a section of the map and click. You will zoom in by a factor of two; but don't stop, total zoom-in/zoom-out parameters let you go up to a factor of 25. Utility features allow you to show country borders and rivers. The project was initially created in June of 1993 and improvements are constantly being made. Technically, links imbedded in the HTML (hypertext markup language) map are controls that change the map rendering. As a result, you can pan or zoom into an area of the map.

Fig, 13.30
Zoom and pan around the world with this interactive global map.

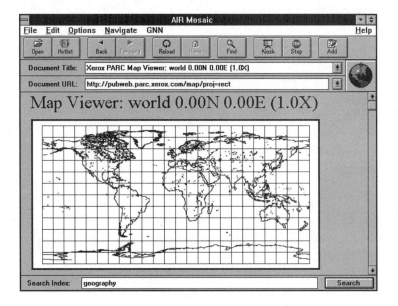

International

Gateway to Antarctica

URL address: **http://icair.iac.org.nz/**

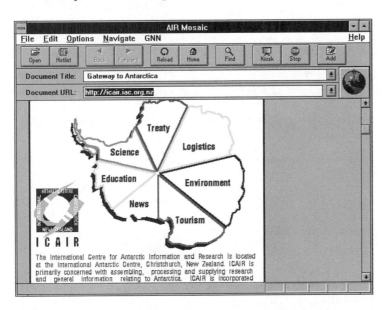

Fig. 13.31
Did you know that less than five percent of Antarctica's land is without permanent ice or snow? This is one of the many interesting facts you'll learn when you visit Gateway to Antarctica.

V

WWW Resources

Covered by 90 percent of the world's ice, which has an average thickness of about 2,000 meters, most people consider the continent of Antarctica to be a cold and mysterious place. Now, thanks to sponsorship by the National Science Foundation, you can visit the South Pole without getting frostbite. This WWW server links you with interesting information about the geological history of the continent, the impact that Antarctica has on the world's environment, opportunities to travel to the continent (physically), and Antarctica gifts.

You will learn that the climate for most of Antarctica is that of a cold desert. In the region of the South Pole, about seven centimeters of snow accumulates annually and it has an annual mean temperature of -49°C. As the ice sheet reflects most of the sun's heat back into the atmosphere, it collects almost no heat and significantly influences world weather patterns. Antarctica received tremendous media attention when it was discovered that ozone depletion, known as the Ozone Hole, was getting larger over the South Pole. This WWW server contains annual program reports for several nations that are involved in experiments on the continent.

If you're even more adventurous, there are links to help you take the next step—a trip to Antarctica. Learn about Southern Heritage Expeditions, a company specializing in expedition cruises to Antarctica and Sub Antarctic Islands; and Arctic Adventures, a Norwegian Company that specializes in Arctic tours. You can also save yourself a trip and just order a free copy of the Antarctic Gift Shop Catalog.

New Zealand

URL address:

http://www.cs.cmu.edu:8001/Web/People/mjw/NZ/MainPage.html

Fig. 13.32
Special tips on hitchhiking and sightseeing are a few of the many useful tidbits you get when you visit the New Zealand WWW home page.

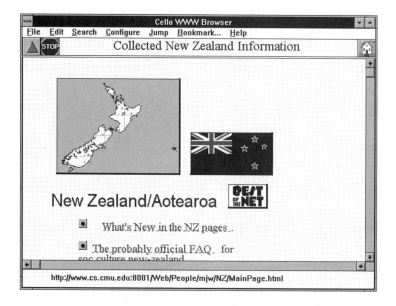

When you visit this home page, you increase your knowledge of this island country as you learn that New Zealand is situated the same distance eastward from Australia as London is to Moscow, and that it is bigger than Connecticut, but smaller than Canada. This just scratches the surface of the many interesting and useful things you will learn about New Zealand. Sports enthusiasts can find out about windsurfing and water-skiing in the beautiful waters surrounding the country. Hikers can receive detailed information about *tramping*, the art of walking in the outdoors. If you are involved in international trade, or simply want to buy a new sweater, you will quickly learn that wool is one of New Zealand's major exports. And, if you enjoy dabbling in international cooking, you can jump to various recipes, including this quick one for Pavlovas:

3 egg whites	1 teaspoon vinegar
3 tablespoons cold water	1 teaspoon vanilla essence
1 cup castor sugar	3 teaspoons cornflour

Beat egg whites until stiff, add cold water, and beat again. Add castor sugar gradually while still beating. Slow beater and add vinegar, vanilla, and cornflour. Place on greased paper on greased tray and bake at 150° C (300° F) for 45 minutes, then leave to cool in the oven.

Other home page links bring you to subdocuments, which offer yet more links to information about New Zealand, such as:

New Zealand News Stories.
Travel and Tourist Information
Physical Environment: Geography, Natural History, Environment
History, People, Language and Culture
Recreation, Entertainment, and Sports
Government and Public Affairs

Singapore Online Guide

URL address: **http://www.ncb.gov.sg/sog/sog.html**

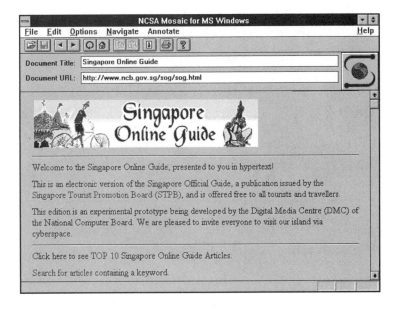

Fig. 13.33
This WWW resource provides an interactive tourist information guide complete with an electronic tour agent.

V

WWW Resources

A travel agent would have a difficult time pulling together this much information about Singapore. This electronic version of the Singapore Official Guide is issued by the Singapore Tourist Promotion Board (STPB) and is free to all tourists and travelers. The first edition is a prototype being developed by the Digital Media Center (DMC) of the National Computer Board.

The hyperlinks on the home page very closely represent the type of information that you would find in a good travel guide: places to visit, hotels, shopping, and more. To make your journey even more interesting, an interactive tour agent gives you a customized mini-tour of Singapore. And if you don't see what you need, you can keyword search articles about Singapore to get more specific information. When you have finished visiting this WWW server, you'll be ready to pack your bags. Here are some of the main selections and topics you can jump to from the home page:

Introduction
What To Expect in Singapore
Multi-Cultural Traditions
Things to See and Do
Shopping in Singapore
Feasting in Singapore
Touring the Region Map of Singapore

Nippon Telephone and Telegraph Corporation

URL address: **http://www.ntt.jp**

Fig. 13.34
Learn about the Nippon Telephone and Telegraph Company and jump to a variety of interesting Japanese resources.

Nippon Telephone and Telegraph Company and its subsidiaries provide a broad range of telecommunication services in Japan, including: telephone, telegraph, leased circuit, data communication, and miscellaneous services. NTT also sells terminal equipment.

In addition to providing general information about its overseas offices and NTT service information, this home page provides linkage to the following 12 laboratories that are part of its R & D department:

Basic Research Laboratories
Software Laboratories
Communication Switching Laboratories
Telecommunications Networks Laboratories
Network Information Systems Laboratories
Human Interface Laboratories
Transmission Systems Laboratories
Radio Communication Systems Laboratories
LSI Laboratories
Opto-Electronics Laboratories
Interdisciplinary Research Laboratories
Communication Science Laboratories

A unique feature of the NTT WWW information is the way it provides Japanese documents. It refers to five browsers that present information in Japanese (all in a UNIX environment).

Window-To-Russia

URL address: **http://www.kiae.su/wwwwtr**

Window-to-Russia is a Moscow-based project created by Relcom Corporation, initiated to give the worldwide network community a means of WWW access to a variety of information resources from and about Russia. Some resources are in Russian. (To view these Russian texts you need to install KOI-8 Cyrillic fonts.) Main menu links offer the following resources:

Arts, Culture, History, and Human Sciences
Business Opportunities
Science, Technology, Computers, and Software
Other Russian Web Servers
Russia-Related Sources Outside Russia

V

WWW Resources

Issues, Politics, and Religion

Amnesty International

URL address:

**ftp://ftp.netcom.com/pub/ariel/www/human.rights/
amnesty.international/ai.html**

Fig. 13.35
The Amnesty
International
home page brings
you to resources
that focus on
global human
rights.

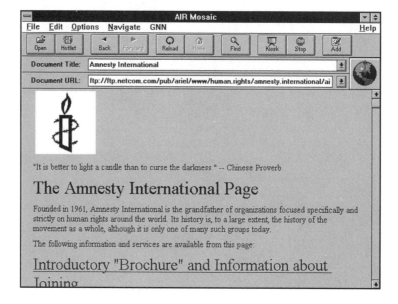

The famous Amnesty International logo, a candle wrapped in barbed wire, tells you a lot about this organization. Founded in 1961, Amnesty International focuses on issues and events that examine and improve human rights around the world. The home page begins with links that provide information about the organization and its goals. You can get fact sheets, obtain an introductory brochure, or learn how to join.

There are also links to the specific information that the organization is known for, such as the Urgent Action Network (UAN), which issues "calls to action" in cases where a person's life is in danger, someone has disappeared, is being tortured, or is not receiving proper medical care. Click the link to Amnesty International Printed Reports and Documentation to bring up a searchable list of all documents including country reports, the Annual Report, and reports on regions or issues. You can then order any of these reports. There is also an electronic directory of Amnesty International offices and contact people around the world.

Legal Information Institute

URL address: **http://www.law.cornell.edu/lii.table.html**

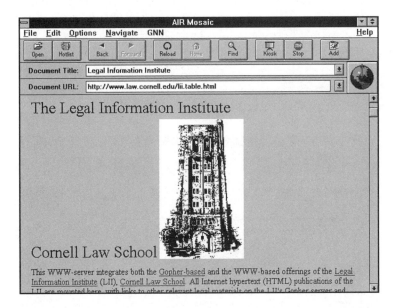

You will enjoy this home page if you are in the legal profession, have ever
used a lawyer, or simply have an interest in the major legal rulings of our
time. The Legal Information Institute connects the resources of the Cornell
Law School with the legal profession, other law schools, and the world via
the Internet. In fact, all LII "publications" are electronic and the LII created
and owns the copyright on the Cello WWW browser.

From the home page, there are links to a variety of hypertext documents
including Supreme Court decisions, issues that relate to civil rights, U.S.
Patent and Copyright Acts, legal proceedings from U.S. states and international cases, an e-mail directory of the faculty of all U.S. law schools, and
links to international legal resources. You can perform keyword searches on
many of the archives.

Click the "Search U.S. Supreme Court Syllabi" link to get an index that allows
you to search all Supreme Court decisions archived at the Case Western Reserve FTP site (URL address **ftp://ftp.cwru.edu**). The result of a search is a
hypertext document that contains links to all the opinions in cases that relate
to your search. Thus, if do a search on the word "gun," you get a list of several cases, one being HAROLD E. STAPLES, III, PETITIONER v. UNITED
STATES (May 23, 1994). You can learn that Justice Thomas delivered the

opinion of the Court, which states that the National Firearms Act makes it unlawful for any person to possess a machine gun that is not properly registered with the Federal Government. You can also jump to other interesting legal resources, such as law schools or "German Legal Materials (in German) from the Juristisches Internetprojekt" and "South African Politics (including Constitution, Interim Flag, and Ballot)."

Jerusalem Mosaic

URL address: **http://shum.cc.huji.ac.il/jeru/jerusalem.html**

Fig. 13.37
When you jump to this home page in Israel, you can take an interactive tour of the sights and sounds of Jerusalem.

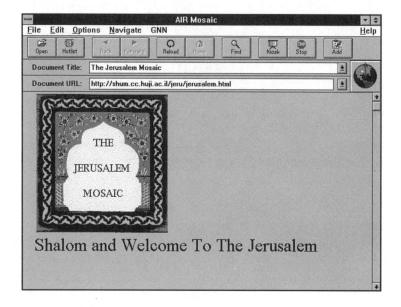

Travel to Israel and take this wonderful guided tour of 4,000 years of Jewish history and religion. Jerusalem Mosaic is a guided tour that gives you the impression that you are actually visiting this great city, the capital of the state of Israel, with its many monuments associated with the great biblical figures of past ages. From this home page, you can see the site of the mystic hill-city founded in the third millennium BC, and the "Urusalim," which appears in pottery inscriptions at the beginning of the second millennium. Listen to the "Song of Jerusalem" or view maps, paintings, and photographs of Jerusalem.

The tour combines these many forms of media in an interactive tour. You travel through an assortment of "gates" to look at and read about different parts of the city. The gates offer categories of images including faces, maps, paintings, and views. There are a number of aerial photographs, which all give you a unique perspective. A passage describes the type of images you will view: "We peek into the different neighborhoods and observe the roofs, squares, streets, and gardens, along with the numerous historical buildings which beautify the city." Other home page links connect you with:

> Main events in the history of Jerusalem
> More information about Jerusalem
> Other Hebrew University information servers

Jobnet

URL address: **http://sun.cc.westga.edu:80/~coop/localhome.html**

Getting a job can be just a little easier with the help of this WWW server. The home page represents a collection of employment resources and job leads collected from the WWW, Usenet news, and listservers. You can access information about employment trends, statistics, and career opportunities. Jobnet also provides links to several employment services and organizations that list jobs, such as Academe This Week from the *Chronicle of Higher Education*, the Academic Position Network, the On-line Career Center, and government databases that list federal employment opportunities. Frequently, the links connect with Gopher servers that you navigate through submenus until you find specific descriptions for job openings.

Periodicals and Books

Gazette Telegraph

URL address: **http://usa.net/gazette/today/Gazette.html**

From the full-color masthead to the icons for different sections, this WWW home page is a great example of an electronic version of a newspaper. Under the banner, you have the current weather conditions, then a headline for the top story of the day, followed by a little, one paragraph teaser to make you want to jump to the story. Next, a few more headlines, then icons for weather, local, nation, sports, world, business, and arts and entertainment news.

You can leave mail for the Gazette staff when you click an icon that opens a form for your name, e-mail address, and an area for your letter. Or, join a reader discussion area where you can either read comments from other readers, like a newsgroup, or leave your own message for other readers. Even though this is a daily publication, you can jump to an archive of the previous week's issues.

Fig. 13.38
The Colorado Springs Gazette Telegraph brings all of the features of a real daily newspaper to the WWW.

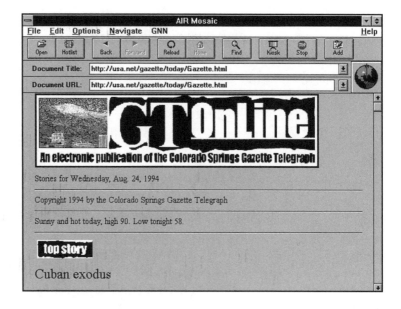

Project Gutenberg

URL address: **http://med-amsa.bu.edu/Gutenberg/Welcome.html**

Gopher: **gopher.tc.umn.edu/Libraries/Electronic Books**

FTP site: **ftp://mrcnext.cso.uiuc.edu/etext/NEWUSER.GUT**

If you enjoy literature, especially the classics, you will love this WWW server. Project Gutenberg began in 1971 when Michael Hart began to enter the text of famous literature into electronic files stored in the mainframe at the Materials Research Lab at the University of Illinois. Between 1971 and today, more than a hundred texts have been added to the collection.

There are two significant features to all the books. First, they are all stored as ASCII text, which means you can easily read and download them to any type of computer system. Second, all the books are in the public domain, which means you don't have to worry about issues of copyright when you download and use the books. Some of the authors represented include Emily Bronte, Edgar Rice Burroughs, Charles Dickens, Nathaniel Hawthorne, Herman Melville, William Shakespeare, Mary Shelley, Henry David Thoreau, Mark Twain, and Jules Verne.

It should be noted that there are three different addresses for this resource. You can use any of these addresses to access Gutenberg publications. The Gutenberg Web server is located at the Medical Library at the Boston University School of Medicine. It began operation in 1993 as a means to facilitate access to the electronic texts available at the main Gutenberg computer—an FTP host. The pages on this server represent links to documents stored on the FTP host. The good news is that, unlike an FTP connection, you don't have to remember file names, directories, or FTP commands—you just point and click to view and download the books. You can also try URL address **http:// info.cern.ch/roeber/fgmr.html** to access an unofficial Gutenberg Master Index.

Electronic Newsstand

URL address: **gopher://gopher.enews.com:70/11**

The Electronic Newsstand was founded in July 1993 to provide Internet users a means by which they could access information created by many different magazine (hard copy) publishers. Like a traditional newsstand, you can browse, at no charge, through these publications.

The subjects cover every area of interest—computers, technology, science, business, economics, foreign affairs, arts, sports, and travel. Each publisher provides an on-line table of contents and a few articles that have been pulled from a current issue. You also can keyword search the archives on specific publications for articles. These articles are really teasers that will hopefully encourage you to order a single copy or a subscription to the publications via The Newsstand e-mail or 800 number. A few of the publications that you will find here include *Animals*, *Business Week*, *Inc. Magazine*, *Computerworld*, *Canoe & Kayak*, *Fiber Optics News*, and *Federal Employees News Digest*.

Center for the Study of Southern Culture

URL address: **http://imp.cssc.olemiss.edu**

For more than 16 years, the Center for the Study of Southern Culture at the University of Mississippi has sponsored educational and research programs about the American South. The Center offers BA and MA degrees in Southern Studies. This WWW home page provides an outlet for information about the cultural activities of the region. From the home page, you can jump to lists of events in each state in the region.

The Center also publishes several periodicals that you can peruse from the home page. These include:

- *Southern Culture Catalog*. Contains videos, sound recordings, and periodicals.

- *The Southern Register*. A Newsletter of the Center for the Study of Southern Culture containing updates on current activities, such as the study of the culture of a 28,000-acre quail hunting reserve.

Fig. 13.39
You'll find a variety of electronic publications that focus on activities and culture of the American South at this home page.

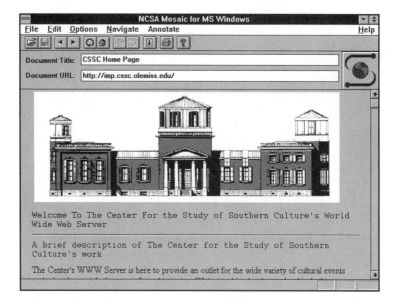

■ *Living Blues.* A journal of the African American blues tradition.

■ *Living Blues: Blues Directory.* A guide to the blues music industry.

■ *Reckon.* The magazine of southern culture.

■ *Rejoice!* A gospel music magazine.

■ *Old Time Country.* The source for traditional country music.

CBC Radio Trial

URL address: **http://debra.dgbt.doc.ca/cbc/cbc.html**

The Canadian Broadcasting Corporation and the New Broadcast Services Laboratory of the Communications Research Centre (CRC), in association with the Communications Development and Planning Branch of Industry Canada, sponsor this WWW radio service.

From the home page you can jump to a list of CBC radio products, an overview of program transcripts that are available, program listings, and samples of digital radio programs. The digital radio program files are in the "au" audio file format. A 10-minute story takes approximately 5 MB. Program samples include:

■ *Quirks And Quarks.* CBC Radio's science program.

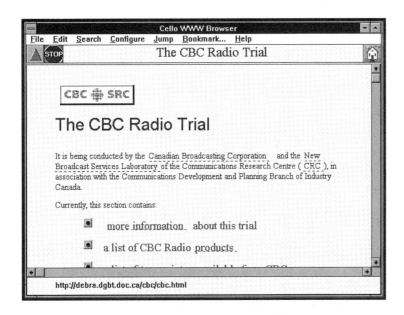

Fig. 13.40
From this home page, download a variety of audio programs from the Canadian Broadcasting Company.

V

WWW Resources

■ *The Idea of Canada*. A program where Canadians talk about what Canada means to them.

■ *Sunday Morning*. A current affairs program.

■ *Basic Black*. This program features people who have unusual jobs and hobbies.

■ *Brand X*. A pop culture entertainment magazine.

Another WWW site, **http://www.cs.cmu.edu:8001/Web/Unofficial/ Canadiana/CBC-News.html**, maintains audio files of the daily Canadian Broadcast News programs.

Science

National Aeronautics and Space Administration (NASA)

URL address: **http://hypatia.gsfc.nasa.gov/NASA_homepage.html**

WWW Telnet address: **telnet://spacelink.msfc.nasa.gov/**

NASA, the U.S. National Aeronautics and Space Administration, is the undisputed world leader in the exploration of space. The NASA mission statement located at the WWW home page declares "As explorers, pioneers, and innovators, we boldly expand frontiers in air and space to inspire and serve America and to benefit the quality of life on Earth.... We explore the universe to enrich human life by stimulating intellectual curiosity, opening new worlds of opportunity, and uniting nations of the world in this quest."

Fig. 13.41
The NASA home page is the definitive source of information and links to other resources about space science, technology, and flights.

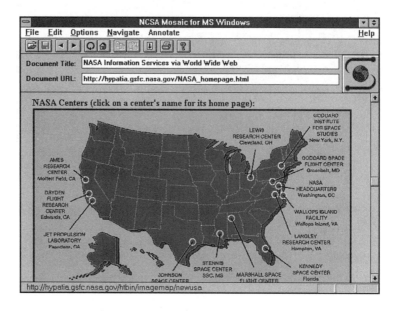

Because it is federally funded, NASA makes information about its programs available to the public. Many of the NASA materials are designed for use by educators and students who access information about NASA's scientific projects, space missions, educational programs, and newsletters. NASA Spacelink, which is a Telnet site, provides lesson plans, GIF digital images, educational software, and schedules for NASA Select TV, a television channel that NASA makes available to cable companies and others who have access to a satellite downlink system.

Delving into NASA's resources on the Web is similar to exploring outer space—it is enormous, and one destination quickly opens up new avenues for discovery. NASA's WWW home page contains a map of the United States that highlights the primary NASA-connected institutions. Each of the *hot buttons* for the locations on the map links users to these institutions.

Here are a few of the WWW sites available from the NASA home page. You can also go to them directly.

NASA Jet Propulsion Laboratory

URL address: **http://www.jpl.nasa.gov/ftps.html**

NASA Langley Research Center Home Page

URL address: **http://mosaic.larc.nasa.gov/larc.html**

NASA Spacelink (interactive session). This is probably the site most used by public school teachers and students.

Telnet address: **telnet://spacelink.msfc.nasa.gov/**

NASA Headline News

URL address:
http://cs.indiana.edu/finger/gateway?nasanews@space.mit.edu

NASA/Kennedy Space Center Home Page

URL address: **http://www.ksc.nasa.gov/ksc.html**

Dinosaurs—Honolulu Community College

URL address: **http://www.hcc.hawaii.edu/dinos/dinos.1.html**

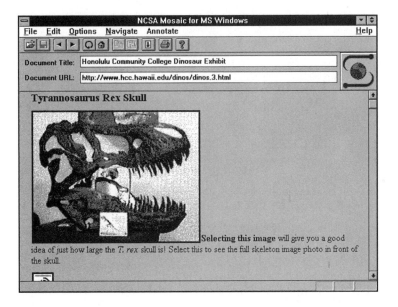

Fig. 13.42
When you jump to this home page you travel to the time of the dinosaurs. See images of T. Rex and other prehistoric creatures.

Dinosaurs are everywhere—movies, television programs, t-shirts—and now on the Web. Did you know that the Triceratops lived 70 million years ago, grew to be 30 feet long, and weighed seven tons? Take this wonderful trip to the WWW server at Honolulu Community College where you can learn (or teach) about dinosaurs. There are some terrific images of these prehistoric creatures and the exhibits in this electronic museum contain artifacts from around the world.

From the home page you begin a guided tour that you can either read or hear (by clicking on the audio icon). You get the feeling that a real guide stands beside you as a voice says, "We could not afford, nor did we have the space for the full Tyrannosaurus Rex skeleton, so we did also purchase, here on the right, a full Tyrannosaurus Rex hind leg. It stands 12 to 13 feet tall as you can see there, and as you look at this leg, the bones of the feet and the leg, you can see very much the connection with birds...."

Australian National Botanic Gardens

URL address: **http://155.187.10.12:80/index.html**

Australia has a lot more to offer than kangaroos and beer. The logo for this WWW home page, a Banksia branch with one flowering and one fruiting inflorescence superimposed over a map of the Australian continent, gives you some idea about the topic—plant life in Australia. This WWW site is a valuable resource for both the serious gardener and the professional botanist.

Fig. 13.43
Go down under and learn about the thousands of plants that grow in Australia.

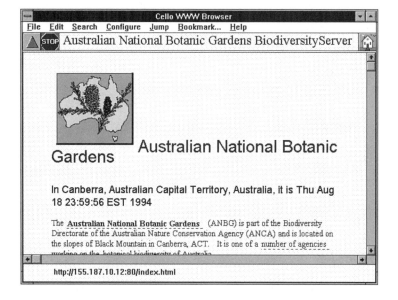

Located in Canberra, the Australian National Botanic Gardens maintain a collection of some 90,000 native plants from all parts of the continent. Learn about the science and the gardening requirements for flowers, plants, and trees. The "Flower of the Week" link provides information about a specific flower that is in bloom at the Gardens. You can almost smell the aroma as you read the descriptions—"The perfume of golden wattles pervades through-

out the gardens, whilst banksias, grevilleas and hakeas continue to flower."
Other home page links bring you to:

ANBG Integrated Botanical Information System (IBIS)
Bibliography of plant identification
A selection of botanical glossaries
Australian Nature Conservation Agency Libraries
Centre for Plant Biodiversity Research (CPBR)
Australian Biological Resources Study (ABRS)
Australian Network for Plant Conservation (ANPC)

National Renewable Energy Laboratory

URL address: **http://www.nrel.gov**

Scientific research plays an important role in the understanding and application of resources and technologies that simultaneously provide energy and improve the environment. NREL, a national laboratory of the U.S. Department of Energy, is renowned for its research activities in renewable energy.

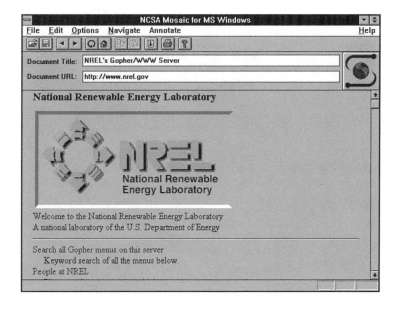

Fig. 13.44
Wind power, photovoltaics, biofuels—these are some of the renewable energy technologies that you find at the NREL home page.

V

WWW Resources

NREL's WWW server provides information about the laboratory and research activities, which encompass photovoltaics, wind energy, biofuels, biomass power, fuels utilization, solar industrial and building technologies, and solar thermal electric and waste management. From the home page you can access information about these research, commercial and experimental applications, energy resource maps, publications, business partnerships—even job opportunities at the lab.

Shopping

Internet Shopping Network

URL address: **http://shop.internet.net**

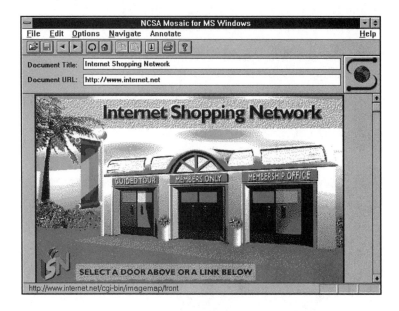

The Internet Shopping Network (ISN) began on-line operation in 1994. The major purpose of this electronic mall is global merchandising. The Internet Shopping Network (ISN) on-line catalog contains products from more than 800 high-technology companies. The home page offers a fantastic image of a shopping center with three doors—door number one is a guided tour of the service, door number two is for members only, and door number three is a membership office. Membership, which is free, means that you have the privilege of ordering, downloading demos, or accessing reviews. Non-members can only window-shop. There is an on-line form for membership, but you must fill it out and fax it back to the company. This is a security measure to protect your credit card information.

Because this service is graphics-intensive, you may want to disable your inline images when you browse. The merchandise in the various stores consists of approximately 20,000 computer hardware and software-related products.

When you enter the service, a series of product category icons appear, such as Macintosh products or modems. Jump into a category and begin a search for individual products. It doesn't take long to find the product you're looking for, complete with the ISN price.

Slovenian Wine Shops

URL address: **http://www.ijs.si/vinoteke.html**

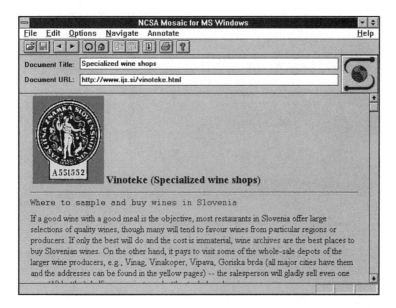

Fig. 13.46
When you visit this home page you can learn about rare Slovenian wines and visit vineyards in this European country.

"Vinoteka" is the Slovene word for wine, and this home page is a fantastic guide for information about where you can sample and purchase wines in Slovenia. Learn about Vinoteka Bradesko, a store located at the City Fairground in Ljubljana that offers the largest selection of wines in Slovenia and will let you taste them. If you get a bit tipsy, try the in-store restaurant to help you get your legs back.

In addition to reviews of wine stores, there is a database, called the "wine archives," that provides information about the country's best wineries and wines. There is, for example, the Wine Tabernacle in Maribore that sports a collection of almost all post-1945 Slovenia vintages—some bottles that can't be found anywhere else. You may want to remember that the Master Cellarer keeps a secret mini-tabernacle with 50 of the most precious bottles. Click the name of this or any other highlighted winery and you get a JPEG image of the vineyards, wine cellar, or some other aspect of wine production. The home page also has links to information about wholesale depots and wine specialty shops.

Downtown Anywhere

URL address: **http://awa.com**

Downtown Anywhere provides a good example of an electronic town. A bit of amusing self-promotion begins at the home page, which states: "Conveniently located in central cyberspace, Downtown Anywhere is a great place to browse, earn, share, and trade. Everything you can think of is available; just think of making it available. We offer choice real estate and all the amenities to anyone seeking a virtual office, a virtual showroom, or a virtual laboratory in the heart of the new marketplace of ideas."

Fig. 13.47

The Downtown Anywhere home page has the look and feel of a real town. Do some window shopping!

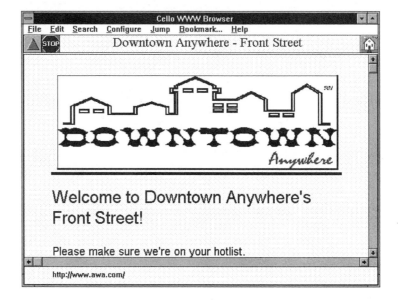

Like a "real town," Downtown Anywhere has icons that bring you to different locations in the cybertown. For example, you can go to real estate to learn how to sell services and products in this village. There is a library, a financial district, museums, and Main Street with its many shops and services. The jump to Main Street opens the door to a variety of stores, which you can then select to go to their home pages and begin your on-line shopping. For music lovers, there is CDnow!, which claims to have "The largest selection of music CDs on the Internet." If you need to upgrade your computer, try Compusource International—a discount supplier of computer products. If you want to help save the planet, there are at least 140 products in the catalog by Environmentally Sound Products, Inc. And if you just want to make a fashion statement, try T-shirts by Mighty Dog Designs.

Shopping in Singapore

URL address: **http://www.ncb.gov.sg/sog/6.shop.html**

Before you plan your next shopping trip to Singapore, check out this home page. Singapore is a duty-free port and shopping is a major activity. Products range from hand-crafted Asian carpets and jewelry to cameras and electronic goods. There are outdoor bazaars and indoor shopping centers, with most establishments open 12 hours every day. If you are looking for an interesting gift, jump from the home page to the section on Singapore Handicrafts. This describes the Singapore Handicraft Center at Chinatown Point that has more than 60 shops that specialize in oriental treasures like scroll paintings, jade carvings, and embroidered quilts.

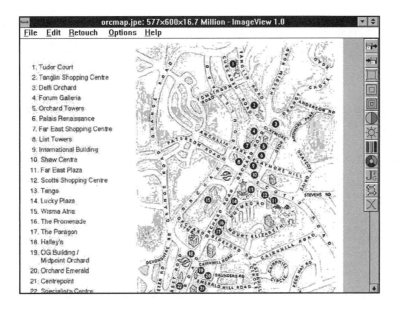

Fig. 13.48
Exotic jewelry, hand-made rugs, and spices are a few of the offerings you can sample via the Singapore Shops Web site.

Here is an example of the in-depth descriptions that you can access: "Orchard Road, so-called because of the fruit trees and spice gardens that grew here in former days, is the Fifth Avenue, the Champs Elysees, the Via Veneto of Singapore. For sheer volume, quality, and choice, it can rival any one of them. Every shopping center along the stretch from Tanglin Road to Orchard Road to Marina Bay is filled with a myriad of goods from around the world." In addition to inline images of the shops and shopping districts, you can click icons to bring up full-screen JPEG maps of the shopping areas. Individual stores are highlighted.

Recreation

Professional Football Server

URL address: **http://www.mit.edu:8001/services/sis/NFL/NFL.html**

It's third down and four to go. From this home page, by Eric Richard, you can get enough NFL information to become a sports commentator. In fact, the WWW Sports Information system (of which this is part) won the 1994 Best of the Web Contest for "Best Entertainment Site." Divided into conferences, there are team-by-team schedules, round-by-round draft selections, and information on proposed NFL realignments. You can quickly look up statistics from years gone by—choose from the following:

Fig. 13.49
Interested in team by team NFL schedules or any other football information? This is the definitive Web site on football.

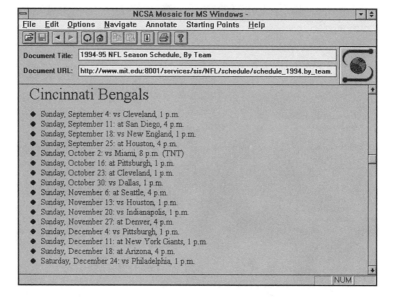

■ *Super Bowl History.* Remember Super Bowl XII when Pittsburgh beat Dallas 35 to 31?

■ *Super Bowl Standings By Team.* "The Kansas City Chiefs are 1 and 1."

■ *Team History and Information.* "The Buffalo Bills Rich Stadium can handle a screaming crowd of 80,290."

Or, try the Year-By-Year NFL Awards to see a listing of Heisman Trophy Winners dating back to 1935—when Jay Berwanger, a Chicago halfback, took honors. If you like football you'll love this Web site. (Note that the NFL has no connection with this service.)

Games

URL address: **http://wcl-rs.bham.ac.uk/GamesDomain**

You want to know the difference between a Cheat and a Crack in the game *Crusaders of the Dark Savant*? Popular is an understatement for this WWW site. In one month, there were some 55,727 requests for different HTML documents—the equivalent of about 151 requests every hour! After all, this server has more than 140 game-related links.

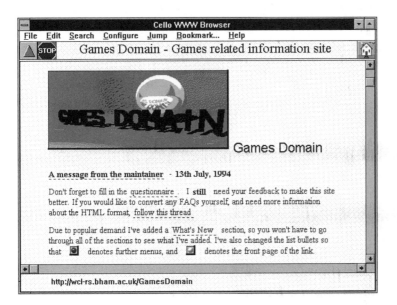

Fig. 13.50
From Checkers to Samurai Showdown, the Games Domain server has information about the rules, clubs, and contests for every game imaginable.

Not only is Game Domain huge, it's also an easy site to navigate. There are nice features, like a What's New section that instantly tells you about new resources or links that have been added and color-coded bullets in front of menu selections that tell you if there are further submenus. If you start your visit by jumping to Usenet, GamesFAQs will give you basic questions and answers for all sorts of games (many of these documents use hypertext).

For the next stop, jump to the Games Related Link: you find at least 50 links to other specific WWW game home pages—from titles like "The World At War: Operation Crusader" to "Othello" (possibly helpful if you play Microsoft Windows game Reversi). There is also a large selection of Games Related FTP links. So if you're into board games, or even bored with games, then get onto this Web site!

Golf Links

URL address: **http://www.gdol.com/golf.links.html**

GolfData is the sponsor of this WWW site. They offer great hyperlinks to golf courses and resources on the Web—and around the world. Here is a quick review of some of the links on this page:

■ *Southern Utah Golf Courses*

URL address: **http://sci.dixie.edu/StGeorge/Golf/golf.html**

Fig. 13.51
Visit the Golf Links page to find challenging golf courses around the world or simply to get pointers from the pros.

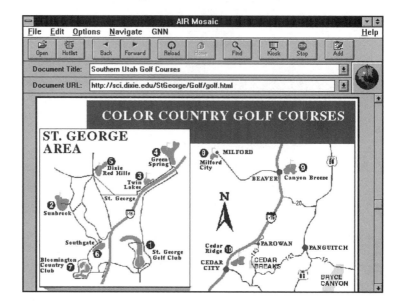

If you've never thought of Utah as a golf paradise, this server will change your mind. Many fine courses are located near areas of incredible natural beauty, such as Zion National Park, Bryce Canyon, and Lake Powell. The home page has a fantastic color map of the area with courses indicated. You can click a course to get more information.

■ *Alberta*

URL address: **http://bear.ras.ucalgary.ca/brads_home_page/ CUUG/golf.html**

If you're planning a golf trip in Alberta, Canada, this WWW site has detailed descriptions of many courses such as the Kananaskis course—it has the Rocky Mountains for a backdrop and consists of two 18-hole championship courses.

■ *The 19th hole*

URL address: **http://dallas.nmhu.edu/golf/golf.htm**

Lots of good golf information here: equipment sources, a golf digest record book, golf associations, and—if you don't already know them—the rules of golf.

■ *Princeton golf archives*

URL address: **http:/dunkin.princeton.edu/.golf**

A site for the serious golfer, this archive has documents that will tell you how to design a club or calculate slope and handicaps. It also has GIF and BMP images.

Finally, you can learn about the GolfData On-Line service. It is a commercial, electronic bulletin board that contains a database of more than 14,000 golf courses, discount coupons, tips from PGA pro Jeff Maggert, information on golf schools (300 of them), golf resort real estate, and an electronic golf shop—need anything else?

Railroads

URL address:

http://www-cse.ucsd.edu/users/bowdidge/railroad/rail-home.html

From single gauge trains of old to modern passenger trains to information about model railroads, this Web site has it all. The home page offers 17 different areas for exploration. Here is a brief summary of several of the links and some examples of the resources they may open for you:

■ *Link of the Week.* As it states, a new link each week that, for example, may connect to a JPEG image of a model railroad in Australia.

■ *What's New.* Recent additions to the Internet/WWW—possibly a list of hotels that are next to rail road tracks (who needs sleep?).

■ *Mailing Lists.* Like the Transit Issues Discussion List.

■ *Commercial On-line Services.* Like CompuServe's TrainNet or GEnie's Travel by Rail.

■ *Databases.* A database of existing diesels or steam locomotive rosters for Canadian railroads.

■ *Railroad Maps.* JPEG, GIF, and Postscript images of the French Metro or the San Francisco BART system.

V

WWW Resources

Fig. 13.52
Whether you
enjoy traveling by
train, have an
interest in old
railroad lines, or
want to build a
model railroad,
this Web site will
serve your needs.

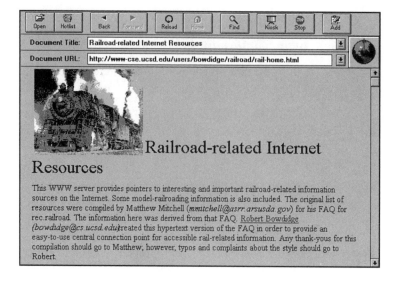

Rec.Travel Library

URL address:

ftp://ftp.cc.umanitoba.ca/rec-travel/README.html

If you are planning a trip, this is a great resource. The site maintains a library
of documents for travelers and tourists. Brian Lucas at the University of
Manitoba in Canada operates the site. Links at the home page offer access to
more than 15M of travel information and you can find a file on just about
any country in the world. There is also useful information on airfare, cruise
reviews, tour operators, and travel agents. There is an electronic newsletter on
Caribbean travel. Or, click the *tourism offices* link and access a database of
more than 680 tourist offices worldwide. You keyword search by entering a
company name and the database retrieves the address and phone number of
the tourist offices in that country.

Chapter 14

Hot FTP and Gopher Sites

You often can locate specific information and files on the Internet by browsing the large anonymous FTP sites and Gopher servers.

This chapter lists:

- Some of the most interesting and important sites on the Internet that provide anonymous FTP services, with information on what files can be found there.

- Some major sites providing Gopher services, including descriptions about what information is available on each site.

Major Internet FTP Sites

In the following sections, the file locations for directories and files are given from the top of the anonymous FTP area for each site. The directories are shown in a UNIX format (/directory), and subdirectories are indented under the upper-level directories. When you log in through anonymous FTP, you can click the corresponding folder to move to the directory listed. From there you can click the corresponding next level folder to get listings of the individual files in each area.

ftp.uu.net

Site name: **ftp.uu.net**
Contact: **archive@uunet.uu.net** or **tale@uunet.uu.net**

UUNet, an Internet service provider, is also one of the central distribution sites for all netnews traffic across the Internet. The FTP archive at **ftp.uu.net** is one of the largest and most complete on the Internet—almost everything can be found here! It has a very broad collection of programs and informational files. It's essential that you get the index files and search them for the information you want.

Location	Description
/index	Lists of what files are available
/systems	Software for various types of systems
/amiga	Software for Amiga computers
/apple2	Software for Apple II computers
/gnu	Free Software Foundation software
/mac	Info-mac mailing list archives, mainly
/msdos	Lots of software for MS-DOS machines
/unix	Software for UNIX systems (LINUX, etc.)
/ibmpc	Software for PC computers
/vendor	Information from many computer vendors
/info	Information about UUNet and the FTP area
/index	Index files for this FTP site
/published	Information from publishers
/pub	Miscellaneous software and information
/archiving	Compression and archiving software
/database	Information on different databases
/economics	Information on economics
/games	Game software for various computers
/security	Security software packages (COPS, etc.)
/text processing	Editors and text-processing systems
/window sys	Window system software (X Window, etc.)
/inet	Information on the Internet
/aups	Acceptable use policies from sites
/ddn news	DDN management bulletin archives

Location	Description
/doc	General network documentation
/isoc	Internet Society documents
/maps	Maps of the Internet and subnets
/netinfo	General network information
/resource guide	The Internet Resource Guide
/rfc	All Internet Request For Comments documents
/networking	Different network software packages
/news	Software for netnews transport and reading
/mail	Software for mail reading and transport
/doc	Documents of general interest
/dictionaries	Various language dictionaries
/libraries	Lists of libraries on the Internet
/music	Musical scores for various instruments
/patents	Patent documents
/political	Political documents (U.S. Constitution, for example)
/security	Computer security related documents
/standards	Standards documents (IEEE, ISO, etc.)
/style	Written style documents
/supreme court	U.S. Supreme Court decisions
/graphics	Graphics software and documentation
/languages	Computer language software

V

WWW Resources

wuarchive.wustl.edu

Site name: **wuarchive.wustl.edu**

Contact: **postmaster@wuarchive.wustl.edu**

This site, at Washington University at St. Louis, is one of the biggest FTP sites on the Internet. It mirrors software archived at many different Internet sites. It holds very large collections of PC and Apple Macintosh software, as well as software and documents covering almost every topic.

Location	Description
/systems	Software for different computer systems
/ibmpc	Huge amount of PC software
/mac	Huge amount of Macintosh software
/newton	Software for Apple Newton machines
/novell	Software specifically for Novell NetWare
/info	Information about this site
/languages	Information about various computer languages
/packages	Different software packages
/NCSA	Copies of files from the FTP site **ftp.ncsa.uiuc.edu**
/OAK	Copies of files from the FTP site **oak.oakland.edu**
/benchmarks	Different computer benchmark software
/compression	Compression and archiving software
/dialslip	Serial Line IP dialup software
/dist	Software distribution software
/gopher	Gopher client and server software
/mail	Mail-reading software
/news	Netnews software
/wuarchive ftpd	The special FTP server software written here
/www	The World Wide Web software system
/graphics	Different computer graphics packages
/usenet	Archives of some USENET groups
/doc	General documents
/EFF	Electronic Frontier Foundation information
/bible	The Bible in electronic form
/graphics formats	Different graphics formats
/nsfnet stats	Network statistics collected by NSF
/rfc	Network Request For Comments documents
/techreports	Reports from various universities

Location	Description
/edu	Software and information for educational sites
/multimedia	Multimedia data files
/audio	Internet Talk Radio files
/images	Pictures in different formats

sunsite.unc.edu

Site name: **sunsite.unc.edu**

Contact: **ftpkeeper@sunsite.unc.edu**

Sunsite is run by the University of North Carolina as a major site for academic information. It contains collections of software and information for many academic areas, and also is a central site for information about computers manufactured by Sun Microsystems, Inc.

> **Note**
>
> All directories listed for this site are under the /pub directory. You should click the /pub folder after logging in.

Location	Description
/academic	Software for academic use, arranged by area of knowledge
/agriculture	
/astronomy	
/athletics	
/biology	
/business	
/chemistry	
/computer science	
/data_analysis	
/economics	
/education	

(continues)

V

WWW Resources

Location	Description
/engineering	
/environment	
/geography	
/geology	
/history	
/languages	
/library	
/literature	
/mathematics	
/medicine	
/music	
/pharmacy	
/physics	
/political science	
/psychology	
/religious_studies	
/russian studies	
/water	
/archives	Archives of mailing lists, USENET newsgroups, and publications
/docs	Written materials, Internet documents, computers, literature, politics
/electronic publications	Archives of various electronic newsletters, magazines, and other publications
/gnu	All Free Software Foundation software
/languages	Compilers and interpreters of computer languages
/micro	Software for microcomputers
/games	Archives of various games

Location	Description
/mac stuff	Archives of Mac software
/pc stuff	Archives of PC software
/multimedia	Software and information about computer-based video and sound
/talk radio	Audio files from Internet Talk Radio

oak.oakland.edu

Site name: **oak.oakland.edu**

oak.oakland.edu is a major mirror site. Because Oak is very well connected to the Internet, retrieving the software is very easy.

Location	Description
/pub	
/misc	Simtel20 miscellaneous software (lots!)
/msdos	Very large archive of MS-DOS software
/pc blue	PC-BLUE archive of PD and user-contributed PC software
/pub2	
/macintosh	Very large Macintosh software archive

rtfm.mit.edu

Site name: **rtfm.mit.edu**

This important site holds the archives of all the Frequently Asked Questions (FAQ) informational postings made to various netnews groups. If you have a question about a topic covered by a netnews group, check here to see whether it's covered by one of the FAQ postings.

> **Note**
>
> All directories listed for this site are under the /pub directory. You should click the /pub folder after logging in.

V

WWW Resources

Location	Description
/pcm	A PC emulator package
/popmail	The Post Office Protocol mail package
/usenet by group	FAQ postings organized by newsgroup
/usenet by hierarchy	FAQ postings organized by news hierarchy
/usenet addressed	Database and information on the USENET address server

ftp.cica.indiana.edu

Site name: **ftp.cica.indiana.edu**

This archive, a central site for Microsoft Windows applications, is run by the Center for Innovative Computer Applications at Indiana University. If you are looking for a Windows application, check here first.

Note

All directories listed for this site are under the /pub directory. You should click the /pub folder after logging in.

Location	Description
/pc	PC software
/borland	Software and information from Borland International
/misc	Miscellaneous PC software and information
/starter	Important first software (UNZIP, uudecode, etc.)
/win3	Microsoft Windows applications
/unix	Miscellaneous UNIX software

ds.internic.net

Site name: **ds.internic.net**

The InterNIC sites (ds, is, and rs) collectively form the InterNIC services. They provide different types of information, but ds is the most useful for new users. This site has collections of all Internet documents and information; it is a good site to look for answers to questions about the Internet.

Location	Description
/dirofdirs	Pointers to information at different sites, organized by category
/fyi	Internet FYI (informational) documents
/internic.info	Information about the InterNIC
/isoc	Internet Society documents
/nsf	National Science Foundation documents
/policies procedures	Network policies and procedures from sites
/pub	Other information
/conf.announce	Conference announcements
/netpolicy	NSFNET acceptable use policy
/the scientist	On-line issues of *The Scientist*
/z39.50	Databases available using the Z39.50 protocol
/resource guide	The Internet Resource Guide
/rfc	Internet Request For Comments standards
/std	Internet Activities Board standards

ftp.eff.org

Site name: **ftp.eff.org**

This site is maintained by the Electronic Frontier Foundation, an organization interested in exploring the legal aspects of computers and networks.

> **Note**
>
> All directories listed for this site are under the /pub directory. You should click the /pub folder after logging in.

Location	Description
/Alerts	Information about important topics
/EFF	Electronic Frontier Foundation information

(continues)

V

WWW Resources

Location	Description
/CAF	The Computers and Academic Freedom mailing list articles
/Groups	Information about various computer and network organizations
/Publications	Various journals on-line
/net info	Copies of Internet documents

ftp.cso.uiuc.edu

Site name: **ftp.cso.uiuc.edu**

This large, general-purpose site, run by the University of Illinois at Champaign-Urbana, holds a good variety of programs and information, including an especially large collection of software for Amiga, PC, and Macintosh computers.

Location	Description
/bbs	Information on local bulletin board systems
/doc	General computing-related documentation
/pcnet	Lists of compression and network software
/mac	
/MUG	Champaign-Urbana Macintosh User Group collection of software
/eudora	E-mail package for Macintosh computers
/virus	Antivirus software for Macintosh
/mail	sendmail and smail packages
/math	PD math software and source code
/mrc	Index to materials available at the CSO resource center
/pc	IBM personal computer software and files
/adf	IBM Adapter Description Files and other PS/2-related items
/exec pc	Index and sample files from Exec-PC BBS
/local	Collection of local files and software

Location	Description
/pbs	Disks from Public Brand Software
/pcmag	*PC Magazine* files from Exec-PC or PC-Magnet
/pcsig	Files from the largest PC-SIG (Special Interest Group) CD-ROM
/scripts	Kermit and other login scripts
/virus	UICU collection of antivirus files

wiretap.spies.com

Site name: **wiretap.spies.com**
Contact: **archive@wiretap.spies.com**

This site collects interesting information that flows over the Internet. It has a large and eclectic collection of documents ranging from jokes to White House press releases. If you are looking for an official document (such as a government charter or report), this is the place to look.

Location	Description
/Clinton	White House press releases
/Economic_Plan	Clinton's economic plan
/Etext	Electronic documents
/Gov	Government and civics archives from around the world
/Aussie	Australian Law Documents
/Canada	Canadian documents
/Copyright	Copyright laws
/Economic	Clinton's economic plan
/Forfeit	Civil Forfeiture of Assets laws
/GAO Report	GAO miscellaneous reports
/GAO Risk	GAO high-risk reports
/GAO Tech	GAO technical reports
/GAO Trans	GAO transition reports
/Maast	Maastricht Treaty of European Union

(continues)

Location	Description
/NAFTA	North American Free Trade Agreement document
/NATO	NATO press releases
/NATO HB	NATO handbook
/Other	Miscellaneous world documents
/Patent	Patent office reform panel final report
/Platform	Political platforms of the United States
/Treaties	Treaties and international covenants
/UCMJ	Uniform code of military justice
/UN	United Nations resolutions (selected)
/US Docs	U.S. miscellaneous documents
/US Gov	U.S. government today
/US History	U.S. historical documents
/US Speech	U.S. speeches and addresses
/US State	Various U.S. state laws
/World	World constitutions
/Library	Wiretap on-line library of articles
/Articles	Various articles
/Classics	Classic literature
/Cyber	Cyberspace documents
/Document	Miscellaneous documents
/Fringe	Fringes of reason
/Humor	Funny material of all types
/Media	Mass media
/Misc	Miscellaneous unclassified documents
/Music	Music scores and lyrics

Location	Description
/Religion	Religious articles and documents
/Techdoc	Technical information of all sorts
/Untech	Non-technical information
/Zines	Magazines

ftp.microsoft.com

Site name: **ftp.microsoft.com**

ftp.microsoft.com is run by Microsoft corporation to provide support for their products. There is a lot of information here concerning Microsoft products, including patches, bug reports and demonstration software.

Location	Description
/advsys	Information about Advanced Systems including Lan Manager, Windows NT and MS Mail
/deskapps	Microsoft Desktop applications (Word, PowerPoint, etc.)
/developr	Developer tools and Information
/peropsys	Personal Operating Systems (MS-DOS, Windows, etc.)

ocf.berkeley.edu

Site name: **ocf.berkeley.edu**

ocf.berkeley.edu is a site that holds a lot of non-serious information as well as a lot of useful information. The OCF site is run by students, so the files here tend to be eclectic. All files are under /pub, so you should click that folder to find the following directories:

Location	Description
/Comics	Information about various local comics
/FTP_Sites	Directory of other FTP sites
/Library	Large collections of materials on various subjects (such as fiction, literature, etc.)

V

WWW Resources

Internet Gopher Sites

Because Gopher is based in a hierarchical structure, you easily can browse among many sites. The following sections list a few of the major Gopher sites to get you started.

gopher.micro.umn.edu

URL: **gopher.micro.umn.edu**

This is the Gopher home site, where the Gopher software was developed. As such, it has the complete list of all available Gopher sites around the world and keeps the most recent information about Gopher on-line.

> **Menu Items**
> Information About Gopher
> Computer Information
> Discussion Groups
> Fun & Games
> Internet file server (FTP) sites
> Libraries
> News
> Other Gopher and Information Servers
> Phone Books
> Search Gopher Titles at the University of Minnesota
> Search lots of places at the University of Minnesota
> University of Minnesota Campus Information/Information about Gopher

boombox.micro.umn.edu

URL: **boombox.micro.umn.edu**

This site, also run by the University of Minnesota, holds the source code for most of the Gopher servers and clients. If you don't already have Gopher client code running, you can anonymous FTP to this machine to retrieve the current versions.

wiretap.spies.com

URL: **wiretap.spies.com**

Also described under the earlier anonymous FTP section, wiretap contains many interesting documents that have moved over the Internet. All the following headings have more categories under them—there are too many interesting files to list.

Menu Items
About the Internet Wiretap
Electronic Books at Wiretap
GAO Transition Reports
Government Documents (US & World)
North American Free Trade Agreement
Usenet `alt.etext` Archives
Usenet `ba.internet` Archives
Various ETEXT Resources on the Internet
Video Game Archive
Waffle BBS Software
Wiretap On-Line Library
Worldwide Gopher and WAIS Servers

gopher.internic.net

URL: **gopher.internic.net**

The InterNIC site is the central Network Information Center for the Internet.
The site allows you to find information about the Internet and many of its
resources.

Menu Items
Information about the InterNIC
InterNIC Information Services (General Atomics)
    README
    About the InfoGuide
    About InterNIC Information Services
    About the Internet
    Getting Connected to the Internet
    Beginners: Start Here
    Using the Internet
    Internet Resources
    Advanced Users: NIC Staff, System Administrators, Programmers
    Frequently Asked Questions at InterNIC IS
    Scout Report
    WAIS search InfoGuide (and elsewhere) by keyword
    InfoGuide INDEX
InterNIC Registration Services (NSI)
    InterNIC Registration Archives
    Whois Searches (InterNIC IP, ASN, DNS, POC Registry)

V

WWW Resources

InterNIC Directory and Database Services (AT&T)
    About InterNIC Directory and Database Services
    InterNIC Directory of Directories
    InterNIC Directory Services ("White Pages")
    InterNIC Database Services (Public Databases)
    Additional Internet Resource Information
    Internet Documentation (RFCs, FYIs, etc.)
    National Science Foundation Information

gopher.nsf.gov

URL: **gopher.nsf.gov**

This server—the main Gopher server run by the National Science Foundation—is a central clearinghouse for many scientific reports and documents. This server also provides pointers to many other government Gopher servers; if you are looking for information from a government office or department, look here.

Menu Items
About this Gopher
About STIS
Index to NSF Award Abstracts
Index to NSF Publications
NSF Phone Directory
NSF Publications
BIO—Director for Biological Sciences
CISE—Director for Computer and Information Science & Engineering
Cross Directorate Programs
EHR—Director for Education and Human Resources
ENG—Director for Engineering
GEO—Director for Geosciences
MPS—Director for Math & Physical Sciences
NSB—National Science Board
OIG—Office of the Inspector General
Office of the Director
SBE—Director for Social, Behavioral and Economic Sciences
SRS—Science Resources Studies Division
On-Line STIS System (login as "public")
Other US Government Gopher Servers

FTP and Gopher Sites by Topic

This section lists a few of the many special-interest topics that have information available on the Internet through FTP and Gopher. Each individual entry lists the URL used to reach the FTP or Gopher server. For FTP servers, the location of the file or directory of interest is shown as a directory path. Once you have connected to the server, you can locate the item by clicking the folders corresponding to each piece of the path shown in the location.

For some tips on finding information that is of interest to you, see the section "Search Pages" in Chapter 6, "Shortcuts to Favorite Places."

Note

This section is by no means complete; it's intended simply to give a feel for the types of information available and how to get access to them. There are a number of different locations on the Internet that contain lists of Gopher and FTP sites. One of these is the Monster FTP list, a comprehensive listing of FTP servers you can find at the URL **http://hoohoo.ncsa.uiuc.edu:80/ftp-interface.html**. A quick way to access this list is to Open the Starting Points menu and choose Other Documents. From the walking menu that appears, choose FTP Sites. Another place to find a large selection of Internet resources is the Internet Services list at the URL **http://slacvx.slac.stanford.edu:80/misc/internet-services.html**. A quick way to access this list is to open the Starting Points menu and choose Other Documents. From the walking menu that appears, choose Internet Services List. This list is organized by topic.

One final suggestion for finding Gopher servers: Open the Starting Points menu and choose Gopher Servers. From the walking menu that appears, choose Gopherspace Overview. This will connect you to the University of Minnesota's Gopher server, which contains a listing of all of the Gopher servers that exist. From here, you can browse through the lists of Gopher servers (organized by geographical region), and connect to servers that are in interesting places or that have interesting names.

Gopher and FTP sites are listed for the following topics:

- Agriculture
- Aviation
- Books
- Computer Networking

- Computer Security

- Education

- Genealogy

- Health

- History

- Law

- Mathematics

- Music

- Recipes

- Religion

- Science (General)

- Weather

- ZIP Codes

Agriculture

Several different services offer agricultural information on the Internet. Some services are weather- and crop-related; others provide information related to health.

URL: **gopher://esusda.gov**

This Gopher server, run by the Extension Service of the USDA, provides access to various educational and information services of the Cooperative Extension System, as well as providing links to other agricultural Gopher servers around the country. This Gopher also provides information such as White House press releases, the Clinton health plan, the Federal budget, and more.

URL: **ftp://ftp.sura.net**
location **/pub/nic/agricultural.list**

This document, titled "Not Just Cows—A Guide to Internet/Bitnet Resources in Agriculture and Related Sciences," contains pointers to many resources on BITNET and the Internet for the agricultural sciences. This document is fairly large (about 2,700 lines), so you should peruse it on-line when you retrieve it.

Aviation

URL: **gopher://av.eecs.nwu.edu**

This site is run by Northwestern University as a repository for aviation information. Some information is from the USENET `rec.aviation` group, but quite a bit is contributed from individual pilots on the Internet. Stories, pictures, and flight-planning information are available.

Books

URL: **ftp://mrcnext.cso.uiuc.edu**
    location **/pub/etext**

This site maintains an archive of the Project Gutenberg files. Project Gutenberg is aimed at producing 10,000 of the most widely read books in electronic form. Some books already available at this site are *Alice in Wonderland*, *The CIA World Fact Book*, *Roget's Thesaurus*, and *Moby Dick*.

Macmillan Computer Publishing

URL: **http://www.mcp.com/**

Find information on the best computer book publishers in the world. Books from Que, Sams Publishing, New Riders, Alpha, Brady, and Hayden are featured here. You can review a sample chapter or table of contents from current books. This site also contains a wealth of reference articles pulled from these leading books to answer your questions about computer software and hardware. You can order a Macmillan Computer Publishing book directly from this Web site. Download software associated with best selling titles. (This site will become available in December, 1994.)

Computer Networking

URL: **ftp://dhvx20.csudh.edu**
    location **global_net**

This site maintains an archive of documents pertaining to the effort to bring network access to lesser-developed nations and the poorer parts of developed nations.

> ### Note
> Many other networking documents are available, as described in the host-specific section earlier. The site `ds.internic.net` is a primary source for all documents and information about the Internet and networking in general.

V

WWW Resources

Computer Security

URL: **ftp://ftp.cert.org**
location **/pub**

The Computer Emergency Response Team (CERT) is a federally funded organization that acts as a clearinghouse for computer security information. On its FTP site are archives of all its security bulletins, some computer security tools, computer virus information, and other computer security related items.

Education

URL: **gopher://nysernet.org**

The Empire Schoolhouse is one option under the Nysernet Gopher server (under the K-12 special collection), but is accessed directly through Telnet. This server has information about education from grades kindergarten through 12, including the Educational Resource Information Center and the Empire Internet Schoolhouse.

Genealogy

If you are looking up your roots and need some help, the following sites may be just what you need. They provide information on genealogy, including database programs.

URL: **ftp://wood.cebaf.gov**
location **genealogy**

This site contains a large amount of information on genealogy, including information on the PAF genealogy program, genealogy database programs, and text files relating to genealogy.

URL: **ftp://vm1.nodak.edu**
location **roots l**

This site contains a very large number of text files relating to genealogy. Retrieve the file FAQ.INDEX for a beginning on how to use the information in this directory.

Health

URL: **gopher://gopher.nih.gov**

Run by the National Institutes of Health, this Gopher site has health and clinical information, grants and research information, molecular biology databases, and links to the National Institute of Allergy and Infectious Disease and National Institute of Mental Health Gopher sites. This site also features information about cancer- (CancerNet) and AIDS-related information. Access to the National Library of Medicine is also available.

History

URL: **ftp://byrd.mu.wvnet.edu**
   location **/pub/history**

This site offers documents on many different historic categories, including diplomatic, ethnic, maritime, and U.S. history.

Law

Several law schools offer extensive resources on the Internet for lawyers and others interested in the law.

URL: **gopher://fatty.law.cornell.edu**

This site, run by the Cornell University law school, features information such as a directory of legal academia, discussion and LISTSERV archives, U.S. law (primary documents and commentary), foreign and international law (primary documents and commentary), and other legal resources (such as government agencies and Internet sources). This site is very complete and valuable for all legal references.

URL: **gopher://gopher.law.csuohio.edu**

This site, run by the Cleveland State University law school, features information such as electronic versions of many legal sources, legal sources on the Internet, course schedules, and links to other Gopher sites.

Mathematics

URL: **gopher://e math.ams.com**

This site is run by the American Mathematics Society to provide an electronic forum for AMS members and others interested in mathematics. Topics include mathematical publications, mathematical reprints, mathematical discussion lists and bulletin boards, general information of interest to mathematicians, and professional information for mathematicians.

Music

Musicians have access to several archives of information, including scores, guitar tabulator, and lyrics of popular songs.

URL: **ftp://ftp.nevada.edu**
location **/pub/guitar**

This directory contains tabulator or chords written for guitar. People from all over the world submit songs that they have transcribed into tabulator form; if you submit something, however, please make sure that it isn't copyrighted.

URL: **ftp://ftp.uwp.edu**
location **/pub/music**
or **gopher://ftp.uwp.edu**

This server has archives of information about music, including articles about music composition, archives of music by artist name, classical music buying guide, folk music files and pointers, lyrics archives, and more.

Recipes

Several Internet mailing lists and USENET groups are devoted to cooking and recipes. Over quite a few years, these recipes have been collected into several archives on the Internet.

URL: **ftp://gatekeeper.dec.com**
location **/pub/recipes**

The archive at **gatekeeper.dec.com** has many different items of interest. The recipes area has hundreds of items submitted by users over a period of several years. This archive is organized by recipe title.

URL: **ftp://mthvax.cs.miami.edu**
location **/pub/recipes**

This site holds the archives for the USENET group **rec.food.recipes**. Recipes here are organized by food type—that is, fish, chicken, etc.. Programs for indexing and reading the **rec.food.recipes** archives are also available on this site (for Macintoshes and PCs); see the file **/pub/recipes/readme** for information.

Religion

Many different religious texts and informational files are available on Internet servers. These sites are a good place to find many of these texts.

URL: **ftp://wuarchive.wustl.edu**
location **/doc/bible**

Complete editions of the King James Version of the Bible, including cross-references, are available for PCs and Macintoshes. You probably want to get the README file first to understand how to use the files.

URL: **ftp://quake.think.com**
location **/pub/etext/koran**

This directory contains an electronically scanned version of M.H. Shakir's translation of the Holy Qur'an, as published by Tahrike Tarsile Qur'an, Inc. There are files for each chapter, and you can retrieve each one individually.

URL: **ftp://nic.funet.fi**
location **/pub/doc/bible/hebrew**

This directory contains the Torah from the Tanach in Hebrew, the Prophets from the Tanach in Hebrew, and the Writings from the Tanach in Hebrew. Also included is a program to display Hebrew letters on a PC monitor and a Hebrew quiz with biblical Hebrew-language tutor. This site is in Europe, so you may want to limit your file transfers somewhat.

Science (General)

URL: **gopher://gopher.hs.jhu.edu**

This server is run by the History of Science Department at Johns Hopkins University. Available topics include "scientists on disk"—that is, a collection of important documents by scientists; the history of science (including departmental information such as memos and correspondence); classes about the history of science; and other information in the "grab bag" category. The scientists on disk collection includes papers by Darwin and Oppenheimer and information about the Royal Society of Science.

Weather

URL: **gopher://wx.atmos.uiuc.edu**

This server is the University of Illinois Weather Machine. It gives Gopher access to weather information for many different regions, including many major cities in the United States. It also allows access to image files from different satellites. These images are in GIF format and may be displayed on your local machine after you retrieve them.

ZIP Codes

URL: **ftp://oes.orst.edu**
location **/pub/almanac/misc/zipcode**

This file gives a list of all ZIP codes for the United States (and territories) as of the current date of the file. The file is of the form `zipcode:city, state` (that is, `15001:Aliquippa, PA`), which allows for easy searching.

V

WWW Resources

Index

Symbols

* (asterisk) wild card, 150
16-bit versions of NCSA
Mosaic, 212-214

A

Abdominal Training FAQ,
316-317
aborting
document loads, 86
transactions (Web
Navigator), 252
About Mosaic command
(Enhanced NCSA Mosaic
Help menu), 211
absolute URL references, 38
Add Current to Hotlist
command (Enhanced NCSA
Mosaic Navigate menu), 207
Add Document command
(AIR Mosaic Navigate menu),
196
Add This Document
command
Macintosh Navigate menu,
123
MacWeb Hotlist menu, 264
addresses
host names, 16-17
IP addresses, 17
Advanced Research Projects
Agency network (ARPANET),
8-9
agriculture FTP/Gopher sites,
368
AIR Mosaic
browsing, 193
configuring, 199-203

console, 191-192
features, 189-190
hotlists, 194-195
creating, 195
folders, 196
importing NCSA menus,
197-198
inserting documents,
196-197
installing, 190-191
Kiosk mode, 192-193
opening documents, 193
proxies, 202-203
purchasing, 188-189
saving files, 198-199
starting, 191
Aladdin Systems, 68
alt Usenet hierarchy, 27
American Mathematics
Society, 371
Amnesty International, 330
Anarchie, 70, 73
anchors (hypertext links), 36,
89
and operator, 150
Annotate command
(Windows Annotate menu),
125
Annotate menu commands
Macintosh
Audio, 127
Text, 126
Windows (Annotate), 125
annotations
audio annotations
(Macintosh), 127
inserting, 125-126
setup, 124-125

anonymous FTP servers, 17-18
Archie, 20
connecting, 139
navigating, 140-143
saving files, 145-146
summary, 138
viewing files, 144
ANS Archie server, 136
Apple Computers, Inc.,
301-302
Archie, 19-20, 134-137
sites, listing, 166
Telnet access, 166-169
Archie Request Form
command (Windows
Starting Points menu), 134
archie.ans.net, 166
archie.au, 166
archie.cs.mcgill.ca, 166
archie.doc.ic.ac.uk, 166
archie.internic.net, 166
archie.rutgers.edu, 166
archie.sura.net, 166
archie.switch.ch, 166
archie.th-darmstadt.de, 166
archie.unl.edu, 166
archie.wide.ad.jp, 166
ARPANET (Advanced Research
Projects Agency network),
8-9
asterisk (*) wild card, 150
AT & T, 10
audio annotations
(Macintosh), 127
Audio command (Macintosh
Annotate menu), 127
Australia Archie server, 136,
166

J-K

L

M

X-Y-Z

15 Hour Free Trial*

Internet access doesn't have to be expensive or difficult. Now you can enjoy **professional quality access** to the Internet for a **reasonable price**. We staff our network site **24 hours a day** 7 days a week 365 days a year to keep the network up and running.

We have also put together a collection of shareware programs for our Windows and Macintosh users to make getting started on the Internet a breeze. You'll get all the software you need and installation instructions when you subscribe.

Billing Options for Every User

Dial-up SLIP or PPP Internet Accounts

- Regular: $0.75 per hour with a $20.00 per month minimum.

- High Volume: $30.00 flat rate per month for up to 70 hours. $0.75 per hour for additional hours.

High Speed Lines

All of our modems are 14.4kbps or faster. No waiting for a slow 9600 baud connection. We also have new 28.8K V.34 modem lines for the ultimate in SLIP and PPP speed.

To Get an Account Now:

Call (317) 259-5050 or (800) 844-8649
and tell us you saw our ad in *Using Mosaic*.

We'll set up your account immediately and send you all the information and software you need so that you have your Internet access working with no hassles and no delays.

*Some restrictions apply. Call for details.

Easily Navigate the Vast Resources of the Internet

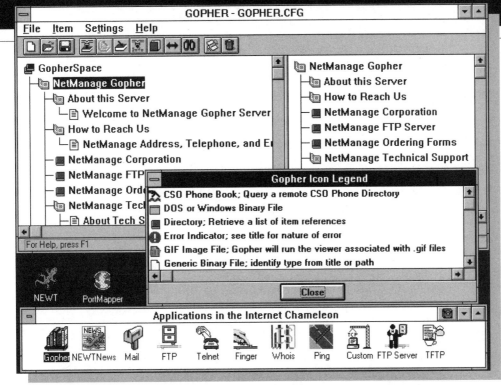

With Internet Chameleon™

othing makes cruising the Internet easier than Internet hameleon. A Windows graphical user interface makes ding information resources easy. The Library of ongress, weather maps, art, history, games. Meet new ends and converse with old friends. Read the latest ws as soon as it's written, or cruise through a web of omputer networks with information resources so merous that no other on-line service comes close! ith Internet Chameleon, you can navigate the largest iverse of information with the click of a button.

pplications Included:

ectronic Mail (SMTP, POP) with MIME and les, Internet News Reader, Gopher Client, le Transfer: FTP, TFTP, and FTP Server, Telnet; tilities: Ping, Finger, WhoIs, SLIP, CSLIP, PPP d ISDN Dial-Up Connections

- More Internet access tools than any other package
- Easy to use point-and-click interface
- Dial into the Internet
- Support for SLIP, CSLIP, PPP and ISDN Internet access
- Pre-configured connections for popular Internet providers
- Easy 5 minute installation
- Native Windows installation and ease of use

MICROSOFT WINDOWS COMPATIBLE

NETMANAGE™
(408) 973-7171
e-mail: sales@netmanage.com
WorldWideWeb: www.netmanage.com
10725 North De Anza Blvd., Cupertino, CA 95014 USA